ASCENT
CENTER FOR TECHNICAL KNOWLEDGE

Autodesk® Fusion 360®
Introduction to Sculpting with
T-Spline Surfaces

Learning Guide
1ˢᵗ Edition
Software Version: 2.0.6670

AUTODESK.
Authorized Publisher

ASCENT - Center for Technical Knowledge®
Autodesk® Fusion 360®
Introduction to Sculpting with T-Spline Surfaces
1st Edition - Software Version: 2.0.6670

Prepared and produced by:

ASCENT Center for Technical Knowledge
630 Peter Jefferson Parkway, Suite 175
Charlottesville, VA 22911

866-527-2368
www.ASCENTed.com

Lead Contributor: Jennifer MacMillan and Paul Burden

ASCENT - Center for Technical Knowledge is a division of Rand Worldwide, Inc., providing custom developed knowledge products and services for leading engineering software applications. ASCENT is focused on specializing in the creation of education programs that incorporate the best of classroom learning and technology-based training offerings.

We welcome any comments you may have regarding this guide, or any of our products. To contact us please email: feedback@ASCENTed.com.

Contents

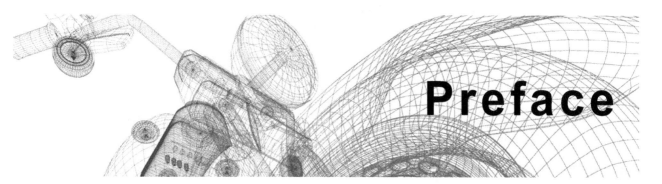

Preface

The Autodesk® Fusion 360® software combines locally installed and cloud-based tools. It enables users to use parametric modeling and surface modeling techniques to create 3D designs. The *Autodesk® Fusion 360®: Introduction to Sculpting with T-Spline Surfaces* guide focuses on surface modeling and how to effectively use the FORM contextual environment of the *DESIGN* workspace. Through a hands-on, practice-intensive curriculum, you will learn the key skills and knowledge required to create organic, highly shaped, and visually appealing models.

Software Version

As a cloud-based platform, updates are frequently available for the Autodesk Fusion 360 software. This guide has been developed using software version: 2.0.6670. If you are using a version of the software later than version 2.0.6670, you might notice some variances between images and workflows in this guide and the software that you are using.

Topics Covered

- Describing the differences between solid and T-Spline surface modeling.

- Creating new projects, loading files into projects, and opening files for use in the Autodesk Fusion 360 software.

- Using the Autodesk Fusion 360 interface, navigating a design, locating commands, and controlling a design's visual display.

- Creating T-Spline surface geometry using the Box, Plane, Cylinder, Sphere, Torus, and Quadball quick shape tools.

- Creating planar and non-planar flat surfaces.

- Attaching a canvas image to a plane and using it to create T-Spline geometry.

- Editing the shape of a T-Spline's control frame by manipulating its points, edges, and faces.

- Assigning or clearing symmetry on T-Spline geometry.

- Creating, constraining, and dimensioning 2D sketches.

- Creating and using construction features in a design.

- Creating extruded T-Spline geometry by extruding a sketch.
- Creating revolved T-Spline geometry by revolving a sketch around a centerline.
- Creating swept T-Spline geometry using appropriate path and profile entities.
- Creating lofted T-Spline geometry using appropriate profile and reference entities.

Note on Software Setup

This guide assumes a standard installation of the software using the default preferences during installation. Lectures and practices use the standard software preferences unless they are specifically changed as prescribed in practice steps.

Students and Educators can Access Free Autodesk Software and Resources

Autodesk challenges you to get started with free educational licenses for professional software and creativity apps used by millions of architects, engineers, designers, and hobbyists today. Bring Autodesk software into your classroom, studio, or workshop to learn, teach, and explore real-world design challenges the way professionals do.

Get started today - register at the Autodesk Education Community and download one of the many Autodesk software applications available.

Visit www.autodesk.com/education/home/

Note: Free products are subject to the terms and conditions of the end-user license and services agreement that accompanies the software. The software is for personal use for education purposes and is not intended for classroom or lab use.

Co-Lead Contributor: Jennifer MacMillan

With a dedication for engineering and education, Jennifer has spent over 20 years at ASCENT managing courseware development for various CAD products. Trained in Instructional Design, Jennifer uses her skills to develop instructor-led and web-based training products as well as knowledge profiling tools.

Jennifer has achieved the Autodesk Certified Professional certification for Inventor and is also recognized as an Autodesk Certified Instructor (ACI). She enjoys teaching the training courses that she authors and is also very skilled in providing technical support to end-users.

Jennifer holds a Bachelor of Engineering Degree as well as a Bachelor of Science in Mathematics from Dalhousie University, Nova Scotia, Canada.

Jennifer MacMillan is the Co-Lead Contributor for this edition of the *Autodesk®
Fusion 360®: Introduction to Sculpting with T-Spline Surfaces* guide.

Co-Lead Contributor: Paul Burden

Paul Burden is the Director of Product Development for ASCENT – Center for Technical Knowledge. He has been in the business of technical training and support for CAD systems since 1995. During that time, he has led courseware projects for CAD and PDM software from most of the major developers of this type of software.

Paul holds a Bachelor of Engineering degree from Memorial University in Newfoundland, Canada, and is a licensed Professional Engineer in Ontario, Canada. Paul's latest projects include implementation of digital formats for learning guides, including eBooks and online learning portals.

Paul Burden is the Co-Lead Contributor for this edition of the *Autodesk®
Fusion 360®: Introduction to Sculpting with T-Spline Surfaces* guide.

In this Guide

The following images highlight some of the features that can be found in this guide.

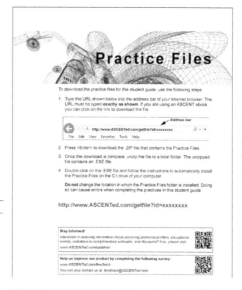

Practice Files

The Practice Files page tells you how to download and install the practice files that are provided with this guide.

Link to the practice files

Learning Objectives for the chapter

Chapters

Each chapter begins with a brief introduction and a list of the chapter's Learning Objectives.

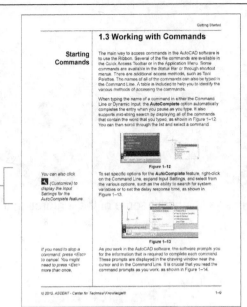

Side notes

Side notes are hints or additional information for the current topic.

Practice Objectives

Instructional Content

Each chapter is split into a series of sections of instructional content on specific topics. These lectures include the descriptions, step-by-step procedures, figures, hints, and information you need to achieve the chapter's Learning Objectives.

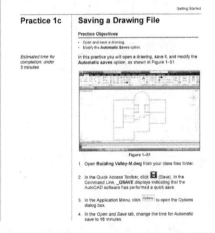

Practices

Practices enable you to use the software to perform a hands-on review of a topic.

Some practices require you to use prepared practice files, which can be downloaded from the link found on the Practice Files page.

Chapter Review Questions

Chapter review questions, located at the end of each chapter, enable you to review the key concepts and learning objectives of the chapter.

Command Summary

The Command Summary is located at the end of each chapter. It contains a list of the software commands that are used throughout the chapter, and provides information on where the command is found in the software.

Practice Files

To download the practice files for this guide, use the following steps:

1. Type the URL shown below into the address bar of your Internet browser. The URL must be typed **exactly as shown**. If you are using an ASCENT ebook, you can click on the link to download the file.

Address bar

https://www.ASCENTed.com/getfile?id=kabomani

File   Edit   View   Favorites   Tools   Help

2. Click **DOWNLOAD NOW** to download the .ZIP file that contains the practice files.

3. Once the download is complete, unzip the file to a local folder.

- For **Windows** users: To ensure that these practice files work correctly on your computer, move the *Autodesk Fusion 360 Surfacing Practice Files* folder directly onto your C:\ drive.

- For **Mac** users: To ensure that these practice files are easily accessible on your computer, move the *Autodesk Fusion 360 Surfacing Practice Files* folder into your *Documents* folder.

  Do not change the location where the practice files folder is placed. Doing so can cause errors when completing the practices.

https://www.ASCENTed.com/getfile?id=kabomani

Stay Informed!

Interested in receiving information about upcoming promotional offers, educational events, invitations to complimentary webcasts, and discounts? If so, please visit:

www.ASCENTed.com/updates/

Help us improve our product by completing the following survey:

www.ASCENTed.com/feedback

You can also contact us at: *feedback@ASCENTed.com*

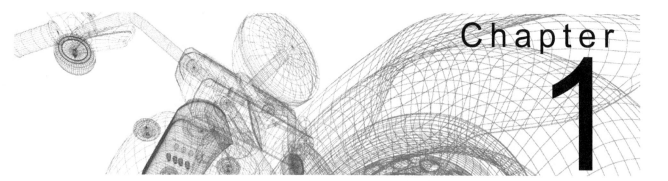

Introduction to Autodesk Fusion 360

The Autodesk® Fusion 360® software is an application that combines locally installed software and cloud-based tools. It enables users to use parametric modeling and surface modeling techniques to create 3D designs. The focus of this learning guide is on surface modeling using the FORM contextual environment. To successfully begin creating geometry using the Autodesk Fusion 360 software, you must install the software, access your Autodesk user account, create a project in the cloud, and become familiar with the interface and navigation tools.

Learning Objectives in this Chapter

- Describe the differences between solid and T-Spline surface modeling.
- Identify the key areas of the Autodesk Fusion 360 interface.
- Create a new project for use in the Autodesk Fusion 360 software.
- Load files into an Autodesk Fusion 360 project.
- Open files in the Autodesk Fusion 360 software.
- Use the design orientation commands to pan, zoom, rotate, and view a design.
- Change the Visual Style, Environment, and Effects settings to customize the display of a design.

1.1 Modeling Techniques in Autodesk Fusion 360

The Autodesk Fusion 360 software includes a number of different modeling tools to support the design of a wide range of manufacturable products. The choice of whether to use the solid modeling tools or the surfacing tools depends on your modeling preference as well as the type of geometry that is being created. It is often difficult and time-consuming to create organic, highly shaped, and visually appealing models using conventional, solid parametric modeling techniques; for these situations, surface modeling is often the better approach. The following is a brief explanation of the available modeling tools to help you understand when each technique is generally used.

Solid Modeling

In traditional solid modeling, features are added one after another, building upon each other to create the overall geometry. The complete parametric history of all of the features that are added to the design is captured and retained in the model's Timeline. The history includes the relationships defined between features to fully define the shape, size and position of the geometry. They can be in the form or dimensions, parameters, or equations, all of which define the design intent of the model. The parameters that describe the geometry can be accessed at any time, enabling you to edit values and easily make changes to the model. Figure 1–1 shows the feature list (Timeline) of solid features used to create the geometry.

Figure 1–1

Surface Modeling

A surface is a non-solid, zero-thickness feature that can define a contoured shape. Surfaces help capture the design intent of complex shapes that are not easily defined using solid features.

Surfaces can also be used as references to help create other features (both solid and non-solid). The term "quilt" is often used to describe surface geometry and can refer to either a single surface entity or a group of stitched (combined) surfaces. Surface modeling in the Autodesk Fusion 360 software is done using the *DESIGN* workspace, *Surface* tab and FORM contextual environment. Once the surface geometry is designed and made air-tight, it generates a solid body. Solid modeling tools (e.g., fillets, shells, chamfers, etc.) can also be used to complete the design after the surface has been converted to a solid body.

Surface Topology: T-Splines

Autodesk acquired T-Spline Inc. in 2011. The Autodesk Fusion 360 software incorporates the T-Spline software for surface creation. T-Spline modeling technology is an alternative to NURBS (Non-uniform rational B-spline) modeling for surface boundary representation.

T-Spline and NURBS technologies are mathematical models that are used to generate and represent complex curves and surfaces that are difficult (if not impossible) to design using solid modeling tools. The surfaces that are generated are defined by a network of points, edges, and faces. Any of these entities can be manipulated to refine and reshape a design.

When using solid modeling tools, features are generally created parametrically, with the location, shape, and size of the features are defined by dimensions (parameters). Surfaces can also be created parametrically, but with surface modeling, the flexibility of T-Splines enables a more freeform approach to design, where entities on the surface can be easily manipulated to control the surface's shape.

Figure 1–2 shows the Timeline for the creation of a form feature that consists of T-Spline surfaces which were created to derive the initial shape of a hairdryer model.

This learning guide focuses on surface modeling using the FORM contextual environment of the DESIGN workspace that is available in the Autodesk Fusion 360 software.

Figure 1–2

Hybrid Modeling

Both surface and solid modeling techniques can be used alone to generate a solid body, but they can also be used in combination to create the final geometry. Figure 1–3 shows the Timeline where a combination of T-Spline forms, surface patches and solid features were used to create the overall shape of a hairdryer model. Additional features are still required to shell and split the model into two halves for manufacturing definition.

Figure 1–3

Direct Modeling

Direct Modeling is commonly used to make changes to imported geometry that does not have any feature history. This modeling technique is not discussed in this learning guide.

Direct modeling is also available in the Autodesk Fusion 360 software. Direct modeling provides the flexibility to edit solid designs without manipulating a feature's parameters.

Non-parametric operations (such as Move and Offset) are used to manipulate faces, as shown in Figure 1–4.

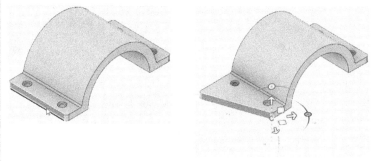

Figure 1–4

1.2 Getting Started

Understanding Workspaces

The Autodesk Fusion 360 software combines related tools and functions into groups called workspaces. When a workspace is activated, you are only able to access the tools from that workspace until another workspace is activated. This learning guide focuses on T-Spline modeling, which can be done using commands in the FORM contextual environment of the *DESIGN* workspace.

- To access the FORM contextual environment, click

  (Create Form) in the CREATE panel, as shown in Figure 1–5.

Figure 1–5

- Once the FORM contextual environment is active, the form tools display with purple icons (as compared to blue icons for solid modeling), as shown in Figure 1–6.

Figure 1–6

Understanding Projects

The Autodesk Fusion 360 software uses projects to manage and organize data. This is done in the Data Panel by selecting

  (Show Data Panel) option in the Quick Access toolbar. At the top-level of the data panel, you can select **New Project** to create a new project and create folders in the project. Each project only contains data that is specific to that particular project. If you create a project, you are designated as the owner, administrator, and moderator.

- Projects include permissions that restrict who can access the data, and what they can do with it.

- Projects can be used for communication and collaboration. In your project, you can post comments, use a shared calendar, publish documents to a project-specific wiki, and generate polls to gather input from project members.

- Open your project in you personal hub to further manage the project files and members, as shown in Figure 1–7. To easily access this page, select the project name at the top of the project's *Data* panel.

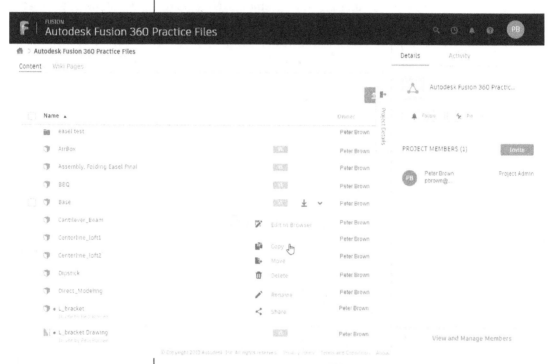

Figure 1–7

1.3 The Autodesk Fusion 360 Interface

When you launch the Autodesk Fusion 360 software, one of the first things you might note is that the interface has a minimalistic layout that presents only the information needed, when it is required. Figure 1–8 shows an example of the interface once a design is opened, including the toolbar, panels, BROWSER, and other interface elements. Multiple designs can be opened at once.

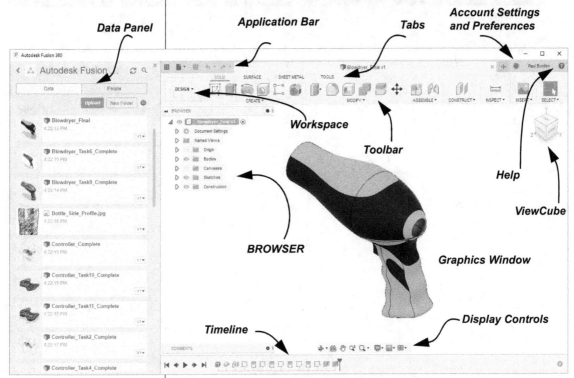

Figure 1–8

Toolbar

The toolbar (shown in Figure 1–9) is a dynamic interface that provides access to many of the tools and options available in the Autodesk Fusion 360 software.

Figure 1–9

BROWSER

The BROWSER is where all of the design data is organized in a tree-like structure, as shown in Figure 1–10. The BROWSER can contain design information, features, work features, folders and more.

Figure 1–10

Accessing Commands

The majority of commands are located in panels opened from the toolbar. Additional tools are also available in context menus or contextual tabs.

Timeline

The Timeline (shown in Figure 1–11) is displayed along the bottom of the graphics window. The Timeline records and displays the modeling history for the design. Each icon represents the feature type that has been added to the design.

Playhead

Figure 1–11

- The playback tools on the left side of the Timeline are used to rewind or fast-forward the Timeline entries to review the design.

- The playhead that displays at the end of the Timeline can be dragged and dropped within the list to return to a specific point in the design history to review the design and insert new features. Any features to the right of the playhead are displayed in gray, indicating that they are suppressed in the design.

- Right-clicking on a feature's icon accesses a context menu that enables you to change the feature by editing, deleting it, renaming it, etc.

- The colors of the feature icons can help you identify the type of feature. Blue icons ( ) indicate solid modeling features and that the SOLID environment is active. Purple icons ( ) indicate form features.

Accessing Help

The Help tool enables you to access resources, such as online help, tutorials, and forums. To access these tools. expand the menu in the top right corner of the software and select from the available options.

Preferences

There are a number of preferences you can set to configure the Autodesk Fusion 360 environment. To access these settings, expand your user name in the top right corner of the software and select **Preferences**. Expand and select each preference type to access the customization options. To return to the defaults, click **Restore Defaults**.

1.4 Design Navigation and Selection

Design Navigation

There are many ways that you can navigate around the Autodesk Fusion 360 interface, which can make working with your designs easier. This includes techniques for zooming, panning, and orienting the design using the mouse or the on-screen tools.

- The on-screen tools can be found at the bottom of the screen in the Navigation Bar.

- The setting that controls the mouse is the **Pan, Zoom, Orbit shortcuts** setting under Preferences. It is set to **Fusion** by default. Hold down the middle mouse button to pan the model. To zoom the model, roll the middle mouse button or press <Ctrl>+<Shift>+middle mouse button. To orbit the model, press <Shift>+middle mouse button.

ViewCube

One of the most convenient ways to change orientation is using the ViewCube, as shown in Figure 1–12. It is located in the top right corner and enables you to quickly snap to standard orthographic views, such as Front, Top, Side, and Bottom.

Figure 1–12

Named Views

Named views can also be used to quickly orient your design to specific views that are predefined in the software, or to views that you have created and saved. The *Named Views* folder is listed at the top of the BROWSER for each model. The four views shown in Figure 1–13 are provided by default when you start a new design.

Figure 1–13

To create a custom named view, right-click on the *Named Views* folder and select **New Named View**. The new view is added to the list. To rename the new view, select its default name and enter a new one.

Geometry Selection

When working in a design, you work with faces, features, bodies, components, work features, etc. To make this process easier, you can use selection filters to enable control over which items are selectable. The selection filter tools are available in the SELECT panel.

Selection techniques include the following:

- Items in the graphics window highlight as you move the cursor over them. By default, faces and edges are selectable.

- To select an entire body, click on the body or component in the BROWSER.

- You can use the **Selection Filters** options to customize exactly what can or cannot be selected. The options that are available change depending on the design and items that are being used.

1.5 Design Display

To make a design easier to work with, its display can be customized by changing its visual style. These options are located in the **Display Settings** menu at the bottom of the interface. The **Visual Style** settings are an application setting and are not saved with the design file. The visual style options are the same whether you are working with a surface or solid model. Figure 1–14 shows examples of the display styles that can be used.

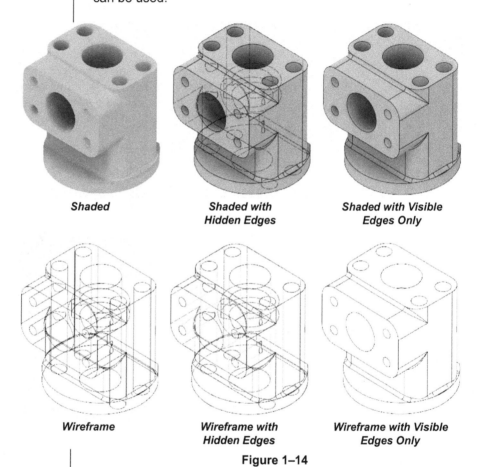

| *Shaded* | *Shaded with Hidden Edges* | *Shaded with Visible Edges Only* |

| *Wireframe* | *Wireframe with Hidden Edges* | *Wireframe with Visible Edges Only* |

Figure 1–14

Environment and Effects

The Autodesk Fusion 360 software has a variety of environments and effects that can be used to improve the display of your model. These options are located in the **Display Settings** menu at the bottom of the interface. Similar to the visual style options, environments and effects are application settings that are not saved with the design file and can be used whether you are working with a surface or solid model.

Form Display Styles

When working with T-Spline surfaces in the FORM contextual environment, you can use the six standard visual styles to control how the model is displayed. Similar to solid geometry, these styles control the shaded and wireframe displays, and sets whether hidden edges or visible edges are displayed. In general, **Shaded with Visible Edges Only** is the most commonly used option. This setting enables you to view and select the control mesh for easy manipulation.

In addition to with any edges that might be displayed based on the active visual style, a mesh is displayed on any active form feature that is being created or edited in the FORM contextual environment. The mesh (shown for the box shape in Figure 1–15) is known as a control frame. It overlays the T-Spline geometry and is used for editing and manipulating the shape of the geometry. The control frame consists of points that are connected by edges. Areas enclosed by edges are called faces. While editing, you can select points, edges, faces, loops, or bodies for editing.

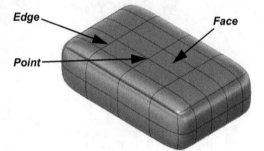

Figure 1–15

Hint: T-points vs. Star Points

- Star points exist when 3, 5, or more edges come together, as shown in Figure 1–16.

- T-points are a t-junction of edges, as shown in Figure 1–17. They enable you to add complexity only where it is needed. T-points are generally created using the modify tools.

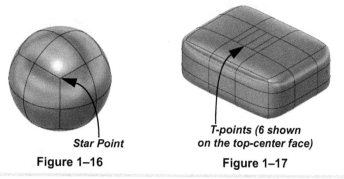

Star Point

Figure 1–16

T-points (6 shown
on the top-center face)

Figure 1–17

As multiple shapes are added, combined, and edited within a sculpted form feature, the shape creates more complex geometry, and a more complex control frame. As a sculpted T-Spline model becomes more complex with multiple shapes interacting, you might notice a drop in computer performance. To improve performance, consider changing the Display Mode option. In the UTILITIES panel, click (Display Mode). The DISPLAY MODE palette opens, as shown in Figure 1–18.

Figure 1–18

The Display Mode options include **Box** (⬚), **Control Frame** (⬚), and **Smooth** (⬚), as shown in Figure 1–19. Each body in a design can have different display model settings. To assign a mode to a individual T-Spline body, select one of its entities to activate it (e.g., face, edge, or point) and then select the mode.

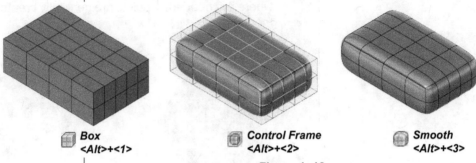

⬚ **Box**
<Alt>+<1>

⬚ **Control Frame**
<Alt>+<2>

⬚ **Smooth**
<Alt>+<3>

Figure 1–19

- The **Smooth** and **Control Frame** display modes require the same processing power.

- The **Box** display mode provides the best performance, but sacrifices the ability to display the true shape of the model.

When editing the shape of the model, consider using the Control Frame mode to learn the relationship between the box and smooth results.

Performance options can also be used to improve performance. In the UTILITIES panel, the **Enable Better Display** and **Enable Better Performance** options can further help with system performance when in the FORM contextual environment. These options toggle between a better display or better performance, respectively.

- **Enable Better Display:** Displays bodies at the highest quality display (applies G1 conditions).

- **Enable Better Performance:** Displays bodies at a lower quality to improve computer performance (applies G0 conditions).

Once the form is finished, the control frame no longer displays.

- If the form feature creates a closed, air-tight shape, the design is converted to a solid and displays as shown on the left in Figure 1–20.

- If the form feature creates a non-air-tight shape, the design remains a surface and displays as shown on the right in Figure 1–20. The color of the normal side of the surface is gray, and the other is beige.

Form features, regardless of whether they become solids, display the same in the Timeline

Figure 1–20

- Once you have completed the form feature in the FORM

  contextual environment, a ⬚ icon displays in the Timeline
  to identify the feature.

Practice 1a

Getting Started

Practice Objectives

- Create a new Autodesk Fusion 360 project and upload files to the project.
- Open a file from an Autodesk Fusion 360 project.
- Use the BROWSER to control the visibility of components in the design.
- Practice orienting the design using several different methods.
- Change the visual style of a design.
- Create a new Autodesk Fusion 360 design.

In this practice, you will begin by setting up an Autodesk Fusion 360 project that will be used with this learning guide, and you will then upload files to the project. To become familiar with the software's interface and navigation controls, you will then open one of the provided designs and practice using all of the navigation tools that are available in the software. To complete the practice, you will create a new file that will be used when you begin learning how to create geometry in the Autodesk Fusion 360 software.

Task 1 - Setting up the practice files.

If the software has not been updated recently, you might be prompted to update it to the latest version of the software.

1. Launch the Autodesk Fusion 360 software.

2. Log into your Autodesk account, if not already logged in. If you do not have an Autodesk account, create one using the **Create Account** option.

3. Verify that the *Autodesk Fusion 360 Surfacing Practice Files* folder exists and contains the files that are required for this learning guide. If it does not, return to the Practice Files page at the beginning of the learning guide to download and extract the files to your local computer to prepare the files for upload.

4. At the top of the interface, in the Application Bar, click

   ▦ (Show Data Panel).

5. At the top of the Data Panel, click **New Project**.

6. Create a new project called **Autodesk Fusion 360 Surface Practice Files**. This project should now be included in your list of projects, as shown in Figure 1–21.

Figure 1–21

7. Double-click on the new project.

8. Ensure that the *Data* tab is selected at the top of the project page.

There are a number of methods that can be used to upload and open files in the Autodesk Fusion 360 software. The following method involves uploading files directly to the project. In an upcoming chapter you will learn how to open files directly in the software and then save them to the project file.

9. Click **Upload** and select **Select Files**.

10. Using the Open dialog box, navigate to the *Autodesk Fusion 360 Surface Practice Files* folder. Select **Blowdryer_Final.f3d** and then click **Open**.

11. In the Upload window, click **Upload**. The blowdryer design uploads to your project.

Files can be displayed in the Data Panel in either List or Grid view. To select the view type,

*click ⚙ and select either the **View as List** or **View as Grid** options.*

12. Once the file has been uploaded, in the Job Status window, click **Close**. The new project and the file should display as shown in Figure 1–22.

Figure 1–22

You will learn how to create the Hairdryer design later in this learning guide.

Task 2 - Opening a file in the Autodesk Fusion 360 software.

1. In the Data Panel, ensure that the *Autodesk Fusion 360 Practice Files* project is active and displayed. In the list of files, double-click on **Blowdryer_Final** to open the file.

2. Close the Data Panel by clicking (Hide Data Panel). The design displays as shown in Figure 1–23.

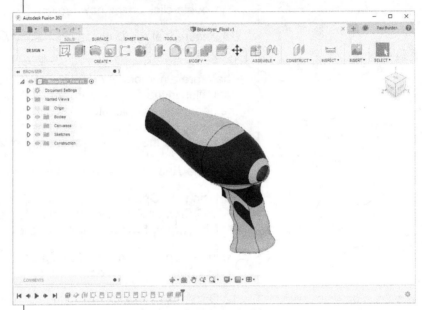

Figure 1–23

3. In the interface, note the following:

    *   The *DESIGN* workspace is currently active, as shown at the left end of the toolbar.

    *   The BROWSER contains the default folders (*Named Views* and *Origin*) and the additional folders (*Bodies*, *Canvases*, *Sketches,* and *Construction*). These additional folders were automatically created as they were required during the design.

4. The Timeline displays at the bottom of the interface and lists all of the features used to create the design. In the Timeline, right-click on and select **Edit**, as shown in Figure 1–24.

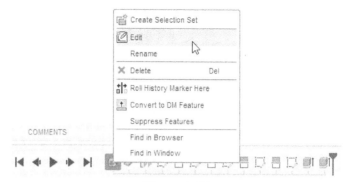

Figure 1–24

5. Note how the FORM contextual environment is now active. The form feature that was used to create the overall shell of the blowdryer model was created in this workspace. This is T-Spline surface geometry. In the remainder of this learning guide, you will learn how to use the tools to create this type of shape in the FORM contextual environment.

6. In the FINISH FORM panel, click (Finish Form) to return to the completed design in the SOLID environment of the *DESIGN* workspace. Note that the form feature (T-Spline surface geometry) was created first and then additional solid modeling tools were used to complete the design. This is a common workflow when modeling complex surface geometry using the Autodesk Fusion 360 software.

Task 3 - Learning to use the BROWSER.

1. On the right of the BROWSER bar, click to collapse the BROWSER. Click to expand the BROWSER.

2. On the left of the BROWSER bar, click to compress the BROWSER. The collapse and compress options can be used individually or together to provide additional space for manipulating and viewing a design.

3. In the expanded BROWSER, adjacent to the *Named Views* folder, click ▷ to expand the folder. Select the **TOP**, **FRONT**, **RIGHT**, and **HOME** views to reorient the design to the preset views.

4. Change to the FRONT view to continue with this task.

5. Expand the *Bodies* folder, and then complete the following steps in this folder:

   1. Observe the three bodies that are listed. Note that two of the bodies are identified with a 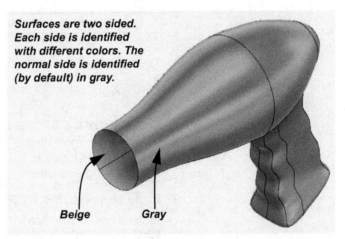, which indicates that they are solid bodies. The other body (i.e., **Body6**) is identified with a ⊞, indicating that it is a surface body.

   2. Hover the cursor over **Body7** and **Body8**. Note that these represent the solid housing and the button in the design.

   3. Click ◉ (Show/Hide) adjacent to **Body7** to hide it from the display.

   4. Click ◉ (Show/Hide) adjacent to **Body8** to hide it from the display. All bodies are now removed from the display and are listed with ◈ (Show/Hide), indicating that they not currently being displayed.

   5. Click ◈ (Show/Hide) adjacent to **Body6** to return it to the display. In the *Named Views* folder, select **Custom**. In this view (shown in Figure 1–25), note that the body is a T-Spline surface that was used to create the solid geometry.

Surfaces are two sided. Each side is identified with different colors. The normal side is identified (by default) in gray.

Beige   Gray

Figure 1–25

6. Hover the cursor over the surfaces on the design to highlight the surfaces that were built and shaped to create the design.

7. Return the solid bodies to the display and hide the surface body.

8. Click ◢ adjacent to the *Bodies* folder to collapse the folder.

6. In the BROWSER, expand the *Canvases* folder. This folder contains any sketched image files that were imported into the design. Note that **BlowDryer01** has a 👁 (Show/Hide) adjacent to it, indicating that it is displayed, and that a

   👁 (Show/Hide) is displayed adjacent to the *Canvases* folder name. By toggling the icon adjacent to the folder name, you can control all items in the folder without needing to individually control their display.

7. Click 👁 (Show/Hide) adjacent to the *Canvases* folder name to display the conceptual sketch that was used in the design. Figure 1–26 shows the sketch and the solid design together. Note that the design very closely matches the sketched conceptual design for the product.

You will learn how to insert an image to be used as a modeling guide for creating the hairdryer design later in this learning guide.

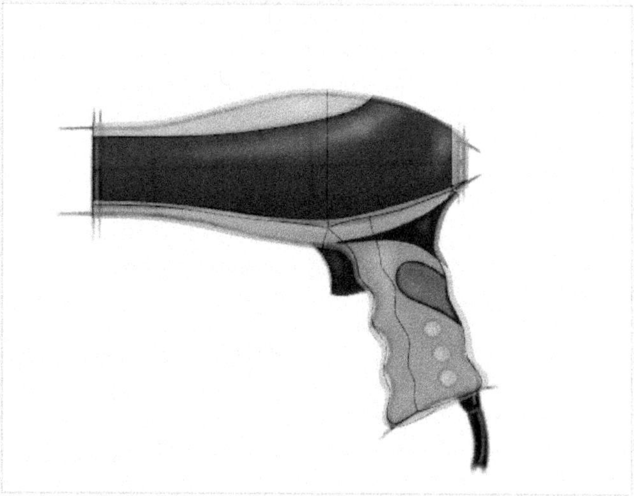

Figure 1–26

8. Change the view to the **RIGHT** view. Note how the sketch was inserted on the center of the design.

9. Return the design to the **HOME** view.

10. Hide the **BlowDyer01** sketch from the display.

Task 4 - Navigate the design using the mouse scroll wheel.

1. To zoom in and out, scroll the mouse scroll wheel forward and backward. Note that the view zooms based on the position of the cursor in the design.

2. To pan, hold the mouse scroll wheel down as you move the cursor around the design.

3. Reposition and zoom the design as required.

Task 5 - Navigate the design using the ViewCube.

1. In the top right corner of the graphics window, hover the cursor over the ViewCube. Click 🏠 (Home) to return the design to its default view.

2. Select the top face of the ViewCube (**TOP**) to reorient the design to the top view.

3. Hover the cursor over the ViewCube until the rotational arrows display in the top right corner, as shown in Figure 1–27. Select the left arrow to rotate the view.

Figure 1–27

4. Hover the cursor over the ViewCube until the triangles pointing to the four edges display. Click the bottom △ to switch to the **FRONT** view.

5. Click 🏠 (Home) to return to the **Home** view.

6. Use the ViewCube to orient the design as shown in the two views in Figure 1–28. In addition to selecting faces on the ViewCube, you can also select edges and corners to orient the design, as required.

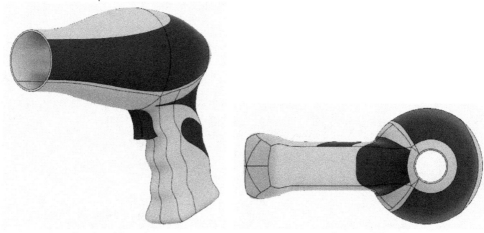

Custom View 1   *Custom View 2*

Figure 1–28

7. Once **Custom View 2** is oriented (as shown in Figure 1–28), expand the *Named Views* folder, if not already expanded.

8. Right-click on the *Named Views* folder and select **New Named View**. Click once on the **NamedView** view to edit its name. Enter **BACK** as the new name.

9. Return to the default Home view using either the Named View or the ViewCube.

10. Hover the cursor over the ViewCube. Select ▽ to expand the ViewCube options, as shown in Figure 1–29.

Figure 1–29

11. Note that **Orthographic** is currently selected. Click **Perspective** to compare the design display.

12. Return the design to the **Orthographic** setting.

Task 6 - Navigate the design using the Navigation Bar.

---

1. In the Navigation Bar at the bottom of the graphics window, activate the Look At tool by clicking 🖻 (Look At), as shown in Figure 1–30.

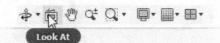

Figure 1–30

Origin planes are three orthogonal planes that are in the XY, XZ, and YZ planes. They are used as references when creating a design. The origin planes can also be selected as references for the Look At tool.

2. Select a planar face on the design to reorient that face parallel to the screen. In this design, there are only three planar faces on the design: at the nozzle, and the two sides of the button. Select any one of these faces to reorient the design.

3. Return to the **Home** view.

4. On the Navigation Bar, click 🖑 (Pan). Hold the left mouse button, and then move the cursor to move the design. The design pans in the same way as pressing the middle mouse button did.

5. On the Navigation Bar, click ⊕ (Zoom). Hold the left mouse button, and then move the cursor to zoom in on the design.

6. On the Navigation Bar, click ⊕ (Constrained Orbit). A circular outline displays around the design and the cursor displays as ⊕ .

You can also start the Orbit command by holding <Shift> and holding the middle mouse button or scroll wheel as you move the cursor.

7. Hold the left mouse button and move the cursor to spin the design in any direction.

8. Hover the cursor over one of the lines that extends horizontally or vertically from the circular outline. The cursor displays as Ⓞ (vertical) or ⬭ (horizontal). Click and drag on these lines to spin the design horizontally or vertically in the current plane.

9. With ⊕ (Constrained Orbit) still active, select a point anywhere on the design. Once selected, that point is centered in the circular outline.

---

10. Practice spinning, panning, and zooming the design using the Navigation Bar.

11. Click  (Zoom Window) and draw a box around the design to zoom into that area.

12. Click ▾ adjacent to 🔍 and then click 🔍 (Fit). Once selected, the design resizes to fit in the graphics window while staying in the same orientation.

13. Return to the **Home** view.

Task 7 - Manipulating the design display.

---

*The **Camera** options on the Display Settings menu enables you to choose between an Orthographic and Perspective display, as an alternative to using the ViewCube.*

1. In the Navigation Bar, click 🖥▾ (Display Settings). Expand **Visual Style**, as shown in Figure 1–31.

Figure 1–31

2. Click on each of the display settings to review how they change the design's appearance. Note: The visual styles are the same for both the SOLID and FORM environments of the *DESIGN* workspace.

3. Return the design to the **Shaded with Visible Edges Only** option.

4. In the Navigation Bar, click 🖥▾ (Display Settings). Expand **Environment**, as shown in Figure 1–32.

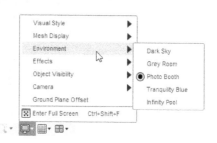

Figure 1–32

---

5. Click on each of the Environment settings to review how they change the appearance of the design.

6. Return the design to the **Photo Booth** option.

7. In the Navigation Bar, click ▭▾ (Display Settings). Expand **Effects**. Toggle the various effect settings to customize the view as required.

8. Clear the **Ground Shadow** option before continuing. The shadow is removed from the ground plane.

The display settings are set for the current Autodesk Fusion 360 session and are not saved with the design.

Task 8 - Create a new design in the Autodesk Fusion 360 software.

1. In the Application Bar, click ▭▾ (File) to access the commands in the **File** menu.

2. Click **New Design**.

3. In the Autodesk Fusion 360 interface, note the following:
   - A new window tab called *Untitled* is added at the top of the window.
   - The *DESIGN* workspace is active.
   - The BROWSER has the *Named Views* and *Origin* folders created by default.
   - Expand the **Document Settings** node. A **Units** node lists the unit of measure for the new design.

4. In the Application Bar, click 🖫 (Save). Enter **SculptPractice** for the filename and then click **Save**. This design will be used in the next chapter of this learning guide when you begin learning about the modeling tools in the Autodesk Fusion 360 software.

5. Click ✕ in the **Blowdryer_Final** window tab to close it. When prompted to save changes to the design, click **Save**.

Chapter Review Questions

1. Match the numbers shown in Figure 1–33 with the interface components listed below.

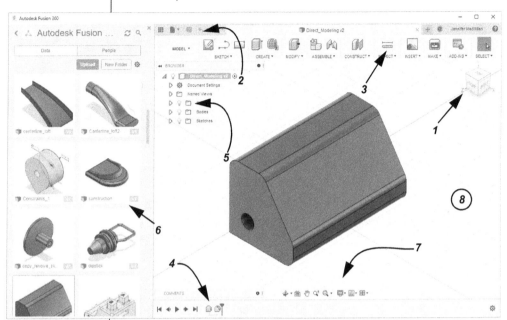

Figure 1–33

Interface Element	Answer
a) Data Panel	
b) BROWSER	
c) Timeline	
d) Display Controls	
e) Toolbar	
f) Graphics Window	
g) ViewCube	

2. You can have multiple designs open in the Autodesk Fusion 360 software at the same time.

    a. True

    b. False

3. Which of the following icons on the toolbar is used to access the FORM contextual environment?

a.

b.

c.

d.

4. The visual styles that are available in both the SOLID and FORM environments of the *DESIGN* workspace provide the same display options.

a. True

b. False

5. Clicking enables you to automatically reorient the display of the design to the **TOP** view.

a. True

b. False

6. Which mouse button do you use to pan the design in the graphics window, without having to use the **Pan** option?

a. Left

b. Middle

c. Right

7. Which combination of items do you select to quickly orient a design face parallel to the screen without spinning? (Select all that apply.)

a. A surface and

b. A planar surface and

c. A surface and

d. A planar surface and

8. Which of the following are selectable entities on the control frame of sculpted geometry? (Select all that apply.)

   a. Points

   b. Edges

   c. Faces

   d. Body

Command Summary

Button	Command	Location
	Constrained Orbit (rotate)	• Display Controls
	Create Form	• **Toolbar:** *DESIGN* Workspace>*SOLID* tab>CREATE panel
	Display Mode	• **Toolbar:** *DESIGN* Workspace>*FORM* tab>UTILITIES panel
	Display Settings	• Display Controls
	Enable Better Display	• **Toolbar:** *DESIGN* Workspace>*FORM* tab>UTILITIES panel
	Enable Better Performance	• **Toolbar:** *DESIGN* Workspace>*FORM* tab>UTILITIES panel
	File	• Application Bar
	Fit	• Display Controls
	Help	• Account Settings and Preferences
	Home View	• ViewCube
	Look At	• Display Controls
	Pan	• Display Controls
N/A	PATCH Workspace	• **Toolbar:** Change Workspace menu
N/A	Preferences	• **Account Settings and Preferences** • expand user name
	Projects	• Application Bar
	Save	• Application Bar
	Show Data Panel	• Application Bar
	Zoom	• Display Controls
	Zoom Window	• Display Controls

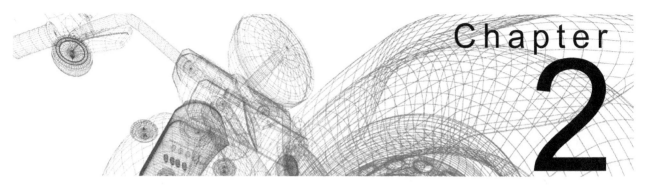

Getting Started in the FORM Environment

To begin the design process in the FORM contextual environment of the *DESIGN* workspace, you create a form feature. The type of form feature used is generally the shape that best represents the overall shape for the required geometry. The form geometry can be selected from an available list of quick shapes, or can be sketched. During creation, you set options that define the overall size and the control frame that define the T-Spline surface. Once created, you have preliminary T-Spline geometry that can be further manipulated to create the overall design.

This chapter discusses getting started and creating the available quick shapes. Sketched forms and the editing tools are discussed further later in this learning guide.

Learning Objective in this Chapter

- Create T-Spline surface geometry using the Box, Plane, Cylinder, Sphere, Torus, and Quadball quick shape tools.

2.1 Design Units and Origin

In addition to the default named views, the BROWSER of a new design also includes the **Document Settings** node (under which units are set) and the *Origin* folder.

Units

The default unit for a new design is millimeters (mm), as indicated in the **Units** node of the BROWSER, shown in Figure 2–1.

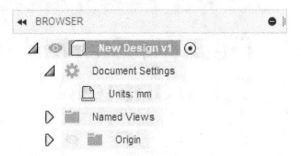

Figure 2–1

To change the active units, in the BROWSER, hover the cursor over the **Units** node and click (Change Active Units). In the CHANGE ACTIVE UNITS palette, you can select one of the unit types shown in Figure 2–2.

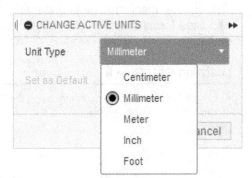

Figure 2–2

You can change the default units for a new design in the Preferences dialog box.

Once a new unit is assigned, you can select **Set as Default** to ensure that all new designs use the set unit type.

Origin

The *Origin* folder in the BROWSER (shown in Figure 2–3) contains the following items:

- Three orthogonal planes: XY plane, XZ plane, and YZ plane

- Three axes: X-axis, Y-axis, and Z-axis

- A center point O at the default (0,0,0) location

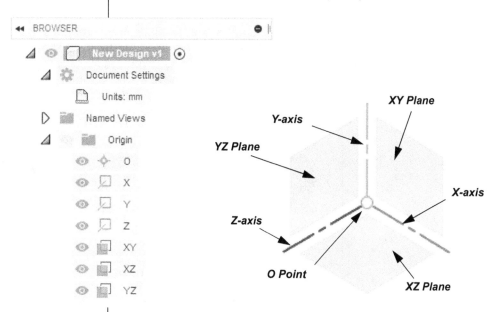

Figure 2–3

By default, when you create a new design, the origin features are not displayed because visibility is set as hidden for the *Origin* folder. Click (Show/Hide) to display the origin features.

2.2 Surface Quick Shapes

Similar to solid quick shapes, the Autodesk Fusion 360 software includes quick shape tools. These tools enable you to create basic, primitive shapes using the T-Spline surface geometry options from the FORM contextual environment of the *DESIGN* workspace. Using these tools, you can draw the sketch and create the 3D surface geometry at the same time.

Form Timeline icon:

The T-Spline quick shapes that can be created are: **Box**, **Plane**, **Cylinder**, **Sphere**, **Torus**, and **Quadball**, as shown in Figure 2–4. Surface geometry represents only the outer shell of the design, and does not have a solid volume. Once surfaces are modeled, they can be converted to a solid if the boundary is completely enclosed.

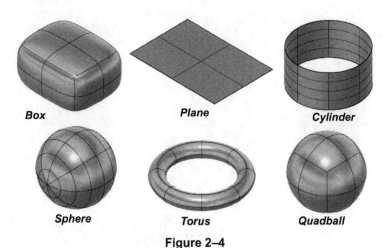

Box   *Plane*   *Cylinder*

Sphere   *Torus*   *Quadball*

Figure 2–4

*The **Quadball** primitive quick shape tool is the only shape that is available in the FORM environment but is not available in the SOLID environment of the DESIGN workspace. Because the quadball is a closed shape, once you return to the SOLID environment, it is automatically converted into a solid.*

The quick shape creation options are located in the toolbar in the CREATE panel, as shown in Figure 2–5.

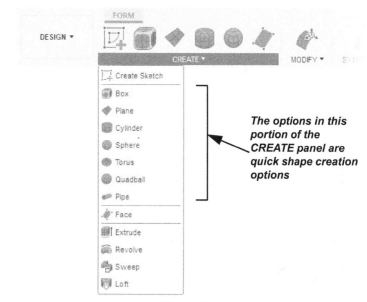

Figure 2–5

How To: Create a Primitive Quick Shape

1. In the CREATE panel, select the type of shape you want to create.
2. Select a plane or planar face to use as the placement plane for the shape.
3. Locate the center point for the shape on the selected plane. You can:

   • Select the projected model origin to locate the shape at the origin center point.

   • Select vertices on existing geometry.

   • Select anywhere on the placement plane.

4. Drag the mouse to define the extent of the shape. To define exact sizes for the shape, enter values in the dimension entry fields that display on the sketch. Click the left mouse button to complete the shape's sketch. The shape's palette opens (as shown in Figure 2–6) to finalize the shape.

- For a **Sphere** and **Quadball**, only the centerpoint needs to be selected before its palette opens to finish the shape.

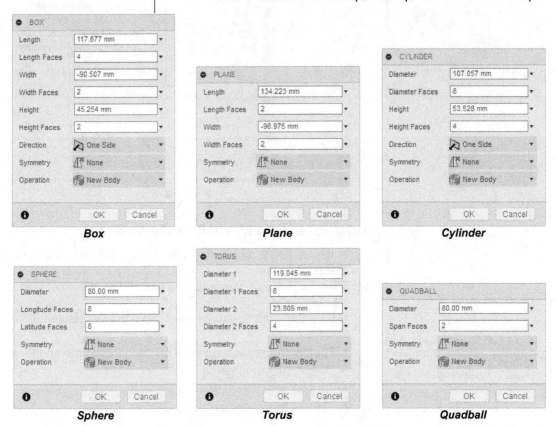

Figure 2–6

5. Define the shape's size using any of the following techniques:

- Drag the arrowheads that display on the model. The active arrowhead is displayed in blue. Select any of the other arrowheads to activate them for dragging. Figure 2–7 shows the default shape and arrowheads available for a Box and Cylinder.
- Enter values in the palette fields (shown in Figure 2–7).

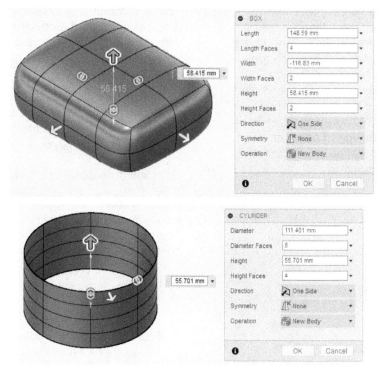

Figure 2–7

6. Enter the number of faces that are to be added in all directions, as shown in Figure 2–8.

The shape is more refined when more faces are added. However, using too many sides can also create too much control.

Length Faces = 6
Width Faces = 4
Height Faces = 2

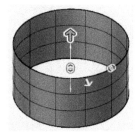

Diameter Faces = 12
Height Faces = 3

Figure 2–8

- For a Sphere, enter the number of faces in the longitudinal and latitudinal directions.
- For the Quadball, only a single face field (Span Faces) is provided.
- For a Torus, enter the number of faces for both diameter values.

Assigning symmetry ensures that changes to the shape that are made after creation affect the control frame in the same way on both sides of the symmetry line. Symmetry can also be assigned after form creation, or deleted, if required.

7. Assign symmetry by selecting **Mirror** in the Symmetry drop-down list, and then select the appropriate axis or directions in the creation dialog box.

   • Once assigned, green edges display as a dashed yellow edge to identify the symmetry lines

   • For a Cylinder, Sphere, Quadball, and Torus, you can define symmetry using the **Mirror** or **Circular** options. **Circular** defines symmetry to each edge within the shape.

8. For the Box and Cylinder shapes, select an option from the *Direction* drop-down list. Select ⬒ (One side) to extend the shape in one direction or ⬔ (Symmetric) to divide its height value equally on both sides of the placement plane.

9. The only Operation available for a shape in the FORM contextual environment is **New Body**.

10. Click **OK**.

   • The palette closes and the shape displays with its control frame.

   • If multiple shapes are added in the form feature, they are listed as individual bodies in the BROWSER, as shown in Figure 2–9 for the box and cylinder shapes. The shapes can be combined using the modification tools, if required.

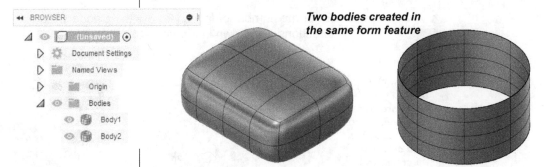

Two bodies created in the same form feature

Figure 2–9

   • Multiple form features can be included in a design. However, note that FORM contextual environment tools cannot be used to combine these features. The FORM tools are only available to combine bodies if they are in the same form feature.

Exiting the FORM Environment

To exit the FORM contextual environment, in the FINISH FORM panel, click ✓. You return to the SOLID environment with access to the solid modeling tools.

- If the form that was created is completely enclosed, a solid is automatically created to fill the volume of the T-Spline surface, as shown for the box in Figure 2–10. A single form icon(🔲) displays in the Timeline, and the *Bodies* folder in the BROWSER displays a 🔲, indicating that the form feature was converted to solid geometry.

*A Box, Sphere, Torus, and Quadball can all be used to create solid geometry once the **Finish Form** option is selected.*

Figure 2–10

*A Cylinder, Plane, and Face are all maintained as surfaces once the **Finish Form** option is selected.*

- If the form is not completely enclosed, the T-Spline surface remains as surface geometry, as shown for the Cylinder in Figure 2–11. A single form icon (🔲) displays in the Timeline, and the *Bodies* folder in the BROWSER displays a 🔲 for surface geometry.

Figure 2–11

Working with Existing Form Features

When working in a design, you might be required to edit an existing form feature or add additional form features.

- To add additional T-Spline surface geometry to an existing form, right-click on 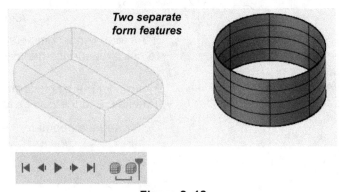 in the Timeline and select **Edit**.

  Alternatively, you can double-click on in the Timeline to access the FORM contextual environment.

- To add a second form, enter the FORM contextual environment again. A second form feature is added to the Timeline, as shown in Figure 2–12. Any existing form features display as transparent.

- A design can contain a single form feature or multiple form features. The choice to work with a single or multiple form features depends on how the two interact. If they are separate pieces of geometry that are only combined using solid or patch tools they can be separate. If the two must be edited to create a single shape that is modifiable in the FORM contextual environment it must be created as one form feature.

Figure 2–12

Practice 2a

T-Spline Surface Modeling: Creating Quick Shapes

Practice Objectives

- Create T-Spline surface geometry using a quick shape primitive.
- Vary the quantity of faces to explore the impact that the control frame size has on future modifications.
- Change the visual display and display mode for T-Spline surface geometry.

In this practice, you will learn how to access the FORM contextual environment of the *DESIGN* workspace and use a quick shape primitive to create a T-Spline surface in the design file. You will then create a second surface with a different quantity of faces and explore the impact that the quantity of faces can have on edits. Once the T-Spline surface geometry is created, you will return to the SOLID environment of the *DESIGN* workspace and review how it displays in the design.

Task 1 - Create a T-Spline Box design.

1. Select the *SculptPractice* tab along the top of the toolbar, if it is not already active, as shown in Figure 2–13.
   - This is the empty design that was created in the first chapter. If you do not have this design, in the Application Bar, click ■▼ (File)>**New Design** and save the design as **SculptPractice**.

Figure 2–13

2. To access the FORM contextual environment of the *DESIGN* workspace, in the CREATE panel, click 🌑 (Create Form).

3. In the CREATE panel, click ⬜ (Box).

4. When prompted to choose a plane, in the BROWSER, in the *Origin* folder, select the XZ plane. Alternatively, you can select the XZ plane directly in the graphics window.

5. Click on the Origin to select it as the center point, and then drag the profile to approximately 75mm x 75mm, similar to that shown in Figure 2–14. Click to finalize the box profile.

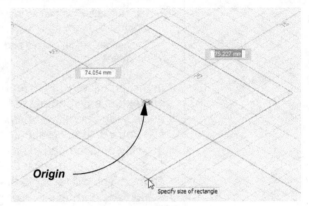

Figure 2–14

6. The BOX palette opens and the shape is automatically given a third dimension, similar to that shown in Figure 2–15. Manipulators on the box enable you to manipulate its size and number of faces.

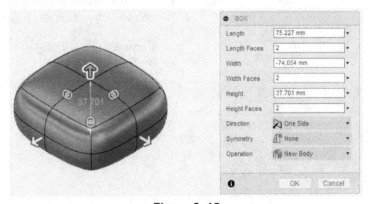

Figure 2–15

7. Select and drag any of the manipulator arrows to free-form adjust the length, width, or height of the box.

8. In the BOX palette, for the *Length*, *Width*, and *Height* fields, enter **75mm**.

9. In each of the three *Faces* fields, enter **3**. This divides each side of the box into 9 faces, as shown in Figure 2–16.

Alternatively, you can drag the  sliders in the model to change the number of faces.

Figure 2–16

10. In the Symmetry drop-down list, select **Mirror** to assign symmetry. Select **Width Symmetry** to ensure that symmetry is maintained in the width direction when faces are modified. The edges along the mirror line in the width direction change to green to indicate that symmetry has been assigned.

11. In the BOX palette, click **OK** to create the box.

12. In the lower left corner of the Autodesk Fusion 360 software window, in the Timeline, hover the cursor over , as shown in Figure 2–17. The icon is identified as **Form1** in the tooltip.

Figure 2–17

13. In the BROWSER, note that **Body1** has been added to the *Bodies* folder, and that the icon associated with **Body1** indicates that it is a T-Spline surface ( ).

14. In the toolbar, note that you are still in the FORM contextual environment of the *DESIGN* workspace. Additional T-Spline surface geometry can be added to this form.

15. To exit the FORM contextual environment, in the FINISH FORM panel, click  (Finish Form). The design file is returned to the SOLID environment and the geometry displays as shown in Figure 2–18. Note how the control edges and points are no longer visible.

Figure 2–18

16. In the BROWSER, note that the icon associated with **Body1** now indicates that it is a solid (⬜). This is because the surface was completely enclosed and automatically converts to a solid when you return to the SOLID environment.

Task 2 - Edit Form1 to create a second body in it.

In this task, you will create a second box that has the same size as the first, but that has a different number of faces.

1. In the Timeline, right-click on ⬜ and select **Edit**, as shown in Figure 2–19. This returns you to the FORM contextual environment where you can continue to edit and add to the T-Spline design.

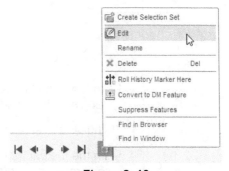

Figure 2–19

2. In the CREATE panel, click 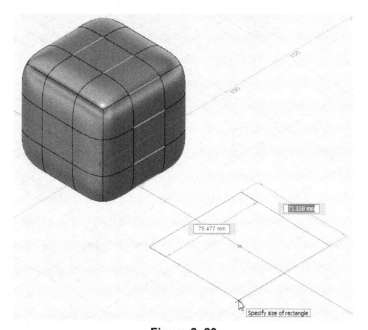 (Box) to create a second body.

3. When prompted to choose a plane, select the XZ plane.

4. Select a location on the XZ plane that is adjacent to the first box that was created, and then drag the profile to approximately **75mm x 75mm**, similar to that shown in Figure 2–20. Click to define the box profile.

Figure 2–20

5. In the BOX palette, for the *Length*, *Width*, and *Height* fields, enter **75mm**.

6. In the three *Faces* fields, enter **5**. This divides each side of the box into 25 faces, as shown in Figure 2–21. Note the slight difference in the rounded edges of the box due to the higher number of faces.

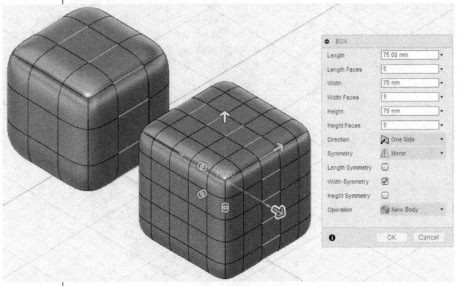

Figure 2–21

7. In the BOX palette, click **OK** to create the box.

8. In the BROWSER, note that **Body2** has been added to the *Bodies* folder.

Task 3 - Review the T-Spline Display Styles.

As a sculpted T-Spline model becomes more complex with multiple shapes interacting, you might notice a drop in computer performance. To improve performance, consider changing the Display Mode option.

1. The T-Spline display modes can only be controlled when working in a form feature.

2. In the UTILITIES panel, click (Display Mode). The DISPLAY MODE palette opens, as shown in Figure 2–22.

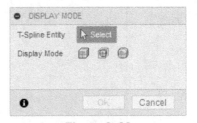

Figure 2–22

3. In the Display Mode area, select ⬚ (Box). The model displays as it does when you are creating T-Spline geometry.

4. Click **OK**. Note that the display setting remains active. Working in this mode can help improve system performance when you are working on complex form features.

5. In the UTILITIES panel, click ⬚ (Display Mode).

6. In the Display Mode area, select ⬚ (Control Frame). The model displays showing both the smooth and box forms. This can help you see the relationship between the lines and the smooth geometry.

7. Return to the **Smooth** display mode and then close the DISPLAY MODE palette.

Task 4 - Edit the two bodies by dragging a face.

1. In the MODIFY panel, click ⬚ (Edit Form). The EDIT FORM palette opens.

2. Select the middle face on the top surface of **Body1**, as shown in Figure 2–23.

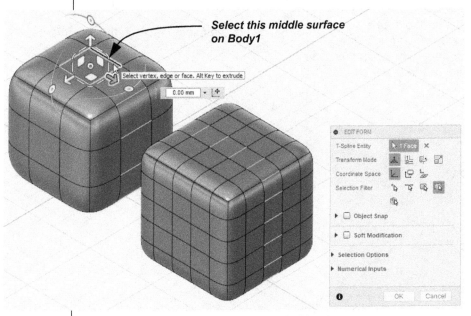

Figure 2–23

3. Select the vertical arrow over the face you selected and drag it above the body. Drag it to a distance of **20 mm**, as shown in Figure 2–24.

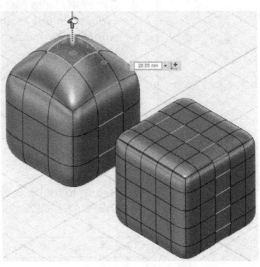

Figure 2–24

The EDIT FORM palette will be discussed in detail in a later chapter. It is being shown here to illustrate how the number of faces change the control frame curve network and how this changed the edits that are made to the shape.

4. In the EDIT FORM palette, click **OK** to complete the edit. Click anywhere in the graphics window to clear the face selection.

5. In the MODIFY panel, click   (Edit Form). The EDIT FORM palette opens.

6. Select the middle face on the top surface of **Body2**, as shown in Figure 2–25.

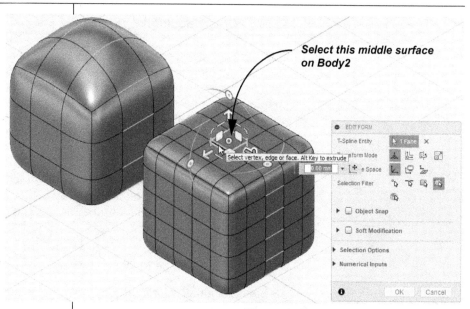

Figure 2–25

7. Select the vertical arrow over the selected face and drag it above the body to a distance of **30 mm**.

8. In the EDIT FORM palette, click **OK** to complete the edit. Note the difference in the shape of the two bodies shown in Figure 2–26. The larger quantity of faces on **Body2** provided a denser network and resulted in finer control over the edit.

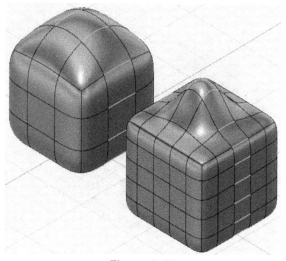

Figure 2–26

9. In the FINISH FORM panel, click 🌀 (Finish Form).

Task 5 - Create additional shapes.

In this task, you will create the cylinder and sphere shapes. The creation workflow for these shapes is similar to the one that you used to create the boxes in the previous task. You will create the shapes using a combination of free-form manipulation and manual entry to define their size.

1. In the CREATE panel, click ![icon] (Create Form).
   - This will create a second, independent form in the design file. Note that the first form is grayed-out, indicating that it is not active and cannot be selected as a reference.

2. In the CREATE panel, click ![icon] (Cylinder).

3. Select the XZ plane to locate the sketch.

4. Select a centerpoint for the cylinder that is adjacent to the boxes, similar to that shown in Figure 2–27.

5. Using the drag handles or entry fields, define the cylinder's *Diameter*, *Height*, and number of faces for each, as shown in Figure 2–27.

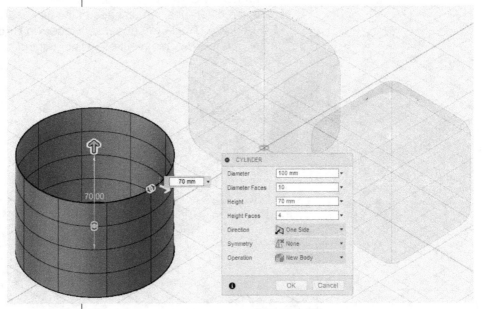

Figure 2–27

6. In the CYLINDER palette, click **OK** to create the cylinder.

7. In the FINISH FORM panel, click ![icon] (Finish Form).

8. In the Timeline, note that there are two forms listed in the design file, as shown in Figure 2–28.

Figure 2–28

9. In the BROWSER, expand the *Bodies* folder. Because the cylinder is not completely enclosed, note that the geometry is identified as surface geometry (⬚) when you are in the SOLID environment.

10. In the CREATE panel, click ⬛ (Create Form). In the CREATE panel, select ⬤ (Sphere).

11. Select the XZ plane.

12. Select a centerpoint for the sphere that is adjacent to the other bodies, as shown in Figure 2–29.

13. Unlike the **Box** and **Cylinder** tools, the **Sphere** tool does not start with a sketch. Instead, as soon as you select the center point, a 3D sphere is immediately added (similar to that shown in Figure 2–29), one arrow displays surrounding the shape, and the SPHERE palette opens.

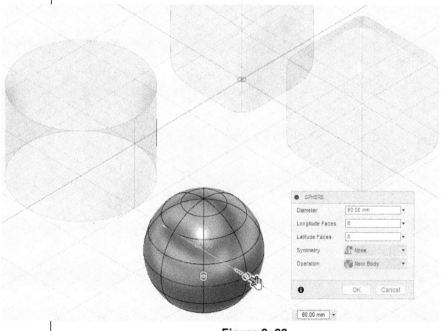

Figure 2–29

14. Drag the arrow to dynamically adjust the diameter, which is the only size value that can be defined for a sphere.

15. Click **OK** to create the sphere.

16. In the FINISH FORM panel, click (Finish Form).

17. Save the **SculptPractice** file.

Task 6 - (Optional) Create additional quick shapes.

1. Continue working in the current design file and create additional form features using the other quick shape primitive options:
   - Create a **Plane** form feature that lies on one of the construction planes.
   - Create a **Quadball**.

2. Save the file. Click in the *SculptPractice* window tab to close the file.

*The **Plane** and **Quadball** shape types are unique commands in the FORM environment that do not exist in the SOLID environment of the DESIGN workspace.*

Chapter Review Questions

1. Which of the following quick shape primitives can be created in both the SOLID and FORM environments of the *DESIGN* workspace? (Select all that apply.)

   a. Box

   b. Plane

   c. Cylinder

   d. Sphere

   e. Torus

   f. Quadball

2. When creating a Quadball T-Spline shape, how many different face entry fields can be modified to define the resulting control frame of the geometry?

   a. 1

   b. 2

   c. 4

   d. None

3. Symmetry can be assigned during the creation of the Box, Cylinder, Sphere, and Quadball quick shape primitives. The remaining quick shape primitives cannot have symmetry assigned during creation.

   a. True

   b. False

4. Which of the following statements are true based on the Cylinder T-Spline form shown in Figure 2–30? (Select all that apply.)

Figure 2–30

a. The ⊜ manipulator can be used to change the diameter of the cylinder.

b. The ⬆ manipulator can be used to change the height of the cylinder.

c. The *Height Faces* value is 6.

d. The *Height Faces* value is 8.

e. Symmetry has been set for the height direction.

5. When in the FORM contextual environment, you can create a second T-Spline surface within a previous form feature (i.e. Form1) by using the CREATE panel, clicking 🟤 (Create Form) and then selecting the required type.

a. True

b. False

Answers: 1.(a,c,d,e), 2.a, 3.b, 4.(b,c), 5.b

Command Summary

Button	Command	Location
	Box	• **Toolbar:** *DESIGN* Workspace>*SOLID* tab>CREATE panel
	Cylinder	• **Toolbar:** *DESIGN* Workspace>*SOLID* tab>CREATE panel
	Finish Form	• **Toolbar:** *DESIGN* Workspace>*SOLID* tab>FINISH FORM panel
	Plane	• **Toolbar:** *DESIGN* Workspace>*SOLID* tab>CREATE panel
	Quadball	• **Toolbar:** *DESIGN* Workspace>*SOLID* tab>CREATE panel
	Sphere	• **Toolbar:** *DESIGN* Workspace>*SOLID* tab>CREATE panel
	Torus	• **Toolbar:** *DESIGN* Workspace>*SOLID* tab>CREATE panel

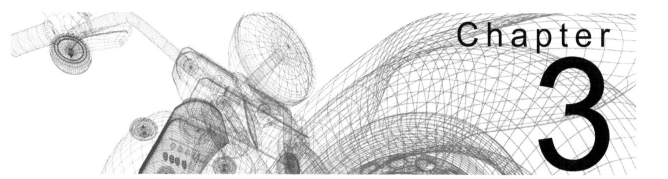

Filling Openings in a T-Spline Surface

To convert into a solid, a T-Spline body must not have any gaps or openings. In this chapter, the Face and Fill Hole options are discussed as ways to create T-Spline surface geometry that fill gaps in a design.

Learning Objectives in this Chapter

- Use the Face option to create planar and non-planar surfaces.
- Use the Fill Hole option to create planar and non-planar surfaces.

3.1 Creating a Face

The Face feature enables you to create irregular, planar, or non-planar surface geometry.

Depending on the existing reference points that are selected, faces can be planar or non-planar. The selection of existing points cannot prevent the model from returning to Smooth display, otherwise the T-Spline geometry will fail when the form is finished.

- Faces can be used to close an opening (as shown in Figure 3–1) by selecting existing points on a form feature. Once you begin selecting existing points, the display mode changes to Box mode to make the selection easier.

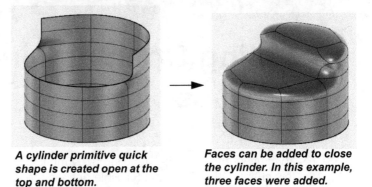

A cylinder primitive quick shape is created open at the top and bottom.

Faces can be added to close the cylinder. In this example, three faces were added.

Figure 3–1

- A face can be created by selecting points on a placement plane. This type of face is planar, as shown in Figure 3–2.

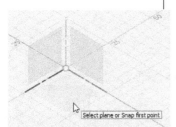

Select a placement plane to begin creation

Select points on the plane to define the corners of the face

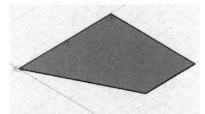

A face that is defined by selecting points on the plane is planar

Figure 3–2

Face features that are created on a plane and do not reference any existing T-Spline entities do not generate a control frame mesh. In the next chapter in this learning guide, you will learn to use the modification tools to add edges and additional vertices to faces.

Hint: Filling Holes Using a Face Operation

You can use a **Face** operation to fill an opening that is planar. However, when the opening lies in a single plane, the **Fill Hole** is a more efficient tool to use.

How To: Create a Face

1. In the CREATE panel, select ✎ (Face). The FACE palette opens, as shown in Figure 3–3.

Figure 3–3

By default, if you select individual points without referencing existing entities, the points create a planar face.

2. Set how the face is to be created using the options in the *Mode* area:

   - ⬚ **(Simple):** Select individual points to define the face.

   - ⊞ **(Edge):** Select an existing edge and two points to define the face.

   - ⬓ **(Chain):** Create additional faces around a chain of edges.

3. Define the number of corners in the face in the *Number of Sides* area:

   - ▢ **(Four Sides):** Creates a face with four boundary points.

   - ⬠ **(Multiple Sides)**: Creates a face with any number of points. To complete the face, you must select the first selected point a second time.

4. Enable the **Object Snap** option, if required, to snap to objects. Once the option is enabled you can define an offset value from a snapped point to aid in creating the face.

5. Select points and edges to define the face.

6. Once you re-select the starting point, the face is defined. You can continue to create additional faces on the defined placement plane, or click **OK** to complete face creation.

3.2 Filling a Hole

When using some of the form quick shape creation options, geometry is often open at the top and bottom when it is created. In addition to using the **Face** option to close the gap, you can also use the **Fill Hole** option. This option enables you to select an edge in a chain to close a hole. The hole can be of any shape, as long as all of the edges are connected to one another.

Examples of surfaces that have been created using the Fill Hole option are shown in Figure 3–4. In each example, the three fill hole mode options are displayed to show how the resulting geometry can vary.

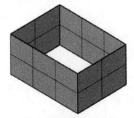
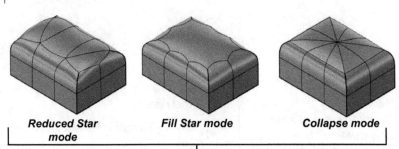

Original Extruded Sketch   **Reduced Star mode**   **Fill Star mode**   **Collapse mode**

Fill Hole option used to close a gap

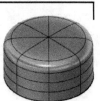

Original Cylinder Quick Shape   **Reduced Star mode**   **Fill Star mode**   **Collapse mode**

Figure 3–4

Consider the following tips when filling a hole:

- Use **Fill Star** mode if minimal distortion of the shape is required. Note that it is good practice to use as few star points as possible. **Reduced Star** mode is recommended if you need to maintain symmetry.

- If **Collapse** mode is selected, enable the **Weld Center Vertices** option to weld the vertices at the center.

- Enable the **Maintain Crease Edges** option to keep any creased edges when filling the hole. An example of how this option affects a model is shown in Figure 3–5.

Maintain Crease Edges

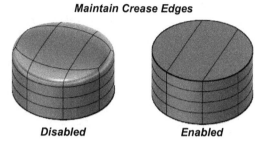

Disabled   *Enabled*

Figure 3–5

How To: Fill a Hole

1. In the MODIFY panel, select  (Fill Hole). The FILL HOLE palette opens, as shown in Figure 3–6.

FILL HOLE	
T-Spline Edge	▶ Select
Fill Hole Mode	ⓘ Reduced Sl... ▼
Maintain Crease Edges	☑

Figure 3–6

2. Select any one of the edges along the chain of edges that is being filled. A preview of the geometry displays. The edge selected as the reference is highlighted in blue.

3. **Reduced Star** is the default *Fill Hole Mode* option. Change this option to **Fill Star** or **Collapse to** vary the shape of the new surface as needed to capture the required shape. The three fill options are shown in Figure 3–4.

4. Depending on the *Fill Hole Mode* that was used, additional options might be available:
   - **Maintain Crease Edges:** Available for all modes, it enables you to fill the hole with a creased edge that creates a flat face.
   - **Weld Center Vertices:** Available for the **Collapse** mode, enables you to weld all of the points that merge together at any one point.

5. Click **OK** to complete the geometry.

Practice 3a

T-Spline Surface Modeling: Closing Gaps

Practice Objectives

- Create T-Spline surface geometry using the quick shape primitives.
- Add T-Spline surfaces to fill gaps in the geometry.

In this practice, you will use multiple options to close gaps in a design. Once the T-Spline surface geometry is created, you will return to the SOLID environment of the *DESIGN* workspace and review how it displays in the design.

Task 1 - Create a T-Spline cylinder design.

1. In the Application Bar, click ![icon] (File)>**New Design** and save the design as **Fill**.

2. In the CREATE panel, click ![icon] (Create Form).

3. In the CREATE panel, click ![icon] (Cylinder).

4. Select the XZ plane to locate the sketch plane.

5. Select the origin point as the centerpoint for the cylinder. Drag outwards click to define the diameter of the cylinder.

6. Using the drag handles or entry fields, define the cylinder size and number of faces as shown in Figure 3–7.

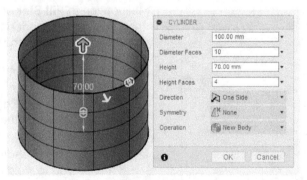

Figure 3–7

7. In the CYLINDER palette, click **OK** to create the cylinder.

Task 2 - Fill gaps in the cylinder form.

In this task, you will use two different T-Spline surface creation options: **Face** and **Fill Hole**. You will use both options so that you can compare the resulting shapes.

1. In the MODIFY panel, click ⬙ (Fill Hole).

2. Select any of the edges along the top chain of edges of the cylinder. In the *Fill Hole Mode* drop-down list, select **Reduced Star**, if not already selected. A preview of the geometry displays similar to that shown in Figure 3–8. Note that the selected edge is highlighted in yellow.

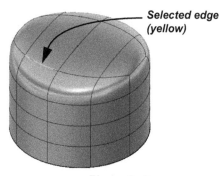

Selected edge (yellow)

Figure 3–8

3. Change the *Fill Hole Mode* option to **Collapse** to vary the shape of the new T-Spline surface. The resulting geometry is displayed as shown in Figure 3–9.

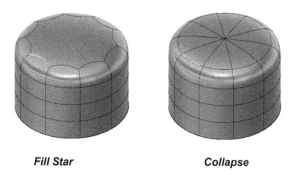

Fill Star   **Collapse**

Figure 3–9

4. Return the *Fill Hole Mode* option to **Reduced Star**.

*When working in the FORM contextual environment, all geometry is additive and no feature history is stored. For this reason, the **Undo** command is the only way to remove individual features in the design. Note that features can only be removed in the reverse order to how they were initially created.*

5. Click **OK** to complete the geometry. Note that a new form is not created, and instead the geometry is combined with the cylinder. The geometry acts as one T-Spline.

6. In the Application Bar, click ↰ (Undo) to remove the face from the display.

7. In the MODIFY panel, click ⬦ (Fill Hole).

8. Select an edge in the same loop of edges. This time, create a flat face is that does not round into the cylinder by selecting the **Maintain Crease Edges** option. This will create the face shown in Figure 3–10.

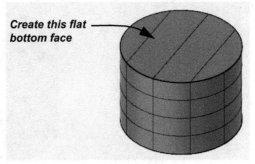

Create this flat bottom face

Figure 3–10

9. Rotate the design so that the opening on the other end is displayed.

10. In the CREATE panel, click ◆ (Face).

11. In the *Mode* area, ensure that ▣ (Simple) is selected.

12. In the *Number of Sides* area, select ⬠ (Multiple Sides).

13. Click to select the first point to start the face shown in Figure 3–11.

14. Click to select the second point shown in Figure 3–11.

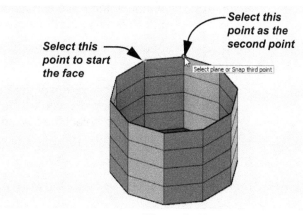

Figure 3–11

15. Continue to select each point around the edge in a clockwise direction. To complete the face, click to select the start point a second time (shown in Figure 3–12).

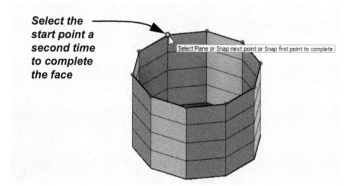

Figure 3–12

16. In the FACE palette, click **OK** to finish the face. The geometry displays as shown in Figure 3–13. This is the same as the geometry that was created using the **Fill Hole** option with the **Fill Star** *Fill Hole* mode.

Figure 3–13

17. Although the **Face** command can be used to fill the hole, the **Fill Hole** option is the more efficient option to use for openings that are planar. Click ↰ (Undo) in the Application Bar.

18. To show the benefit of the **Face** command to close non-planar gaps, you will delete faces in the model. Hold <Ctrl> and select the five adjacent faces shown in Figure 3–14.

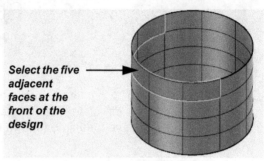

Select the five adjacent faces at the front of the design

Figure 3–14

19. Press <Delete> to delete the faces. The design updates as shown in Figure 3–15.

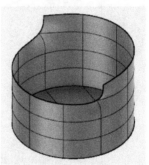

Figure 3–15

20. Restart the **Face** option.

21. In the *Mode* area, ensure that ▣ (Simple) is selected.

22. In the *Number of Sides* area, select ⬠ (Multiple Sides).

23. Select the first point (shown in Figure 3–16) to start the face and continue selecting in a clockwise direction around the top edge of the cylinder.

Select this point to start the face

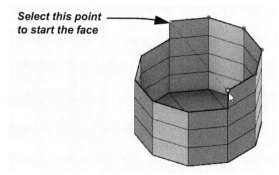

Figure 3–16

24. Select the first point a second time to complete the face. The face displays as shown in Figure 3–17.

- Do not click **OK**. You will add two additional faces before clicking **OK**.

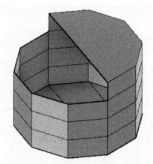

Figure 3–17

25. Once all three faces are completed, the T-Spline control frame will generate and merge all of the faces together.

26. In the *Number of Sides* area, select ▭ (Four Sides).

27. Select the same start point (shown in Figure 3–18) to begin the creation of the next face. Select the three points shown in Figure 3–18 to define the face. When using the ▭ (Four Sides) option the face is generated after the selection of any four points and eliminates you having to reselect the start point to finish the face.

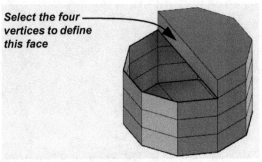

Select the four vertices to define this face

Figure 3–18

Tip: To create 3-sided faces, select the same point for both the 3rd and 4th selection.

28. With the FACE palette still open, use the **Multiple Sides** option to create the final face to close the opening (as shown in Figure 3–19).

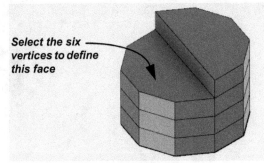

Select the six vertices to define this face

Figure 3–19

29. Click **OK** to complete the face creation. The new faces create the geometry shown in Figure 3–20.

Fill Hole using the Reduced Star option creates a similar face.

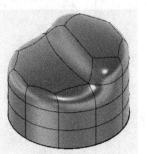

Figure 3–20

30. Undo the creation of the last face. Note how only one of the faces was removed, as shown in Figure 3–21.

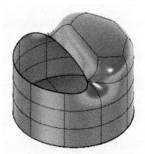

Figure 3–21

31. Use the **Fill Hole** option to fill the gap with the **Reduced Star** Fill Hole mode.

- Note how the **Fill Hole** option provides different control frame shapes (as shown in Figure 3–22) than the single type that is provided with the **Face** option. When choosing whether to use the **Face** or **Fill Hole** options, consider the resulting control frame of points, edges, and faces that are created. In the next chapter, you will learn about the editing tools and how the control frame affects the edits.

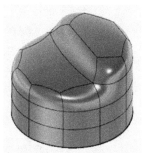

Figure 3–22

32. Click **OK** to finish the face.

33. Finish the form feature and save the design.

Chapter Review Questions

1. Once you begin selecting existing points to locate a Face feature, the display mode temporarily changes to the _____ display style to ease selection.

   a. Box

   b. Smooth

   c. Control Frame

2. The _____ option enables you to create a face by selecting points on an origin plane.

   a. **Fill Hole**

   b. **Face**

3. When using commands to fill gaps in a T-Spline surface design file, which of the following are true? (Select all that apply.)

   a. The **Face** option enables you to create a face by referencing existing vertices in the design file to fill gaps.

   b. The **Face** option can be used to create a simple planar face between points that are placed on a construction plane.

   c. The **Fill Hole** option enables you to select a mode that defines the shape (i.e., control frame) of the new surface.

   d. The **Fill Hole** option enables you to define the area to fill by selecting points on the edges.

4. The _____ option enables you to close an opening on a cylinder with a flat face.

   a. **Face**

   b. **Fill Hole**

Answers: 1.a, 2.b, 3.(a,b,c), 4.b

Command Summary

Button	Command	Location
	Face	• **Toolbar:** *DESIGN* Workspace>*FORM* tab>CREATE panel
	Fill Hole	• **Toolbar:** *DESIGN* Workspace>*FORM* tab>MODIFY panel

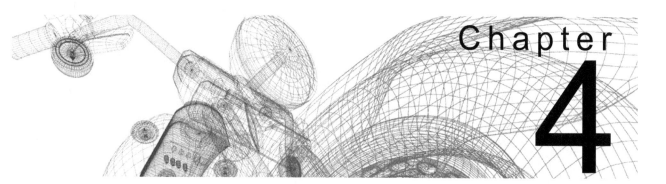

Attaching Canvases

An image can be imported and used as a reference for defining the shape of your T-Spline surface geometry.

Learning Objective in this Chapter

- Attach a canvas image to a plane in the design.

4.1 Working with a Canvas

A commonly used design approach is to insert an image file into your design and then use the image as a guide in creating the required geometry, as shown in Figure 4–1. This is particularly useful when a concept sketch is created on paper, and then translated to a digital image that can be used in design programs like the Autodesk Fusion 360 software. The inserted image is called a canvas.

Sketched Profile of a water bottle design saved as a .JPG file

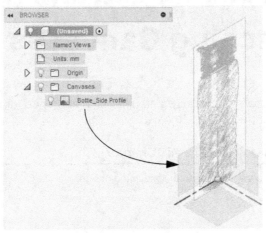

The image file has been attached to the YZ plane in a new design

Completed design based on the conceptual sketch

Figure 4–1

How To: Attach a Canvas

A canvas can be added to the design in any of the SOLID, FORM, or SURFACE environments of the DESIGN workspace using the same process.

1. In the INSERT panel, click ![icon] (Canvas). The CANVAS palette displays as shown in Figure 4–2.

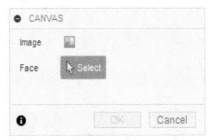

Figure 4–2

2. Expand the *Origin* folder in the BROWSER and select a plane. Alternatively, select a plane in the graphics window.

- Existing planar geometry can also be selected as a placement plane for a canvas.

Supported image file types include .PNG, .JPG, .JPEG, and .TIF.

3. In the CANVAS palette, click 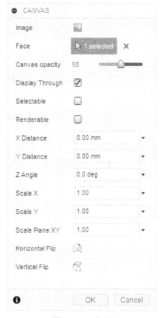. In the Open dialog box, browse to and open the image. The image is placed on the selected plane. The palette updates (as shown in Figure 4–3) with additional options.

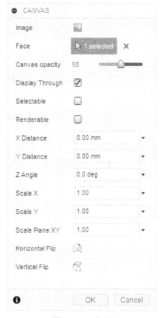

Figure 4–3

4. Customize the visibility and selection options for the canvas:
   - Adjust the *Canvas opacity* slider value to control whether you can see through the image and to what degree.
   - Enable the **Display Through** option so that the image can be seen through any geometry that might be placed on one or the other sides of the image.
   - Enable the **Selectable** option so that you can select the image in the graphics window. If not enabled, you can only select the image in the BROWSER.

Lower opacity values enable you to visualize both the image and the design geometry.

5. To reposition the image on the plane, consider the following:
   - Select the arrow or rotation manipulator to activate it and drag to move or rotate the image, respectively.
   - Enter values in the *X/Y Distance* or *Z Angle* fields to move or rotate the image, respectively.

6. To resize the image on the plane, consider the following:
   - Select the scale manipulator to activate it and drag to resize the image.

- Enter values in the *Scale X, Scale Y,* or *Scale Plane XY* fields to resize the image in an individual direction, or in both directions at the same time.

7. Use the flip buttons to flip the image in the horizontal ( ) and vertical directions ( ).

8. Click **OK** in the CANVAS palette to complete the placement of the image. The canvas is added to the BROWSER in the *Canvasses* folder, and is named using the image file name. Figure 4–4 shows an image placed on the YZ origin plane.

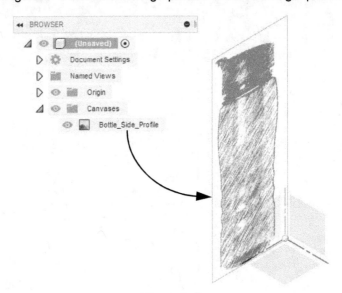

Figure 4–4

Calibrating a Canvas

When an image is attached to a plane, it is automatically fit to the plane. The scaling options that are available when placing the image enable you manipulate its size, but do not provide a method to resize the image to a specific size. Once an image is placed, you can use the **Calibrate** option as a more exact resizing tool. It enables you to measure between two points on the image so that you can enter the required distance. Once the value is entered, the image is scaled accordingly. This is an important step if you are planning to use the image as a reference when creating geometry.

How To: Calibrate an Attached Canvas

1. In the BROWSER, expand the *Canvases* folder. Right-click

   on the image's name and click ⊢ (Calibrate).
2. Select two points on the image to measure the current size of
   the image. The points selected should represent a known or
   desired dimension on the image. The *Dimension Value* field
   displays once the second point is selected. This process is
   shown in Figure 4–5.

*Select a second point on the
canvas plane to complete the
measurement*

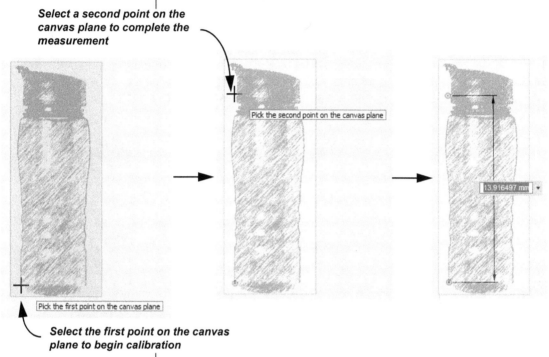

Pick the second point on the canvas plane

13.916497 mm

Pick the first point on the canvas plane

*Select the first point on the canvas
plane to begin calibration*

Figure 4–5

3. Enter a value and press <Enter>. The image resizes so that
   the actual distance between the two selected points in the
   image is updated to the entered value.

Practice 4a

T-Spline Surface Modeling: Modeling from a Sketch

Practice Objectives

- Attach a canvas image to a plane in the design.
- Create T-Spline surface geometry to match a canvas image.

In this practice, you will work in the FORM contextual environment to create the initial shapes of a plastic water bottle. This will be done by importing a canvas image and using the sketch to create two matching cylindrical T-Spline bodies (as shown in Figure 4–6). You will continue the design in the next chapter where you will edit the T-Spline's control mesh to further shape and complete the water bottle design.

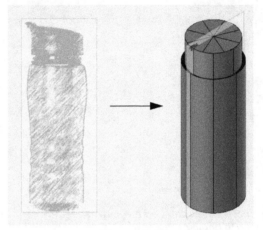

Figure 4–6

Task 1 - Start a new design and insert a canvas image.

1. Click (File)>**New Design**.

2. In the INSERT panel, click (Canvas). The CANVAS palette displays, as shown in Figure 4–7.

Figure 4–7

3. Expand the *Origin* folder in the BROWSER and select the YZ plane, or select it in the graphics window.

4. In the CANVAS palette, click ![icon]. In the Open dialog box, browse to and open the **Bottle_Side_Profile.jpg** image from the practice files folder.

5. Change the *Canvas opacity* slider value to approximately **33**, if not already set. This enables you to see through the image.

6. Zoom in to the image to enlarge it, similar to that shown in Figure 4–8.

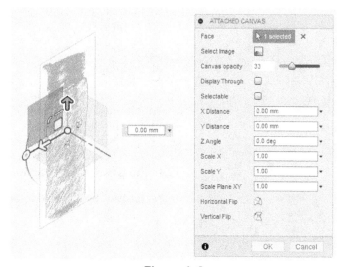

Figure 4–8

7. To reposition the image on the plane, click **RIGHT** on the ViewCube to rotate the image so that it is planar in the graphics window.

8. Click on the arrow manipulator that is currently pointing up (X direction) to activate it. The arrow turns blue when activated.

9. Drag the image up so that the bottom of the bottle approximately aligns with the Z-axis, as shown in Figure 4–9.

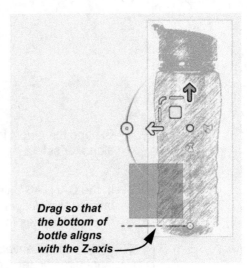

Drag so that the bottom of bottle aligns with the Z-axis

Figure 4–9

10. Click on the arrow manipulator that is currently pointing to the left (Y-direction) to activate it. It will turn blue when activated. Drag the image so that the Origin point is positioned along the central axis of the bottle.

11. Click **OK** in the CANVAS palette to complete the placement of the image.

The overall size of the image is unknown and must be scaled appropriately prior to using it as a reference in your design. In the CANVAS palette there were scale fields, but without knowing the size of the image, it is difficult to ensure that the scale is correct.

12. In the BROWSER, expand the *Canvases* folder. Right-click

on **Bottle_Side_Profile** and click ⊢ (Calibrate).

13. Select the two points on the bottle image shown in Figure 4–10 to measure the current size of the image. The size displays once the second point is selected. This value varies depending on your selection location.

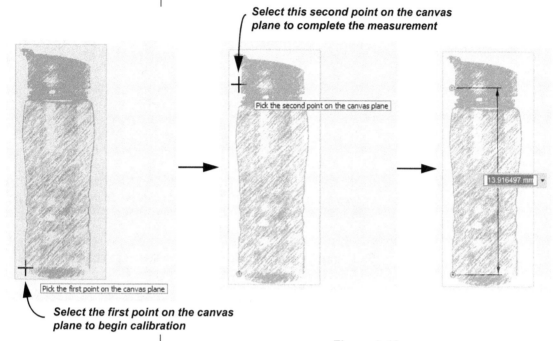

Select this second point on the canvas plane to complete the measurement

Pick the second point on the canvas plane

13.916497 mm

Pick the first point on the canvas plane

Select the first point on the canvas plane to begin calibration

Figure 4–10

14. In the *Dimension Value* field, enter **190mm** as the new value and then press <Enter> to resize the image. This value was used because the design intent requires the bottle to be approximately 190 mm in height.

15. Save the design as **WaterBottle**.

Task 2 - Create cylinder quick shapes to represent the overall design.

---

1. In the CREATE panel, click (Create Form).

2. In the CREATE panel, click (Cylinder).

3. Select the XZ plane to locate the sketch plane. This plane is at the bottom of the bottle image.

4. Select the Origin as the centerpoint for the cylinder, as shown in Figure 4–11.

5. Define the diameter of the cylinder by dragging to the outer edge of the bottle, as shown in Figure 4–11.

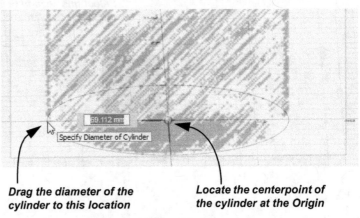

Drag the diameter of the cylinder to this location **Locate the centerpoint of the cylinder at the Origin**

Figure 4–11

6. Using the drag handles or entry fields in the palette, define the cylinder height as shown in Figure 4–12. Extend the cylinder a little ways into the bottle to ensure that the threaded portion of the bottle fits into the cap.

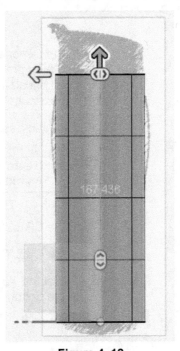

Figure 4–12

7. Drag the diameter slightly inside the bottle so that you can see the outer shape of the bottle. This helps you determine the number of faces to assign.

8. In the *Height Faces* field, enter **10**. Note how the horizontal control lines don't match up with the wavy sketched shape in the lower half of the bottle.

9. Change the *Height Faces* value to **12** value. The control lines line up more closely with the shape, as shown in Figure 4–13. This will make it easier for you to manipulate the cylinder's overall shape.

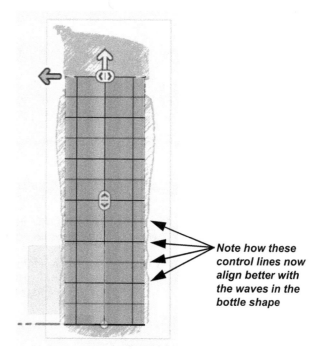

Note how these control lines now align better with the waves in the bottle shape

Figure 4–13

10. Drag the diameter of the cylinder so that it extends to the widest points on the bottle, as shown in Figure 4–14.

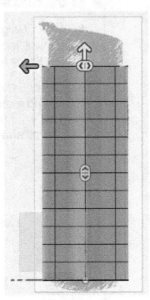

Figure 4–14

11. In the CYLINDER palette, click **OK** to create the cylinder.

12. In the FINISH FORM panel, click (Finish Form) to complete the creation of the first form feature.

13. Expand the *Bodies* folder in the BROWSER and hide the visibility of the cylinder by clicking (Show/Hide) adjacent to **Body1**.

14. In the CREATE panel, click (Create Form). Confirm that you want to enter the FORM contextual environment.

15. To create a workplane for the creation of the lid geometry, in the CONSTRUCT panel, click (Offset Plane). Select the XZ plane at the bottom of the bottle image and drag up to create the new plane at the bottom edge of the lid, as shown in Figure 4–15.

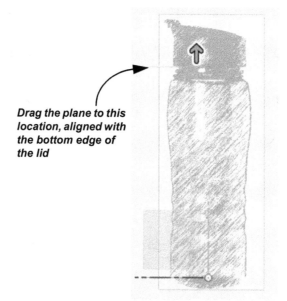

Drag the plane to this location, aligned with the bottom edge of the lid

Figure 4–15

16. Using the same techniques previously discussed, create a new cylindrical body to represent the lid, as shown in Figure 4–16. Remember that only the overall shape of the lid is required. Adjustments to the shape to create the arc and carabiner clip tab will be designed using other tools.

Figure 4–16

17. Once the lid form feature is completed, review the *Bodies* folder in the BROWSER. Toggle on the display of **Body1** by clicking  (Show/Hide) adjacent to it.

18. Rename each body as shown in Figure 4–17. Note that the bracketed numbers (e.g., (1)) are added automatically and cannot be changed.

Figure 4–17

19. Hide the display of the Origin features.

Task 3 - Fill the holes at the bottom of the bottle or top of the lid.

---

1. In the Timeline, right-click on the first form feature in the list, which represents the body of the bottle. Select **Edit**.

2. Rotate the model as shown in Figure 4–18 to view the bottom of the design.

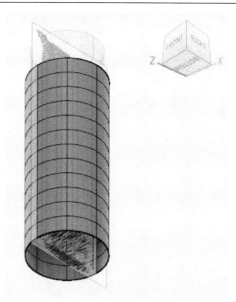

Figure 4–18

3. In the MODIFY panel, use the **Fill Hole** option to close the opening on the bottom of the bottle. The model should display as shown in Figure 4–19.

- Since the bottle is required to have a flat bottom, you must ensure that there are no control frame edges on it. Once the model is converted into a solid, a fillet feature can be added to create a smooth filleted edge.

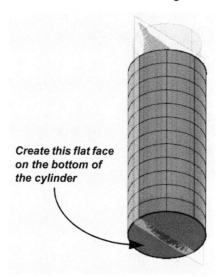

Create this flat face on the bottom of the cylinder

Figure 4–19

4. Finish the form feature that was used to create the Bottle body.

5. Edit the second form feature to add a flat top to the lid, as shown in Figure 4–20.

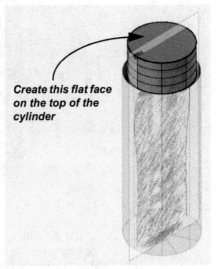

Create this flat face on the top of the cylinder

Figure 4–20

6. Finish the form.

7. Save the design and close the tab. Further changes to the water bottle will be made later in this learning guide once you learn how to use the **Edit Form** option.

Chapter Review Questions

1. Which of the following is not a supported file type for a canvas image?

   a. .PNG

   b. .JPG/.JPEG

   c. .BMP

   d. .TIF

2. Which of the following can be used as a placement reference to place a canvas image? (Select all that apply.)

   a. Origin Center Point

   b. Origin Plane

   c. Planar face on an existing solid

   d. Curved face on an surface

3. Which of the following can be done through the CANVAS palette to customize the canvas image? (Select all that apply.)

   a. Set the canvas' display and opacity.

   b. Set whether the canvas displays through any geometry that is created around it.

   c. Reposition the canvas in the X, Y, or Z directions.

   d. Measure the distance between two points to assign its actual value.

   e. Flip the display of the canvas on the placement plane.

4. The ⊢ (Calibrate) option can be used to resize only the height of the image to a specified value.

   a. True

   b. False

Answers: 1.c, 2.b,c, 3.(a,b,c,e), 4.b

Command Summary

Button	Command	Location
	Attached Canvas	• **Toolbar:** *DESIGN* Workspace>*SOLID* tab>INSERT panel • **Toolbar:** *DESIGN* Workspace>*FORM* tab>INSERT panel • **Toolbar:** *DESIGN* Workspace> *SURFACE* tab>INSERT panel
	Calibrate	• **BROWSER:** Right-click on the image name

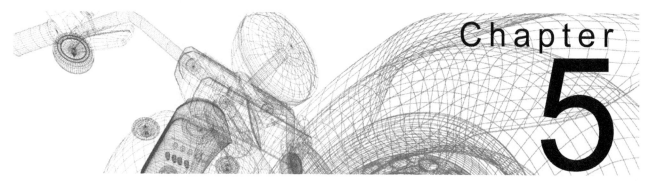

Editing T-Spline Geometry

The FORM contextual environment of the *DESIGN* workspace includes a number of editing tools that enable you to refine sculpted geometry by manipulating the faces, edges, and points that form the geometry's control frame. If the control frame does not provide you with the faces, edges, and points that are required, additional tools are available to create and change these entities.

Learning Objectives in this Chapter

- Manipulate points, edges, and faces in a T-Spline model to define its shape using the Edit Form command.
- Delete points, edges, and faces from a T-Spline body.
- Use specific edge, point, and face commands to manipulate the control frame of a T-Spline body.
- Assign symmetry to a T-Spline body.
- Use the Thicken command to offset a duplicate of the body.

5.1 Editing Form Geometry

To edit a form feature it must be active. To activate it, right-click on  *in the Timeline and select **Edit,** or double-click on its icon.*

When in the FORM contextual environment of the *DESIGN* workspace, the primary command that is used to manipulate geometry is the (Edit Form) option. This option enables you to select points, edges, faces, bodies, or loops on a control frame to enable a manipulator triad which you can drag to change the shape of a T-Spline surface. In the example shown in Figure 5–1, a Box was used to create the geometry shown on the left, and then manipulated using the **Edit Form** option to create the geometry on the right.

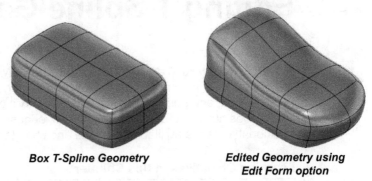

Box T-Spline Geometry   **Edited Geometry using Edit Form option**

Figure 5–1

Feature history is not recorded to account for each of the edits. While you can undo actions during an individual session, the creation history is lost once the model is closed.

To edit a T-Spline control frame using the Edit Form option, complete the following steps.

1. In the MODIFY panel, click (Edit Form). The EDIT FORM palette opens, as shown in Figure 5–2.

Figure 5–2

2. Select an element to edit. Points, edges, faces, bodies, and edge loops can be selected. The triad center is placed on the selected reference entity that is displayed in blue.

- To select multiple entities, hold <Ctrl> while selecting them, or drag a selection window over the entities.
- To select an edge loop, double-click on an edge.
- To select a body, double-click on a face.

Figure 5–3 shows the manipulator triads that display when each element type is selected.

Manipulator triad on a point *Manipulator triad on an edge* *Manipulator triad on a face*

Manipulator triad on a body *Manipulator triad on an edge loop*

Figure 5–3

3. (Optional) Filter and control the selected entities.

- In the *Selection Filter* area, select the element type that is to be selectable. The options include the following:

Icon	Description
	When selected, only points are available for selection.
	When selected, only edges are available for selection.
	When selected, only faces are available for selection.
	When selected, points, edges, and faces are all available.
	When selected, a body is available for selection.

- Expand the *Selection Options* area to further control the entities that are being selected. For example, commands enable you to select next references, invert selections, or select a range of entities.

To change the Display Mode while editing, select the required mode in the Selection Options area.

4. (Optional) Filter the manipulator types that are displayed on the entity's triad using the options in the *Transform Mode* area. The available options enable you to determine whether it displays controls for (⬚) Translation, ⬚ (Rotation), ⬚ (Scaling) or all of the controls at the same time (⬚), as shown in Figure 5–4. The default setting is to show all of the manipulator types.

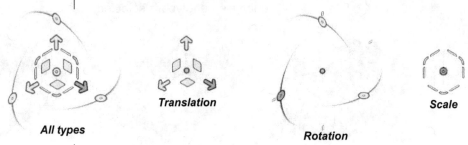

All types   **Translation**   **Rotation**   **Scale**

Figure 5–4

5. (Optional) In the *Coordinate Space* area, define the coordinate space that is to be used. This enables you to control the orientation of the manipulator triad.

- ⬚ (World): Sets the orientation with the model origin orientation. This is the default setting.

- ⬚ (View): Sets the orientation relative to the current view of the model.

- ⬚ (Local): Sets the orientation relative to the selected object.

6. (Optional) Use the remaining options as required:

- Click **Object Snap** to move selected vertices to the closest point on objects in the scene. Vertices can snap to a solid, surface, or mesh body. The Snap Direction setting sets the coordinate space for snapping. Enter an offset value, as required.

- **Soft Modification** causes the edit actions to have a more gradual impact on adjacent surfaces. When enabled, you are provided additional controls to define the *Selection Type* and *Falloff Type* for the modification.

7. Reposition the geometry using any of the following techniques to manipulate the shape of the control frame.

- Select the triad controls to reposition the geometry. Each control on the triad enables you to manipulate the geometry in a different way. Figure 5–5 shows the controls and describes their uses. You can only manipulate one triad at a time.

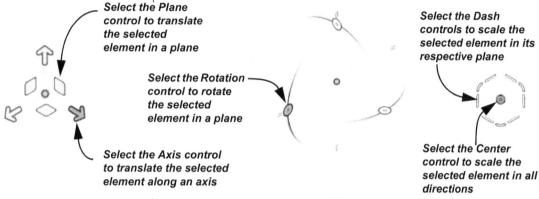

Select the Plane control to translate the selected element in a plane

Select the Rotation control to rotate the selected element in a plane

Select the Axis control to translate the selected element along an axis

Select the Dash controls to scale the selected element in its respective plane

Select the Center control to scale the selected element in all directions

Figure 5–5

- Enter values in the mini-toolbar entry field. The available field depends on the active triad control. This value is not parametric and is not tied to the model.
- Expand the *Numerical Inputs* area to enter values.

8. Continue to select elements on the T-Spline's control frame and make changes, as required.
9. Click **OK** to complete the edit.

Figure 5–6 shows the original and final geometry after multiple edits were made to a Cylinder T-Spline shape.

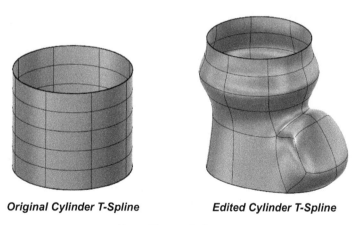

Original Cylinder T-Spline   **Edited Cylinder T-Spline**

Figure 5–6

Hint: Extruding Faces

To extrude a selected face or edge using the **Edit Form** option (as opposed to translating it), hold <Alt> and drag the required translation manipulator. Figure 5–7 shows the difference in a translated face manipulation with and without using <Alt>. Similar results can be obtained using the **Extrude** option that is discussed later in this learning guide.

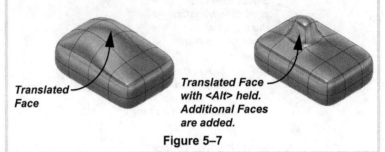

Translated Face

Translated Face with <Alt> held. Additional Faces are added.

Figure 5–7

Hint: Freezing Geometry

Located on the MODIFY panel, the   (Freeze) option enables you to select and lock a face or edge so that it remains in its current position and locks it to prevents movement.

Once frozen, a selected face or edge's color changes to white and a light-blue control frame color displays on its adjacent edges to identify the entities that cannot be edited.

5.2 Deleting Entities

*The **Delete** option can also be used to delete an entire body.*

The control frame layout of a T-Spline shape defines the resulting geometry. You can further modify the shape by deleting points, edges, or faces in the control frame. Once deleted, the control frame is recalculated and changes the geometry. For example, deleting faces can create holes, and deleting points and edges can change the size of the face which might be required for better control when using the **Edit Form** option.

As the feature history is not recorded, consider using undo if an entity is deleted in error.

To delete entities, in the MODIFY panel, click ✖ (Delete) and then select an entity or entities to be deleted. To select multiple entities, hold <Ctrl> as you are selecting the entities. Alternatively, you can select the entities and press <Delete> or right-click and select **Delete**. Figure 5–8 shows the changes caused by using the **Delete** option to delete points, edges, and faces on a T-Spline control frame.

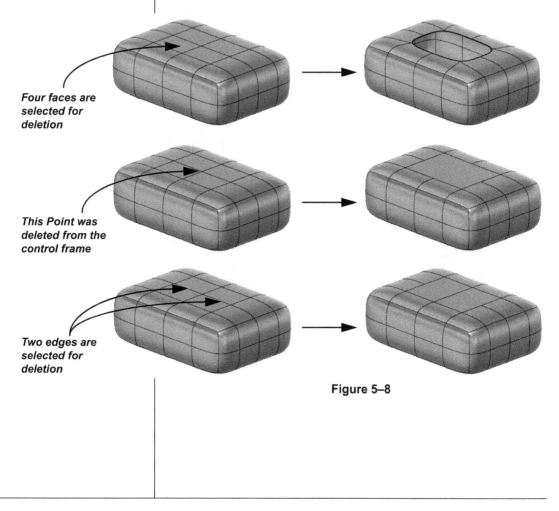

Four faces are selected for deletion

This Point was deleted from the control frame

Two edges are selected for deletion

Figure 5–8

5.3 Working with Edges

There are a number of different editing tools that can be used to modify the edges of T-Spline geometry. These tools are located on the MODIFY panel and include the following:

- Insert Edge
- Slide Edge
- Bevel Edge
- Merge Edges

- UnWeld Edges
- Crease
- UnCrease
- Match Edge

Insert Edge

The ability to add edges provides the flexibility to manipulate the control frame when needed. Note that having too many edges can also adversely affect the amount of control you have when modifying the form's shape.

You can add edges to a T-Spline using the (Insert Edge) option. Adding edges enables you to provide additional references (edges and the points at the end of edges) that can be edited to refine the shape of the model. When inserting edges, there are two modes that can be used:

- **Simple:** Adds a new edge exactly as specified. The shape might change to add the edge.

- **Exact:** Adds edges and maintains the existing shape. Additional edges might be required to ensure that the model retains its current shape.

Additionally, you can select whether edges are added on one or both sides of the selected reference. The images shown in Figure 5–9 show how two edges are inserted and compares how the overall shape changes when the edges are added using the Simple and Exact modes.

This edge is selected as a reference for the Insert Edge option

Edges (Both Sides) added using Simple Mode

Edges (Both Sides) added using Exact Mode

Figure 5–9

Slide Edge

The ![icon](Slide Edge) option slides a selected edge normal to its existing position, as shown in Figure 5–10. Its final location can be defined by either dragging the edge manually, or by entering a value in the entry field. The entry value is entered as a percentage of the distance to the next adjacent edge in the control frame.

These two edges have been selected to be used with the Slide Edge option

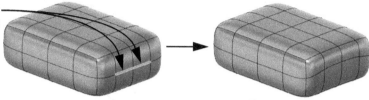

Figure 5–10

Bevel Edge

The ![icon](Bevel Edge) option adds a bevel (chamfer) to an existing edge or edges. When you create the bevel, you are prompted to enter its size (*Bevel Location*) as well as define the number of faces (*Segments*) to be created across the beveled edge. Similar to inserting a new edge, the size of the bevel is defined as a normalized value. Figure 5–11 shows existing edges being selected for beveling and the resulting T-Spline geometry after the **Bevel Edge** option is used.

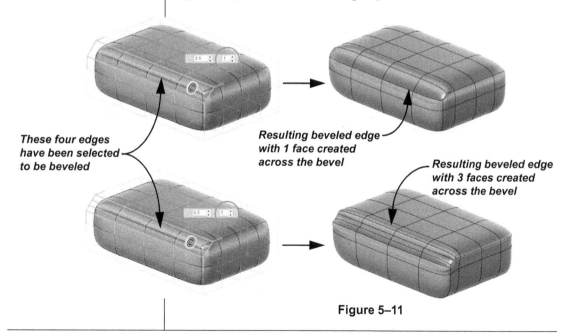

These four edges have been selected to be beveled

Resulting beveled edge with 1 face created across the bevel

Resulting beveled edge with 3 faces created across the bevel

Figure 5–11

Merge Edge

Use the 👆 (Merge Edge) option to merge two open T-Spline edges. This can be used to blend between two T-Spline bodies or two edges in a single body, if the geometry permits. To merge edges, use the MERGE EDGE palette and select the two sets or edges. You can select whether to maintain or ignore crease edges in the generated geometry. The order in which you select the edges affects the resulting geometry.

Figure 5–12 shows two sets of selected open edges and the resulting T-Spline geometry after the edges are merged.

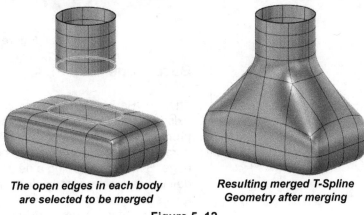

The open edges in each body
are selected to be merged

Resulting merged T-Spline
Geometry after merging

Figure 5–12

UnWeld Edges

The 🪣 (UnWeld Edges) option enables you to select edges to separate them from a T-Spline body. To unweld, simply select the edge or loop of edges and click **OK**. Once unwelded, multiple bodies are created that can be moved independently.

Figure 5–13 shows an example of how the 🪣 (UnWeld Edges) option was used on a box.

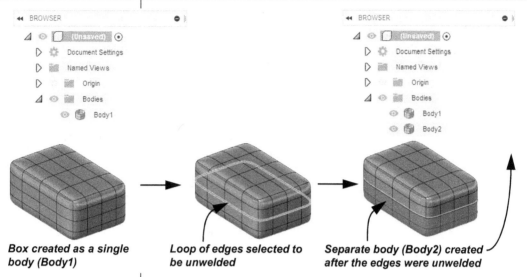

Box created as a single body (Body1)

Loop of edges selected to be unwelded

Separate body (Body2) created after the edges were unwelded

Figure 5–13

Crease/UnCrease Edges

The 🐾 (Crease) option enables you to create non-curvature continuous (sharp) edges on a T-Spline body by selecting and moving an edge. In Figure 5–14, four edges were set to permit creasing. Once set, the edges display as darker black. The image on the right shows how the T-Spline shape reacts to the crease if the edges are moved. Note how the edge is creased after it is moved.

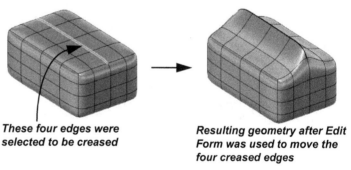

These four edges were selected to be creased

Resulting geometry after Edit Form was used to move the four creased edges

Figure 5–14

To clear the crease setting, click 🐾 (UnCrease) and select the edges to be cleared. The crease is removed and the geometry updates.

Match Edge

When designing a T-Spline shape, you might have a design requirement that the shape must match an existing edge reference. The existing edge reference (target) can be an edge, a solid edge, or a sketch. The edge can be created in the SOLID environment, in the same T-Spline form, or in another T-Spline form. To match the edges, use the 🏴 (Match) command. The number of vertices in each reference should be similar.

If you are matching a fully enclosed entity, the references must also be fully enclosed.

The image on the left in Figure 5–15 shows two T-Spline bodies created as separate features. In the image on the right, the open edge on the box was merged with the edge of the cylinder. Note that T-Spline edges cannot be matched if they exist in the same feature.

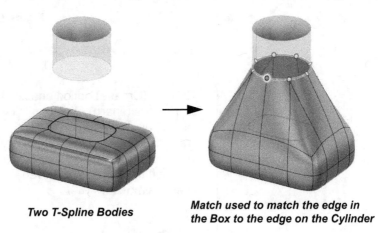

Two T-Spline Bodies   **Match used to match the edge in the Box to the edge on the Cylinder**

Figure 5–15

To prevent movement during editing, you can use the MODIFY panel> Freeze option to freeze entities after matching.

The edges are only temporarily matched and the edge is not fully constrained to the target. For instance, in the example shown above, there are still 2 bodies in the design file and the bodies separate if you edit any of the merged edges.

5.4 Working with Faces

You can manipulate the faces that form a T-Spline control frame to change the shape of geometry. The **Subdivide** and **Bridge** commands enable you to manipulate a face.

Subdivide

The ability to add faces provides the flexibility to manipulate the control frame when needed. Note that having too many faces can also adversely affect the amount of control you have when modifying the form's shape.

The (Subdivide) command enables you to break up a selected face into smaller faces, as shown in Figure 5–16. In general, adding faces helps you to refine the shape of the model and permits more precise editing. When subdividing, you can select one of the following *Insert Mode* options to determine the resulting T-Spline shape:

- **Simple:** Subdivides exactly as specified. The shape might change to add faces.

- **Exact:** Maintains the same existing shape. Additional faces might be required to enable the T-Spline to retain its current shape.

Four faces on a modified Box are selected for subdivision

Resulting faces when using the Simple Insert Mode option

Resulting faces when using the Exact Insert Mode option

Figure 5–16

Bridge

When using multiple T-Spline bodies in a design, you can use

the (Bridge) command to connect the space between the two bodies to create a single body. The Bridge command can also join multiple gaps in a single body. When creating bridged geometry, you can define a curve to follow and assign twists and the number of faces to be generated.

The images in Figure 5–17 show how two separate cylindrical bodies are bridged by new geometry and how it can be used in a single body to create a hole.

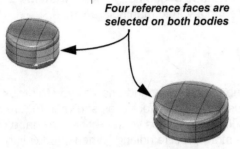

Four reference faces are selected on both bodies

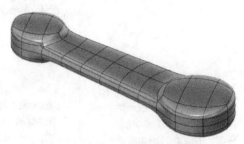

Two bodies in a single form feature

Resulting geometry after the Bridge command was added between the bodies

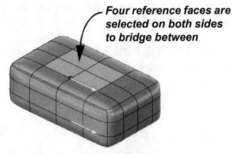

Four reference faces are selected on both sides to bridge between

A single Box T-Spline Body

Resulting geometry after the Bridge command was added

Figure 5–17

5.5 Working with Points

The points that define edges and faces can also be modified using tools on the MODIFY panel. These tools include: **Insert Point**, **Weld Vertices**, **Flatten**, and **Pull**.

Insert Point

Similar to inserting edges, points can be inserted using a similar workflow. An edge is defined when multiple points are inserted, which also defines a new face.

To insert points, complete the following steps:

1. In the MODIFY panel, click (Insert Point).
2. Select points on edges to place new points. Snap points display for endpoint or midpoints of edges, and intermediate points on an edge.
3. Select the *Insertion Mode* type to define the shape of the new points and subsequent edges. The **Simple** and **Exact** options are the same as for inserting edges.
4. (Optional) Enable **Object Snap** to move the new point to the closest point on other objects (solid, surface, and mesh bodies) in the scene.
5. Click **OK**.

The new point (shown in Figure 5–18) breaks the edge and creates multiple edges to fully define any adjacent faces. If subsequent points are selected while the palette is open, an edge is created between the points.

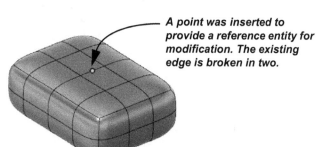

A point was inserted to provide a reference entity for modification. The existing edge is broken in two.

Figure 5–18

Weld Vertices

Once edges are merged, you can use this option to combine vertices to help refine the faces that are generated.

The (Weld Vertices) option enables you to combine two selected vertices. To weld the vertices, select the *Weld Mode* option and select two points on the control frame. The *Weld Mode* options include the following:

- **(Vertex to Vertex):** Merges two selected vertices. The first vertex is moved to the position of the second vertex, as shown at the top in Figure 5–19.

- **(Vertex to Midpoint):** Moves two selected vertices to the midpoint between the selections, as shown at the bottom in Figure 5–19.

- **(Weld to Tolerance):** Combines multiple vertices within a specified tolerance.

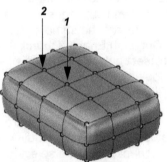

Vertex to Vertex option: Vertex 1 was selected to be welded to Vertex 2

Two vertices welded (Vertex 1 on Vertex 2)

Vertex to Midpoint option: Vertex 1 was selected to be welded to Vertex 2

Two vertices welded and positioned at the midpoint between the two

Figure 5–19

Flatten

If unable to flatten, consider selecting additional vertices as references.

The 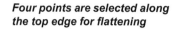 (Flatten) option enables you to select multiple vertices and force them to flatten to a single plane. Once you have selected the points, you must select the *Direction* type. The options include the following:

- **(Fit):** Moves points to a single plane that passes through the vertices.

- **(Select Plane):** Moves points through a specified plane.

- **(Select Parallel Plane):** Moves points parallel to a selected plane.

Figure 5–20 shows how the **Flatten** option was used to flatten multiple vertices so that they are parallel with a selected plane.

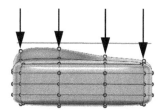

Four points are selected along the top edge for flattening

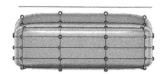

The four points are flattened and remain parallel to the selected plane

Figure 5–20

Pull

*The MODIFY panel> **Interpolate** option can also be used to improve the control frame of a body to smooth out a bodies control points.*

The (Pull) option enables you to snap multiple vertices to a target body. The target body must be a separate form feature or solid. You can manually select the target body, or the system can auto-select based on the closest geometry.

5.6 Controlling Symmetry

The ability to assign symmetry in a T-Spline body can be valuable when using the **Edit Form** command to push and pull a control frame to manipulate its shape. Without the use of parametric dimensions during editing, it is difficult to make the same change on two different sides. By assigning symmetry, you ensure that any edits are copied across symmetric faces.

For example, Figure 5–21 shows the difference between changes made to a Box quick shape without symmetry, and the same change after symmetry has been assigned.

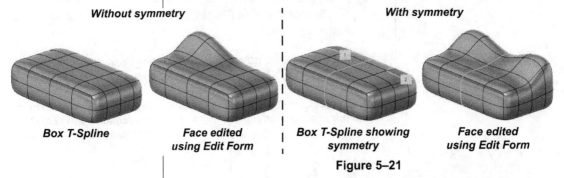

Without symmetry   *With symmetry*

Box T-Spline   *Face edited*   *Box T-Spline showing*   *Face edited*
                    using Edit Form   *symmetry*   *using Edit Form*

Figure 5–21

You can assign symmetry in a T-Spline in several ways:

- Assign symmetry during quick shape creation. For example, for a Box, symmetry can be assigned in length, width, or height, as shown in Figure 5–22.

Figure 5–22

If symmetry cannot be assigned based on the references that you have selected, you are prompted to retry making selections.

- Assign symmetry by selecting faces on the control frame. This is valuable to assign symmetry after form creation. In the SYMMETRY panel, click 🔺 (Mirror - Internal) and select two faces on the geometry. The Autodesk® Fusion 360® software locates the symmetry plane and it displays as a green line, as shown in Figure 5–23.

Figure 5–23

The Circular symmetry option is available when assigning symmetry during the creation of a Cylinder quick shape.

- Circular symmetry can be assigned using the SYMMETRY panel> ✽ (Circular - Internal) option. This enables you assign radial symmetry to geometry, as shown in Figure 5–24. If multiple symmetries can be set when you are assigning circular symmetry, the possible symmetries are listed (e.g., 2-sided, 4-sided, 8-sided, etc.).The availability of the symmetry options is dependent on the number of faces in the control frame. In Figure 5–24, 8-sided symmetry was selected.

Cylinder T-Spline (no symmetry set)

Face edited using Edit Form

Cylinder T-Spline (8-sided symmetry assigned)

Face edited using Edit Form

Figure 5–24

- Symmetry that has been explicitly assigned between faces can be cleared by clicking SYMMETRY panel> 🔺 (Clear Symmetry).

- Use ✤ (Isolate Symmetry) to individually isolate symmetry on faces of symmetry geometry. Isolated faces display in the design as red. Note that isolated faces can still be affected by modifications made to points, edges, and faces on adjacent geometry.

Hint: Duplicating Bodies

The SYMMETRY panel> ▲ (Mirror - Duplicate) and

✤ (Circular - Duplicate) options enable you to mirror an entry body about a plane and pattern a body respectively.

5.7 Thickening Geometry

You can use the (Thicken) command with T-Spline geometry to duplicate and offset an existing body by a specific value. The selected body can have open edges, or it can be a closed body. For open bodies, you can select a *Thicken Type* option to connect the resulting edges and cap the opening. The **No Edge** thicken option leaves the T-Splines as separate bodies.

Figure 5–25 shows some examples of geometry that has been thickened when the selected body is open.

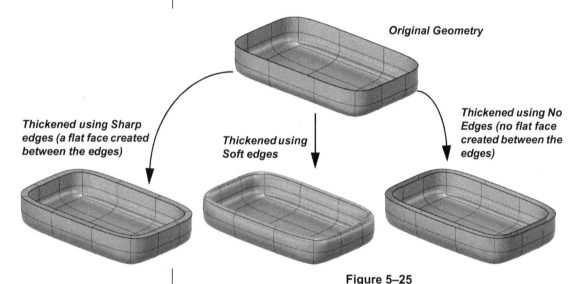

Figure 5–25

To thicken a T-Spline body, complete the following steps:

1. In the MODIFY panel, click (Thicken).
2. Select a T-Spline body to be thickened.
3. In the *Thicken Type* area, select how the thickened geometry is to be capped. Note that these options only affect the geometry results when thickening an open body. The options include:

   • **(Sharp):** Creates a flat face to bridge the offset.

   • **(Soft):** Creates a new face that is rounded to bridge the offset.

   • **(No Edges):** Leaves an open gap between the thickened geometry.

4. Define the offset direction using the options in the Direction drop-down list. The options include:

- ⟩ **(Normal):** Offsets the body normal to the selected body.

- ⟩ **(Axis):** Offsets perpendicular to a selected directional reference.

5. Enter a thickness value.
6. Click **OK** to thicken the selected body.

Practice 5a | Editing T-Spline Geometry

Practice Objectives

- Create T-Spline geometry using the **Cylinder** command.
- Edit T-Spline geometry so that edges and faces are translated, scaled, and rotated.
- Insert and delete edges on the T-Spline geometry.
- Use the **Fill Hole** command to close an open loop of edges.
- Thicken T-Spline geometry to form a fully enclosed surface.

In this practice, you will edit the forms that were created in a previous exercise. The goal is to reshape the two cylinders to more closely match the sketch that was provided for the design, as shown in Figure 5–26. To complete the design, you will refine the shape of the two surface bodies so that they can be used to create solid bodies. To complete the practice, you will convert the bodies into individual solid components, assign appearances, and then render the design.

2D Conceptual Sketch

3D Base Shape Creation

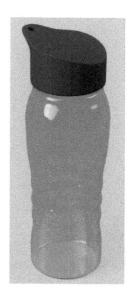

Final 3D Design

Figure 5–26

Task 1 - Create a new design from a file.

1. Click 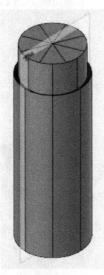 (File)>**Open**. In the Open window, click **Open from my computer**.

2. In the Open dialog box, navigate to the *Autodesk Fusion 360 Surfacing Practice Files* folder. Select **WaterBottle_Initial_Forms.f3d**, and click **Open**. The design displays as shown in Figure 5–27.

   - This is the design that was started in the previous chapter. If you prefer, you can continue in your own design or use the one provided.

Figure 5–27

3. In the BROWSER, expand the *Canvases* folder. Right-click on **Bottle_Side_Profile** and select **Edit Canvas.** The same EDIT CANVAS palette that was used to add the canvas opens.

4. Enable the **Display Through** option.

5. To improve the visibility of the sketch, change the *Canvas opacity* slider to **70%**. Click **OK**.

6. Reorient the design to the **RIGHT** view using the ViewCube. The canvas image is now visible through the two cylinders, as shown in Figure 5–28. This is helpful when editing the shape to match the canvas image.

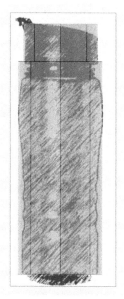

Figure 5–28

Task 2 - Edit the T-Spline geometry for the lid.

In this task, you will shape the lid of the water bottle.

1. In the BROWSER, expand the *Bodies* folder and click

   (**Show/Hide**) adjacent to the **Bottle** body. This hides the body from the display so that you can focus on your edits to the lid.

2. To edit the **Lid** body, double-click on the second in the Timeline. This is the form feature that was used to create the **Lid**.

3. Zoom in on the lid so that you can easily see the image through the cylinder.

4. Rotate the design similar to that shown in Figure 5–29. You will make edits by pushing and pulling points, edges, and faces.

Figure 5–29

5. Rotate the design to the **RIGHT** view using the ViewCube.

6. In the MODIFY panel, click 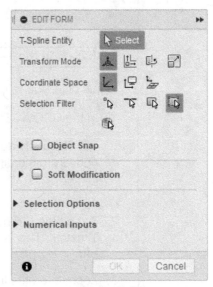 (Edit Form). The EDIT FORM palette displays, as shown in Figure 5–30.

Figure 5–30

7. In the *Selection Filter* area, ensure that 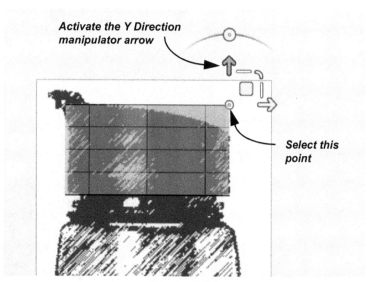 (All) is selected as the default option. This enables you to select points, edges, or faces. Hover the cursor over points, edges, and faces on the form's control frame. Note that you can select any of them.

   • Selecting the other options filters the selection to points only, edges only, or faces only, which can be useful in complex T-Spline geometry with large control frame layouts.

8. In the *Coordinate Space* area, select (View Space), if not already selected. This sets the manipulator to lie planar with the screen. This requires the design's orientation to be set, as required, for the proper manipulation. Ensure that the view is set as **RIGHT**.

9. Select the point shown in Figure 5–31, and then select the Y-direction (up) arrowhead manipulator.

Figure 5–31

To undo the last change, in the Quick Access Toolbar, click

↰ *(Undo).*

10. Drag the manipulator arrow down to align the top right edge of the cylinder with the canvas image of the lid, as shown in Figure 5–32.

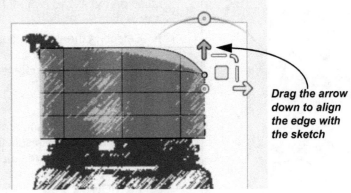

Drag the arrow down to align the edge with the sketch

Figure 5–32

11. Click away from the design to clear the point selection.

12. Rotate the model slightly, hold <Shift>, and then select the two points shown in Figure 5–33.

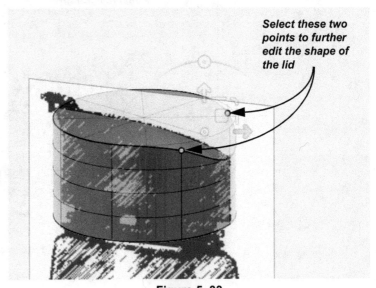

Select these two points to further edit the shape of the lid

Figure 5–33

13. Return the design to the **RIGHT** view.

Manipulations are not exact. You can jump between points, manipulator handles, and views to manipulate the shape as needed.

14. Drag the Y-direction manipulator arrow down to further align the top edge of the cylinder with the canvas image of the lid, as shown in Figure 5–34. Depending on your edit, you might need to reselect the single point that was first moved and adjust it further to match the shape of the sketch.

Figure 5–34

15. Click away from the design to clear the selection of any entities.

16. Click **OK** to complete the edit, and then return to the design's **Home** view.

17. Note that a ghost image of the initial cylinder that was created in the Lid body still displays. To clear this from the display, you can change your Preferences. In the Account Settings and Preferences, click your user name and select **Preferences**.

18. In the Preferences dialog box, select **General>Design** and then clear the **Show ghosted result body** option. Click **OK**.

19. Click ✓ (Finish Form). Based on your edits, you might receive an error that the T-Spline model has failed. This is entirely dependent on the geometry and the resulting shape of the control frame. For example, the Error dialog box in Figure 5–35 is indicating that edges or faces are crossing. This would prevent you from successfully finishing the form. In the example, the top edge was dragged lower than the lower edge, causing edges to cross and faces to fail.

Figure 5–35

20. In the dialog boxes, click **Return>Close** to remain in the form and fix the error, if required.

21. Rotate the design to the **BACK** view.

22. In the MODIFY panel, click 🐿 (Edit Form). Select the two edges shown in Figure 5–36 and drag them down to evenly space the edges between their adjacent edges.

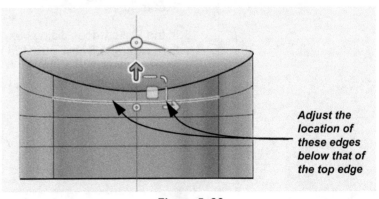

Adjust the location of these edges below that of the top edge

Figure 5–36

23. Complete the edit and finish the form to ensure that the shape can be created. Periodically finishing the form before starting another edit is good practice to ensure that errors do not compound with additional edits.

24. Return to the design's **Home** view.

25. Save the design as **WaterBottle_Edits**.

Task 3 - Edit the left side of the lid.

In this task, you will insert some additional points which will generate additional faces at the top of the bottle. By adding these edges, you will be provided with the references required to edit the left-side of the lid.

1. Double-click on the second form in the Timeline to edit the lid's form feature again.

2. In the MODIFY panel, click ⟋₊ (Insert Point).

3. Set the *Insertion Mode* to **Exact**.

4. Click to insert the point along the top edge shown in Figure 5–37.

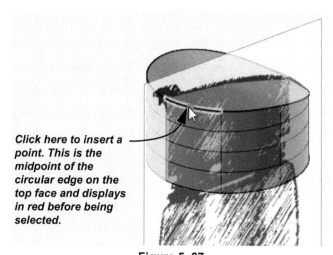

Click here to insert a point. This is the midpoint of the circular edge on the top face and displays in red before being selected.

Figure 5–37

5. A preview of the new control frame displays, as shown in Figure 5–38.

- Additional edges, faces, and points were included because **Exact** mode was used. These additional entities were required to add the point while still maintaining the exact shape of the form.

- Because a symmetric point on the opposite side of the canvas plane was generated, a second point is not required.

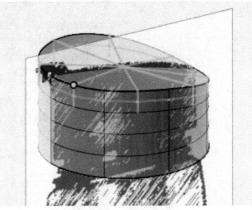

Figure 5–38

6. Click **OK** to complete the point insertion.

7. Hold <Ctrl> and select the two edges shown in Figure 5–39.

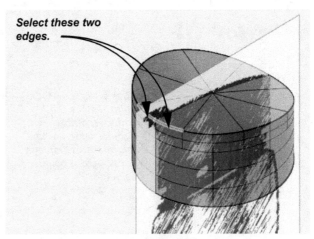

Figure 5–39

8. In the MODIFY panel, click ⬚ (Edit Form).

9. Change the view orientation to **RIGHT** and ensure that the Coordinate Space setting is set to 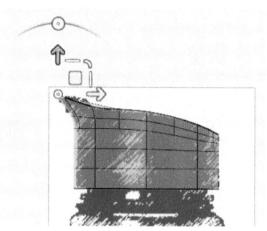 (View Space).

10. Drag the edges using the X- and Y-direction manipulators so that the control frame displays similar to that shown in Figure 5–40.

The drag interval that is used depends on the zoom level. Zoom in closer to reduce the drag interval, or zoom out to make it larger.

Figure 5–40

11. Click away from the control frame to clear the edge selection and return to the default **Home** view.

12. Select the face shown in Figure 5–41 and change the Coordinate Space setting to 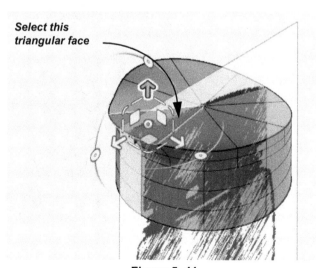 (World Space). Activate the Y-manipulator.

Select this triangular face

Figure 5–41

13. Drag the manipulator up slightly to change the shape of the top of the lid to more closely match the sketch. You can switch to the **RIGHT** view during these edits to ensure that the change matches the image.

14. Select the edge that intersects the canvas plane, as shown in Figure 5–42. With *Coordinate Setting* set to 🖵 (View Space), further manipulate the shape of the lid, as required.

In general, sketches represent a conceptual version of the design. The size and shape does not have to be exact, and might vary from what is ultimately chosen as the final design.

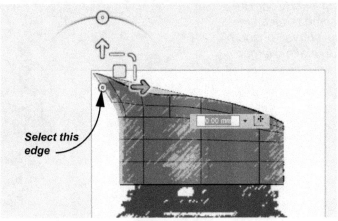

Select this edge

Figure 5–42

15. Click **OK** to close the EDIT FORM palette.

16. Hide the display of the **Bottle_Side_Profile** canvas image.

17. Use the **Fill Hole** option to close the form feature, as shown in Figure 5–43. (Hint: Ensure that the **Collapse** and **Maintain Crease Edges** options are selected.)

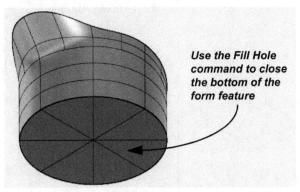

Use the Fill Hole command to close the bottom of the form feature

Figure 5–43

18. Finish the form. In the *Bodies* folder, note that the **Lid** body is now showing as a solid body (🞎).

19. Save the design.

Task 4 - Create a hole in the lid.

In this task, you will use your knowledge of the solid modeling commands to create a hole that can be used to connect a carabiner clip.

1. Create a construction plane using the 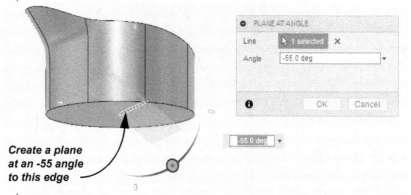 (Plane at Angle) command and select the edge that was generated when the Fill Hole was created, as shown in Figure 5–44. In the *Angle* field, enter an value of **-55**. Click **OK**.

Create a plane
at an -55 angle
to this edge

Figure 5–44

2. Create a sketch on the new plane, add a sketch point, and then dimension it as shown in Figure 5–45.

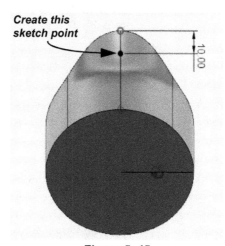

Create this
sketch point

10.00

Figure 5–45

3. Finish the sketch.

4. Create the hole shown in Figure 5–46, referencing the sketched point. Change the *Extents* option to **All** and then enter a *Diameter* value of **8 mm**.

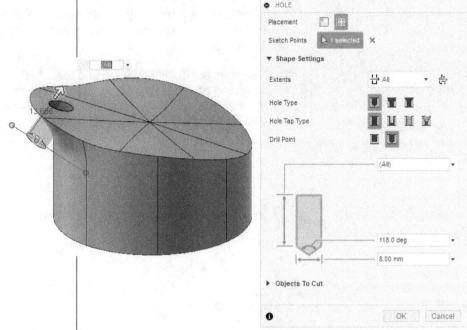

Figure 5–46

5. Click **OK** to complete the hole.

6. Add **1 mm** fillets to the top edge of the lid and the bottom edges of the hole. The model should display similar to that shown in Figure 5–47.

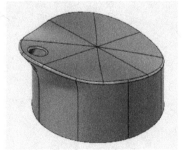

Figure 5–47

7. Save the design.

Task 5 - Edit the Bottle form.

In this task, you edit the Bottle form to match the canvas image.

1. If you successfully completed Task 4, continue using your saved model and go to Step 2. If you did not successfully complete Task 4, open the design from your practice files folder:

    1. Click  (File)>**New Design from File**.
    2. Using the Open dialog box, navigate to the *Autodesk Fusion 360 Surfacing Practice Files* folder.
    3. Select **WaterBottle_Edits1.f3d**, and click **Open**.
    4. Save the design in the current project.

2. Using the BROWSER, toggle on the display of the **Bottle** body and the canvas image, and hide the **Lid** from the display, as shown in Figure 5–48.

Figure 5–48

3. Double-click on the first form feature in the design to edit it. This is the form feature that was used to create the **Bottle**.

4. Change the view orientation to the **RIGHT** view.

5. Start the **Edit Form** command.

6. Hold <Ctrl> and double-click on each of the three horizontal edges shown in Figure 5–49. Double-clicking ensures that the entire loop of edges around the cylinder are selected.

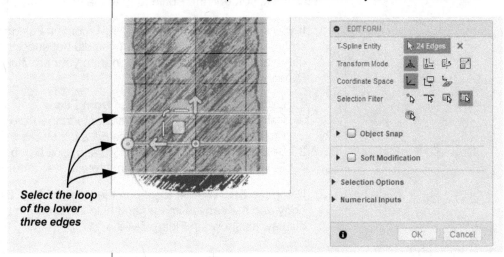

Select the loop of the lower three edges

Figure 5–49

In the Transform Mode area, you can select 🔲 *(Scale) to filter the view to only display the Scale manipulators.*

7. Select the Scale manipulator and reposition the edges similar to that in the canvas image (shown in Figure 5–50).

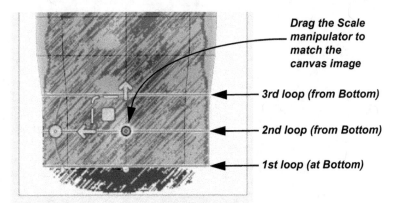

Drag the Scale manipulator to match the canvas image

3rd loop (from Bottom)

2nd loop (from Bottom)

1st loop (at Bottom)

Figure 5–50

8. Click away from the control frame to clear the edge selection.

9. Select the next loop of edges (i.e., the 4th loop working your way up from the bottom). Scale the loop as shown in Figure 5–51.

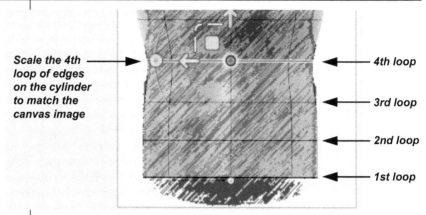

Scale the 4th loop of edges on the cylinder to match the canvas image

4th loop

3rd loop

2nd loop

1st loop

Figure 5–51

10. Click **OK** to close the EDIT FORM palette.

11. To correctly shape the next few loops, additional edges are required. In the MODIFY panel, click (Insert Edge). The INSERT EDGE palette opens.

12. Select the next loop of edges (i.e., the 5th loop working your way up from the bottom).

13. In the *Insertion Side* field, select **Both**. Ensure that the *Insert Location* is **.50**, as shown in Figure 5–52.

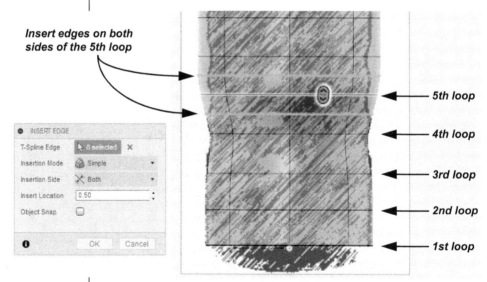

Insert edges on both sides of the 5th loop

5th loop

4th loop

3rd loop

2nd loop

1st loop

Figure 5–52

14. Click **OK** to create the new edges.

15. Insert an additional single edge above the 8th loop of edges, as shown in Figure 5–53.

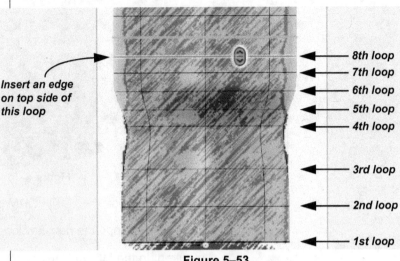

Insert an edge on top side of this loop

8th loop
7th loop
6th loop
5th loop
4th loop

3rd loop

2nd loop

1st loop

Figure 5–53

Hint: Consider selecting and scaling two loops of edges at once to scale them to the same size.

16. Using the scaling technique previously discussed, scale the 5th to 8th loop edges to more closely match the canvas image, as shown in Figure 5–54.

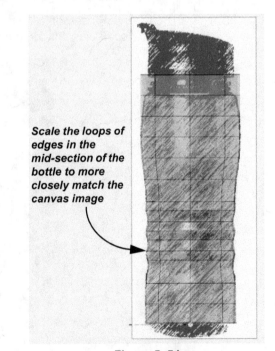

Scale the loops of edges in the mid-section of the bottle to more closely match the canvas image

Figure 5–54

17. Scale the top of the bottle similar to that shown in Figure 5–55.

Scale the loops of edges at the top of the bottle to match the canvas image

Figure 5–55

18. Click **OK** to close the EDIT FORM palette.

19. Save the design to ensure that the edits that you have made to this point are saved.

Task 6 - Edit the opening of the bottle.

In this task, you will insert some additional faces at the top of the bottle to create the top contour.

1. Start the **Edit Form** command and return to the **RIGHT** view.

2. Select the loop of edges at the top of the bottle. Use the Y and Scale manipulators to edit the loop of edges as shown in Figure 5–56.

*To ensure that the entire loop of edges are selected, you can rotate into a 3D orientation to review the edge. Return to the **RIGHT** view before manipulating the shape.*

Use the Y and Scale manipulators to shape the top edge of the bottle

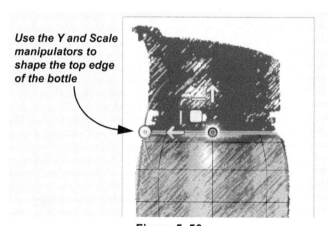

Figure 5–56

3. With the top edge still selected, activate the Y manipulator, hold <ALT> and drag up to create additional edges and faces around the circumference of the cylinder, as shown in Figure 5–57.

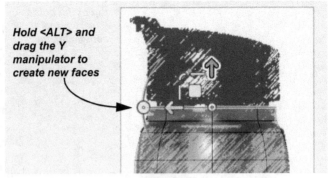

Hold <ALT> and drag the Y manipulator to create new faces

Figure 5–57

4. Return to the default **Home** view.

5. With the loop of edges still selected at the top of the bottle, ensure that the Y-direction manipulator is selected, hold <Alt>, and drag up to approximately **1mm** to create an additional set of faces. Release <Alt>. Enter **1mm** in the entry field to assign the specific value.

6. Enable the scale transform mode manipulator, if not already displayed. Scale the top loop of edges of the new faces similar to that shown in Figure 5–58. Drag to approximately **.8**, or enter the value in the entry field.

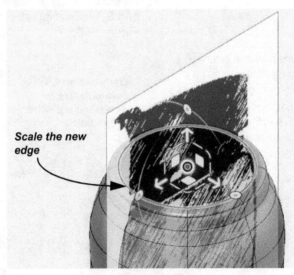

Scale the new edge

Figure 5–58

If the model display automatically changes to the Box display style, it indicates that the geometry is failing. Undo the change and redo it.

7. Continuing to use <ALT>, drag the Y manipulator and scale the edges to create the remainder of the lip of the bottle, similar to that shown in Figure 5–59.

Figure 5–59

8. Click **OK** to complete the edit.

9. Toggle off the display of the canvas image.

10. Return to the **Home** view and fill the hole at the top of the Bottle body with a creased edge.

11. Finish the form feature and note in the *Bodies* folder that the Bottle body is now showing as a solid body (⬚).

12. In the SOLID environment, create a **5mm** constant radius fillet on the bottom edge of the bottle.

13. Toggle on the display of the **Lid** solid body. The design should display in a shaded view similar to that shown in Figure 5–60.

Figure 5–60

14. Save the design.

Task 7 - Complete the design of the two bodies.

To complete the designs of the two solid bodies, the intersecting geometry must be removed to remove material inside the lid, and then the bottle must be shelled. This task explains how the **Combine** and **Shell** commands can be used to do this.

1. If you successfully completed Task 6, continue using your saved model and go to Step 2. If you did not successfully complete Task 6, open the design from your practice files folder:

   1. Click ![File icon] (File)>**New Design from File**.
   2. Using the Open dialog box, navigate to the *Autodesk Fusion 360 Surfacing Practice Files* folder.
   3. Select **WaterBottle_Edits2.f3d**, and click **Open**.
   4. Save the design in the current project.

2. In the MODIFY panel, click 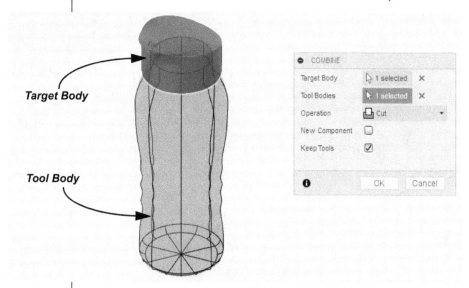 (Combine). Complete the following in the COMBINE palette (as shown in Figure 5–61):

- Select the **Lid** as the *Target Body* reference.
- Activate the *Tool Bodies* field, if it isn't already active. Select the **Bottle** solid body as the reference.
- In the *Operation* field, select **Cut**.
- Enable the **Keep Tools** option to ensure that the tool body reference is not removed after the cut is completed.

Target Body

Tool Body

Figure 5–61

3. Click **OK**.

4. Hide the display of the **Bottle** solid body and verify that the cut was created.

5. Add **2 mm** fillets to the three sharp edges on the lid, as shown in Figure 5–62.

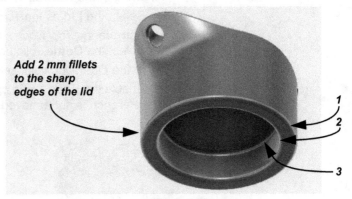

Add 2 mm fillets to the sharp edges of the lid

Figure 5–62

6. Toggle off the display of the Lid solid body and toggle on the display of the **Bottle** solid body.

7. In the MODIFY panel, click (Shell). Complete the following in the SHELL palette (as shown in Figure 5–63).

   - Select the top circular planar face as the *Faces/Body* reference.
   - Enter **2 mm** as the *Inside Thickness* value.
   - Ensure that the *Direction* is set to remove the shell on the **Inside** of the design.

Remove the top planar face to shell the bottle

Figure 5–63

8. Click **OK**.

9. Toggle on the display of the **Lid** solid body.

10. Save the design.

Task 8 - (Optional) Assign appearances to the bodies.

In this task, you will learn to assign appearances and render the model.

1. If you successfully completed Task 7, continue using your saved model and go to Step 2. If you did not complete Task 7, open the design from your practice files folder:

   1. Click 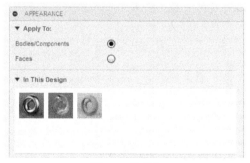 (File)>**New Design from File**.
   2. Using the Open dialog box, navigate to the *Autodesk Fusion 360 Surfacing Practice Files* folder.
   3. Select **WaterBottle_Edits3.f3d**, and click **Open**.
   4. Save the design in the current project.

2. Right-click on the design name at the top of the BROWSER and select **Appearance**. The APPEARANCE palette opens.

3. In the *Library* area at the bottom of the palette, expand the **Plastic>Transparent** categories.

4. Select the **Acrylic (Clear)** appearance and drag and drop it into the *In this Design* area of the palette.

5. Scroll up in the library and expand the **Plastic>Opaque** category.

6. Select the **Plastic - Matte (Blue)** appearance and drag and drop it into the *In this Design* area of the palette. The *In this Design* area of the palette should display as shown in Figure 5–64.

Figure 5–64

7. Select the **Plastic - Matte (Blue)** appearance from the *In this Design* area and drag and drop it onto the **Lid** body in the graphics window.

8. Select the **Acrylic (Clear)** appearance from the *In this Design* area and drag and drop it onto the **Bottle** body in the graphics window.

9. Close the APPEARANCE palette.

10. Expand the **Change Workspace** menu and select **Render** (as shown in Figure 5–65) to launch the *RENDER* workspace.

Figure 5–65

11. Reorient the design as required to fit it in the graphics window.

12. In the IN-CANVAS RENDER panel, click 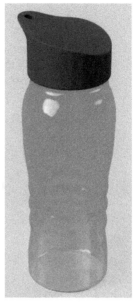 (In-Canvas Render) to launch the rendering process. For this exercise, you will maintain all of the default rendering settings. After rendering, the design should display similar to that shown in Figure 5–66.

The rendering shown in Figure 5–66 was rendered for over 30min. To review a saved version of the rendered design, open **WaterBottle_ Rendering.png** *from the practice files folder.*

A completed design, **WaterBottle_Final.f3d***, has been included in the practice files.*

Figure 5–66

13. Save the design and close the window.

Practice 5b

Connecting T-Spline Geometry

Practice Objective

- Create two T-Spline bodies and use the **Bridge, Merge Edge**, and **Weld Vertices** commands to generate geometry between them.

In this practice, you will create two sculpted T-Spline base shapes in a single form feature and use different editing tools to join them. Once joined, you will compare how each option generates the connected shape. The steering wheel model that you will create is shown in Figure 5–67.

Figure 5–67

Task 1 - Create two T-Spline bodies.

1. Create a new design and save it as **Steering Wheel** in your project folder.

2. Activate the FORM contextual environment.

3. Use the **Torus** quick shape feature to create a T-Spline on the XZ plane that is centered on the origin. Create the shape using the settings shown in Figure 5–68.
   - Ensure that you enter the number of faces as shown in Figure 5–68 to ensure that the correct number of faces are generated to complete the exercise.

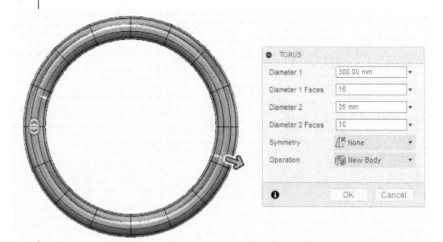

Figure 5–68

4. Use the **Cylinder** quick shape feature to create a T-Spline on the XZ plane that is centered on the origin. Create the shape using the settings shown in Figure 5–69.

   - Ensure that the *Direction* option is set as **Symmetric** and that the *Height* is a total of **30 mm**.

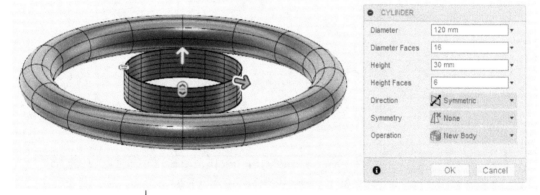

Figure 5–69

5. Switch to the **FRONT** view and verify that the cylinder is not extending above or below the torus. You might need to re-enter the *Height* value to ensure that the height is correct.

Unlike in the previous practice where two separate form features were created, in this practice the two shapes were created in a single form feature. Using this design approach enables the shapes to be combined to generate a final body.

6. Create a sketch on the XZ plane. In the SKETCH panel, click

   A (Text).

7. With the design in the **TOP** view, place a cursor in the 12 o'clock position to locate a text box.

8. In the *Text* field, enter **12**. Change the *Height* value to **30 mm**, and then click **OK**.

9. Continue to add text to identify the 3, 6, and 9 o'clock positions around the Torus, as shown in Figure 5–70. These numbers will help you identify the sides of the models that you will be working with.

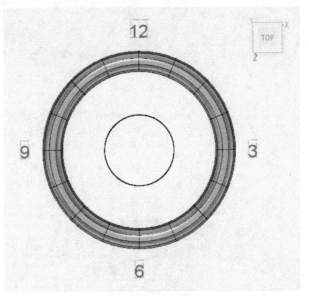

Figure 5–70

10. Finish the sketch.

Task 2 - Modify the geometry on the outer torus to manipulate its shape.

---

1. In the MODIFY panel, click (Insert Edge). The INSERT EDGE palette opens.

2. Select the loop of edges in the 3 o'clock position, as shown in Figure 5–71.

   • Note: Double-clicking on a single edge selects all of the edges that are adjacent to it and form a loop.

3. In the Insertion Mode drop-down list, select **Exact**. This ensures that when the edges are inserted that the Torus remains circular.

4. In the Insertion Mode drop-down list, select **Both**. For the *Insert Location*, enter to **.50**. Click **OK**. The new edges display as shown on the right in Figure 5–71.

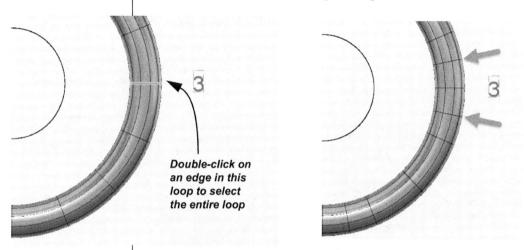

Double-click on an edge in this loop to select the entire loop

Figure 5–71

5. Use the **Insert Edge** option and create the additional edges at the 6 and 9 o'clock positions on the wheel, as shown in Figure 5–72.

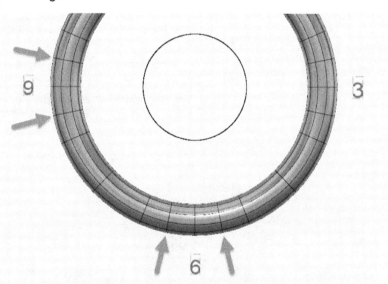

Figure 5–72

6. Rotate the design so that it displays similar to that shown in Figure 5–73.

7. In the SYMMETRY panel, click ▲▲ (Mirror - Internal) and select the two faces on the geometry shown in Figure 5–73 to define a line of symmetry through the Torus. By defining symmetry, any changes to the faces on one side of the symmetry line will also be done to its symmetric face.

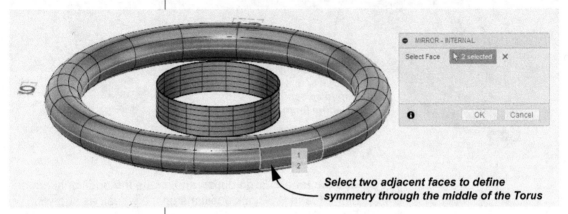

Select two adjacent faces to define symmetry through the middle of the Torus

Figure 5–73

8. Similar to Step 7, assign symmetry to the cylinder.

Hold <Ctrl> to select multiple faces at once.

9. Use 🖱 (Edit Form) to extrude the four faces shown in Figure 5–74. All of the faces should be explicitly selected (i.e., displayed as blue). Ensure that the X-axis manipulator arrow is selected and then hold <Alt> to extrude the faces. Enter **-20 mm** in the entry field to assign the specific value.

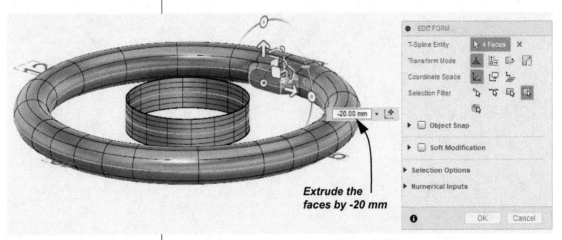

Extrude the faces by -20 mm

Figure 5–74

In the previous step you were asked to select faces on both sides of the symmetry line. This is because an extrude done by selecting only two faces on one side of the symmetry line is executed separately on both sides and will not produce the required geometry.

10. Undo the previous extrude.

11. Select two faces on one side of the symmetry line (they turn blue). The opposite faces turn yellow. Hold <Alt> to extrude the faces. Note the difference in the geometry.

12. Undo the change to return to the previous extruded geometry shown in Figure 5–74.

13. Use the same technique to extrude the similar faces at the 6 and 9 o'clock positions on the wheel, as shown in Figure 5–75. Depending on the positive direction of the manipulator arrows, you might need to enter positive or negative extrude values.

By entering the extrude distance, you are able to ensure that the three extrusions are the same size.

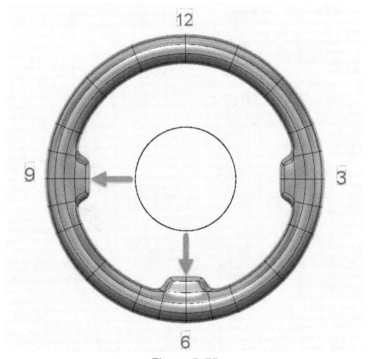

Figure 5–75

Task 3 - Create geometry between the two cylinders.

In this task, you will connect the extruded faces with the interior cylinder. Each of the three extrusions will be done using a different technique. You will use the **Bridge**, **Weld Vertices**, and **Merge Edge** options and compare the resulting geometry.

1. In the MODIFY panel, click 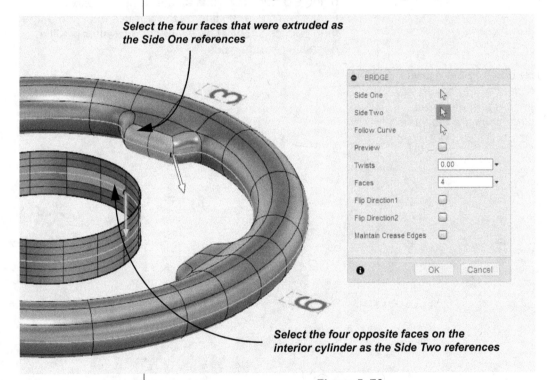 (Bridge).

2. If not already active, select the *Side One* field.

3. Select the four faces on the extrude that were created at the 3 o'clock position on the wheel, as shown in Figure 5–76.

4. Select the *Side Two* field to activate it. Select the four faces on the interior cylinder, as shown in Figure 5–76.

Select the four faces that were extruded as the Side One references

Select the four opposite faces on the interior cylinder as the Side Two references

Figure 5–76

- Maintain the default for the *Twist* field and enter **4** in the *Face* field. Click **OK** to create the bridge geometry. Note that a warning appears indicating that symmetry will be removed as a result of this operation. Symmetry can be used to aid in symmetric modification, but not all commands can use it. The geometry displays as shown in Figure 5–77.

You can use the **Bridge** option to connect existing faces and open edges.

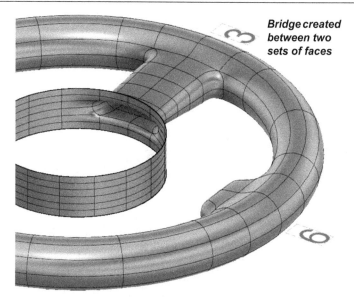

Bridge created between two sets of faces

Figure 5–77

5. Rotate the design so that you can create geometry between the interior cylinder and the extruded faces at the 6 o'clock position.

6. Delete the four extruded faces on the torus and the opposing four faces on the cylinder, as shown in Figure 5–78.

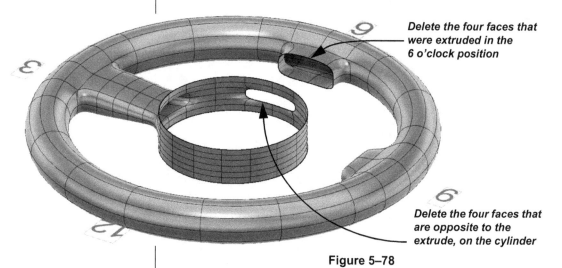

Delete the four faces that were extruded in the 6 o'clock position

Delete the four faces that are opposite to the extrude, on the cylinder

Figure 5–78

*Alternatively, you can use **Vertex to Vertex** to achieve different geometry.*

7. In the MODIFY panel, click ⬙ (Weld Vertices). The WELD VERTICES palette opens and all vertices on the design are highlighted.

8. In the *Weld Mode* field, select ⬙ (Vertex to Midpoint). This ensures that when two vertices are selected, a new vertex is created between them.

9. The eight vertices on each opening are to be matched to one another to fill the gap. Select the two vertices at the bottom-middle of the opening. The vertices should weld as shown at the top of Figure 5–79.

10. Continue selecting opposing vertices until the gap is closed. Click **OK**.

11. Rotate the design so that you can create geometry between the interior cylinder and the extruded faces at the 9 o'clock position.

12. In the BROWSER, expand the *Sketches* folder and hide the visibility of **Sketch1**.

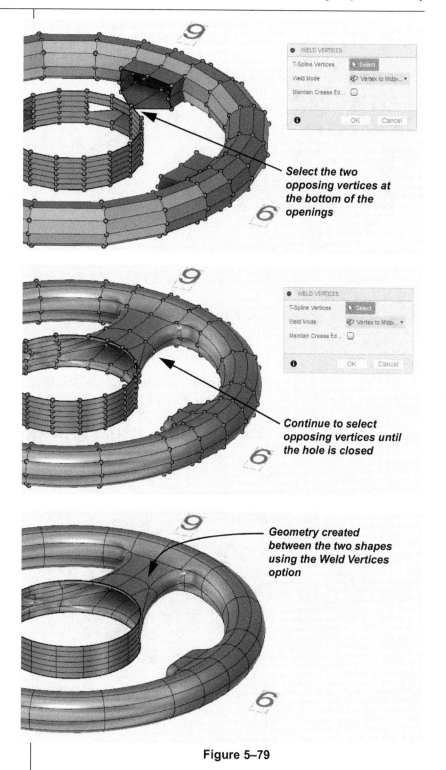

Select the two opposing vertices at the bottom of the openings

Continue to select opposing vertices until the hole is closed

Geometry created between the two shapes using the Weld Vertices option

Figure 5–79

13. Delete the four extruded faces on the torus and the opposing four faces on the cylinder, as shown in Figure 5–80.

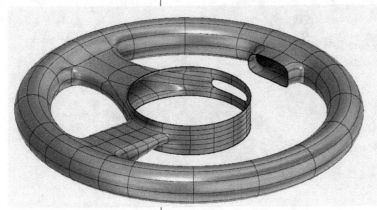

Delete the four faces on the remaining extrude, as well as the faces opposite it on the cylinder

Figure 5–80

14. In the MODIFY panel, click (Merge Edge).

15. Double-click on an edge in the opening on the torus (as shown in Figure 5–81) to select the loop for *Edge Group One*.

16. Activate the *Edge Group Two* field. Double-click on an edge in the opening on the cylinder (as shown in Figure 5–81) to select the entire loop.

   • Note: The order of edge selection when you are merging edges will affect the geometry and how the first edge group is merged into the second.

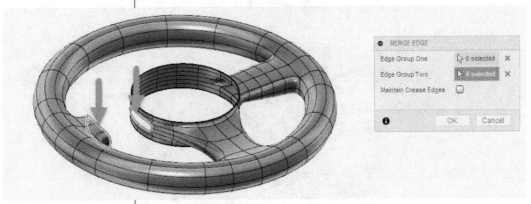

Figure 5–81

17. Click **OK** to merge the two edges. The model displays similar to that shown in Figure 5–82. Note in the highlighted areas in the image that the faces are not smooth. This is because of issues with how the geometry is merging with other faces on the cylinder.

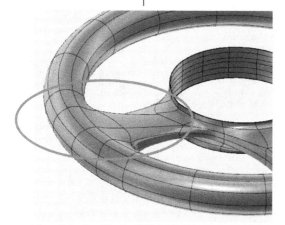

Visual Style: Shaded With Visible Edges Only   *Visual Style: Shaded*

Figure 5–82

Unlike in solid modeling, when sculpting there is no feature list added to the Timeline. The Undo option is simply used to return to a previous point in the design.

18. Undo the **Merge Edge** operation and the deletion of the faces on the cylinder. Depending on the order in which you deleted the faces, you might need to delete the faces on the extrude.

19. Use the **Insert Edge** command to create a new edge on both sides of the edge shown in Figure 5–83. This edge is at the 9 o'clock position on the cylinder and is directly opposite the mid-line of the hole on the extrude.

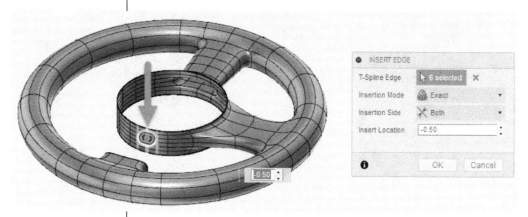

Figure 5–83

20. Delete the four faces on the cylinder as shown in Figure 5–84. Merging to this smaller loop of edges will provide a smoother transition because the **Merge Edge** command affects adjacent faces.

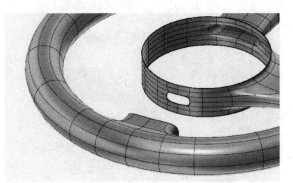

Figure 5–84

21. Use **Merge Edge** to merge the edges of the two loops. Select the loop of edges on the cylinder as the *Edge Group One* references and select the loop of edges on the torus as the *Edge Group Two* references. The resulting geometry is smoother than it was previously, as shown in Figure 5–85. Note that the **Merge Edge** command has a bigger impact on adjacent faces than the **Bridge** option.

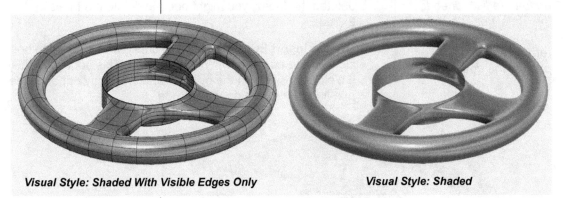

Visual Style: Shaded With Visible Edges Only   *Visual Style: Shaded*

Figure 5–85

22. Undo the **Merge Edge** operation.

*The order of reference selection affects the resulting geometry when using **Merge Edge**.*

23. Use **Merge Edge** again to merge the edges of the two loops, but this time select the references in the reverse order (i.e., select the loop of edges on the torus as the *Edge Group One* references, and select the loop of edges on the cylinder as the *Edge Group Two* references). The resulting geometry is shown in Figure 5–86.

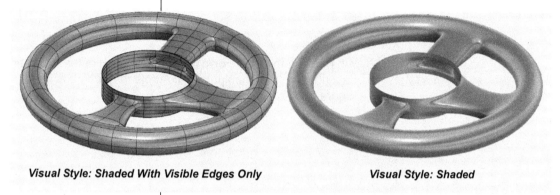

Visual Style: Shaded With Visible Edges Only   **Visual Style: Shaded**

Figure 5–86

24. Use the **Fill Hole** command to close the holes in the top and bottom of the cylinder and finish the form. The model should display in the Shaded display style as shown in Figure 5–87.

This geometry was created with the Merge Edge option

This geometry was created with the Weld Vertices option

This geometry was created with the Bridge option

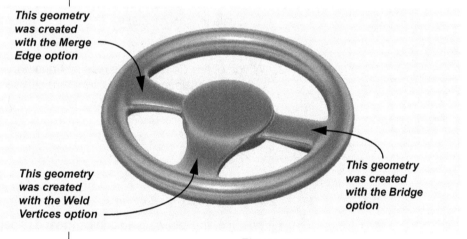

Figure 5–87

25. Review the solid geometry that was created. Note how the results differ to add geometry between the two shapes.

26. Save the design.

Chapter Review Questions

1. When modeling in the FORM contextual environment, you can use the **Match** command to match parametric sketches from the SOLID environment.

   a. True

   b. False

2. When using the **Edit Form** command, which of the following describe the triad manipulator controls that are shown in Figure 5–88? (Select all that apply.)

   Figure 5–88

   a. Translate in X, Y, or Z axis

   b. Translate in plane

   c. Rotate in plane

   d. Scale in X, Y, or Z axis

   e. Scale in plane

3. Which of the *Coordinate Space* settings provides you with only two translation manipulators that can be used to manipulate the form geometry?

   a. ⌊ (World)

   b. ⌐ (View)

   c. ⌐ (Local)

4. Which of the following editing commands enables you to add elements (i.e., points, edges, or faces) to existing form geometry? (Select all that apply.)

   a. **Insert Edge**

   b. **Insert Point**

   c. **Subdivide**

   d. **Crease**

5. The **Flatten** command enables you to select multiple points and make them parallel to a selected plane.

   a. True

   b. False

6. When subdividing a face, (Simple mode) forces the form geometry to remain exactly the same once the faces have been subdivided.

   a. True

   b. False

7. Which of the following commands can be used to create geometry between two form shapes that exist in the same feature? (Select all that apply.)

   a. **Insert Edge**

   b. **Subdivide**

   c. **Merge Edge**

   d. **Bridge**

   e. **Match**

8. For symmetry in T-Spline geometry, which of the following are true?

   a. Symmetry can only be assigned when the base T-Spline geometry is created using quick shapes.

   b. Symmetry can only be assigned using the **Symmetry** command by selecting faces on the T-Spline geometry.

   c. All of the symmetry assigned during quick shape creation can be removed using the **Clear Symmetry** command.

   d. Faces that are adjacent to a face that is a symmetry reference also update to reflect the symmetry.

Answers: 1.a, 2.(a,b), 3.b, 4.(a,b,c), 5.a, 6.b, 7.(c,d), 8.d

Command Summary

Button	Command	Location
	Bevel Edge	• **Toolbar:** *DESIGN* Workspace>*FORM* tab>MODIFY panel • **Context Menu:** (with edge selected)
	Bridge	• **Toolbar:** *DESIGN* Workspace>*FORM* tab>MODIFY panel
	Circular - Internal (Symmetry)	• **Toolbar:** *DESIGN* Workspace>*FORM* tab>SYMMETRY panel
	Clear Symmetry	• **Toolbar:** *DESIGN* Workspace>*FORM* tab>SYMMETRY panel
	Crease	• **Toolbar:** *DESIGN* Workspace>*FORM* tab>MODIFY panel • **Context Menu:** (with edge, point, or face selected)
	Delete	• **Toolbar:** *DESIGN* Workspace>*FORM* tab>MODIFY panel • **Context Menu:** Right-click in the graphics window • **Context Menu:** (with edge, point, or face selected) • **Keyboard:** <Delete>
	Edit Form	• **Toolbar:** *DESIGN* Workspace>*FORM* tab>MODIFY panel • **Context Menu:** Right-click in the graphics window • **Context Menu:** (with edge, point, or face selected)
	Flatten	• **Toolbar:** *DESIGN* Workspace>*FORM* tab>MODIFY panel • **Context Menu:** (with edge, point, or face selected)
	Freeze	• **Toolbar:** *DESIGN* Workspace>*FORM* tab>MODIFY panel • **Context Menu:** (with edge or face selected)
	Insert Edge	• **Toolbar:** *DESIGN* Workspace>*FORM* tab>MODIFY panel • **Context Menu:** Right-click in the graphics window • **Context Menu:** (with edge selected)
	Insert Point	• **Toolbar:** *DESIGN* Workspace>*FORM* tab>MODIFY panel

	Match	• **Toolbar:** *DESIGN* Workspace>*FORM* tab>MODIFY panel
		• **Context Menu:** (with edge selected)
	Merge Edge	• **Toolbar:** *DESIGN* Workspace>*FORM* tab>MODIFY panel
	Mirror - Internal (Symmetry)	• **Toolbar:** *DESIGN* Workspace>*FORM* tab>SYMMETRY panel
	Pull	• **Toolbar:** *DESIGN* Workspace>*FORM* tab>MODIFY panel
	Slide Edge	• **Toolbar:** *DESIGN* Workspace>*FORM* tab>MODIFY panel
		• **Context Menu:** (with edge selected)
	Subdivide	• **Toolbar:** *DESIGN* Workspace>*FORM* tab>MODIFY panel
		• **Context Menu:** (with face selected)
	Thicken	• **Toolbar:** *DESIGN* Workspace>*FORM* tab>MODIFY panel
	UnCrease	• **Toolbar:** *DESIGN* Workspace>*FORM* tab>MODIFY panel
		• **Context Menu:** (with edge, point, or face selected)
	UnFreeze	• **Toolbar:** *DESIGN* Workspace>*FORM* tab>MODIFY panel
		• **Context Menu:** (with edge or face selected)
	UnWeld Edges	• **Toolbar:** *DESIGN* Workspace>*FORM* tab>MODIFY panel
		• **Context Menu:** (with edge selected)
	Weld Vertices	• **Toolbar:** *DESIGN* Workspace>*FORM* tab>MODIFY panel
		• **Context Menu:** (with point selected)

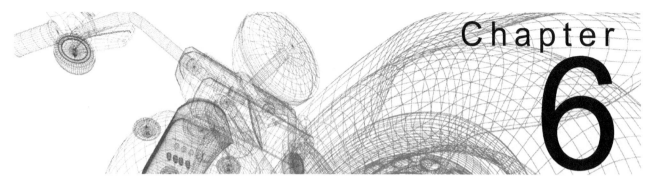

6

Sketching Tools

In addition to using the quick shape tools for T-Spline form creation, you can also reference a sketch to create 3D T-Spline Form geometry. To efficiently create sketches in the Autodesk® Fusion 360® software, an understanding of the sketch workflow, entity creation workflows, and construction geometry is required. This chapter focuses on these sketching tools. In the upcoming chapters, you will learn how to use these sketches to create sculpted geometry.

Learning Objectives in this Chapter

- Describe the general workflow to create a new sketch in an Autodesk Fusion 360 design.
- Use the sketch entity types to create lines, splines, points, rectangles, circles, and arcs.
- Sketch entities so that the required dimensions and constraints are assigned as entities are sketched.
- Add dimensions to sketch entities.
- Assign constraints to a sketch to control the required relationships between sketch entities.
- Create new construction planes, axes, and points in a design.

6.1 Introduction to the Sketching Workflow

A sketch is a key tool in creating T-Spline geometry because not all geometry can be accurately defined using only the quick shape options (e.g., Box, Cylinder, Torus). Incorporating the use of sketches in design enables you to create extruded, revolved, lofted, and swept T-Spline geometry.

The sketch plane for a sketch can be an origin plane, a construction plane, or existing solid face.

To start a 2D sketch, in the toolbar's *SOLID* tab>CREATE panel, select ⬚ (Create Sketch), and then select a sketch plane on which to place the sketch. Sketch tools are located in the CREATE panel drop-down list, or accessed by right-clicking in the graphics window to open the marking menu, as shown in Figure 6–1.

Figure 6–1

A sketch can be created in the SOLID environment prior to entering the FORM contextual environment, or it can be created directly in the FORM contextual environment. Consider the following:

- Sketches created in the SOLID and FORM environments can be used in the other environments, as required, to create geometry.

- Only sketches created in the SOLID environment are displayed as separate Timeline entries (![icon]). Sketches created in the FORM environment are contained within the form feature and don't have a Timeline entry.

In this learning guide, all sketches are created in the SOLID environment prior to beginning form creation so that all of the sketches are easily accessible in the Timeline.

- Sketches created in the SOLID and FORM environments are listed in the BROWSER in the *Sketch* folder.
  - Sketches created in the SOLID environment are editable from the BROWSER, while sketches created in the FORM environment can only be edited with the **Edit Sketch** command if you have the form feature open. For this reason, it is recommended that you rename your sketches to help identify them and where they were created if you intend to create sketches in both environments.

General Sketch Workflow

The following describes the general workflow for creating a sketch. Although the steps to create each sketch entity type varies slightly, the overall workflow for creating a sketch is the same. Each entity type is discussed in more detail later in this chapter.

Sketches can also be created by selecting the sketch plane first, and then initiating the start of a new sketch.

1. Initiate the creation of a new sketch.
2. Select an origin plane, construction plane, or solid planar face on which you want the sketch to be created.
3. Use the available entity creation options to define the shape of the sketch.
4. Assign constraints and dimensions to fully locate and define the sketch.
5. Complete the creation of the sketch.

6.2 Sketch Entities

Line

Use the **Line** tool to create a single line or a continuous series of connected lines, similar to that shown in Figure 6–2.

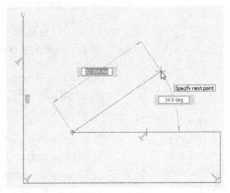

Figure 6–2

Use any of the following methods to start the **Line** tool:

- In the CREATE panel, click ⌐ (Line).

- Right-click in the graphics window and select **Line** from the context menu.

- Press <L>.

Fit Point Spline

Use the **Fit Point Spline** tool to sketch a free-form 2D curve, as shown in Figure 6–3.

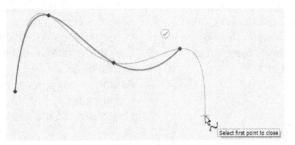

Figure 6–3

To start the **Fit Point Spline** tool, in the *SKETCH* contextual tab>CREATE panel, expand **Spline** and click ⌒ (Fit Point Spline).

Points

Points will snap to grid points if snapping is enabled and the grid is displayed.

Use the **Point** tool to sketch individual points.

To start the **Point** tool, click ┬ (Point) in the *SKETCH* contextual tab>CREATE panel.

Rectangles

Use the **Rectangle** tool to create a predefined rectangular shape, as shown in Figure 6–4, Figure 6–5, and Figure 6–6. To start the **Rectangle** tool, in the *SKETCH* contextual tab> CREATE panel, expand **Rectangle** and select the appropriate creation type.

There are three Rectangle creation types:

*   ⬜ (2-Point Rectangle)

Press <R> to sketch a 2-point rectangle.

Horizontal and vertical constraints are automatically added to the sides of a 2-point rectangle.

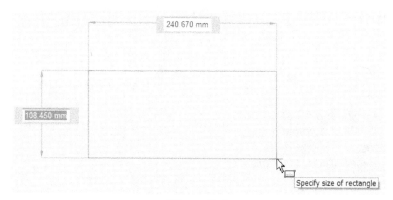

Figure 6–4

- ◇ (3-Point Rectangle)

Parallel constraints are automatically added to the sides of a 3-point rectangle.

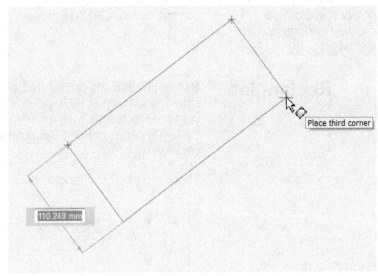

Figure 6–5

- ▢ (Center Rectangle)

A point and construction lines are automatically created to locate the center of the rectangle.

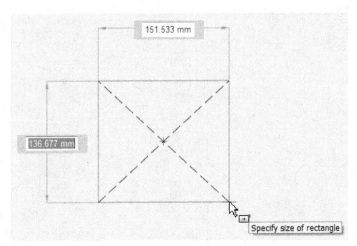

Figure 6–6

Circle

Press <C> to sketch a center diameter circle.

Use the **Circle** tool to create predefined circular shapes, as shown in Figure 6–7 to Figure 6–11. To start the **Circle** tool, in the *SKETCH* contextual tab>CREATE panel, click **Circle** and select the appropriate creation type.

There are five Circle creation types:

- 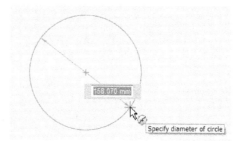 (Center Diameter Circle)

Figure 6–7

- (2-Point Circle)

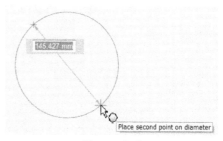

Figure 6–8

- (3-Point Circle)

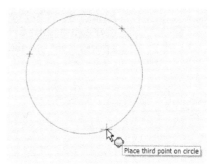

Figure 6–9

- 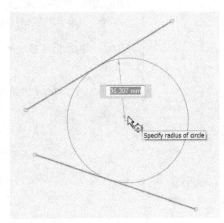 (2-Tangent Circle)

Figure 6–10

- (3-Tangent Circle)

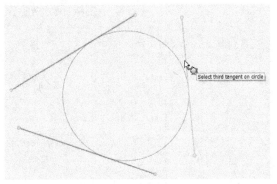

Figure 6–11

Arcs

Use the **Arc** tool to create predefined arc shapes, as shown in Figure 6–12 to Figure 6–14. To start the **Arc** tool, in the *SKETCH* contextual tab>CREATE panel, click **Arc** and select the appropriate creation type.

There are three Arc creation types:

- 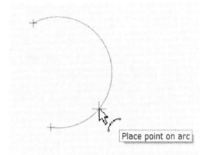 (3-Point Arc)

Figure 6–12

- (Center Point Arc)

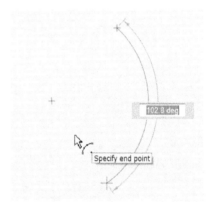

Figure 6–13

- (Tangent Arc)

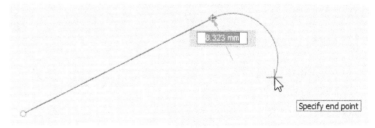

Figure 6–14

Slot

Use the **Slot** tool to create a closed symmetrical shape with two parallel lines enclosed by two arcs of equal radius. To start the **Slot** tool, in the SKETCH contextual tab>CREATE panel, click **Slot** and select the appropriate creation type.

There are five Slot creation types. Three of these types are shown in Figure 6–15, Figure 6–16, and Figure 6–17. To create these three slot types, select three points to fully define the shape. Tooltips display at the cursor explaining what selections are required.

The remaining two types (**Three Point Arc Slot** and **Center Point Arc Slot**) are created using a similar method, but instead of a linear centerline, you create an arc that drives the shape of the slot. To create these two slot types, select four points to fully define the shape. Tooltips display at the cursor explaining what selections are required.

- ⬭ (Center to Center Slot)

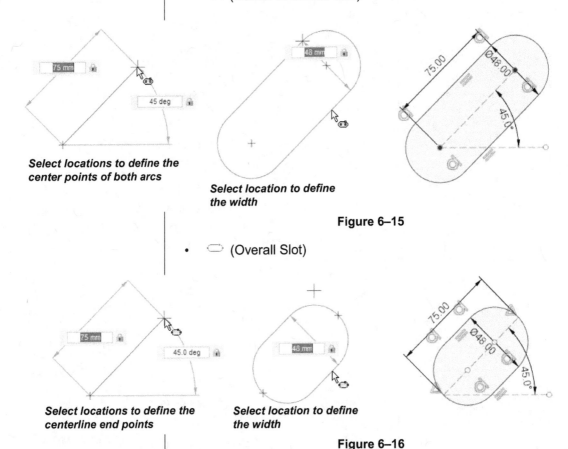

Select locations to define the center points of both arcs

Select location to define the width

Figure 6–15

- ⬭ (Overall Slot)

Select locations to define the centerline end points

Select location to define the width

Figure 6–16

• 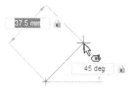 (Center Point Slot)

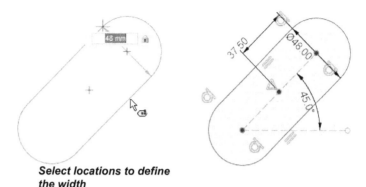

Select locations to define the center point of the centerline and the center point of one arc

Select locations to define the width

Figure 6–17

Polygons

A polygon is defined as a closed shape with at least three straight sides. To start the **Polygon** tool, in the *SKETCH* contextual tab>CREATE panel, click **Polygon** and select the appropriate creation type.

There are three Polygon creation types, shown in Figure 6–18, Figure 6–19, and Figure 6–20. To create any of these polygons, select two points to fully define the shape. Tooltips display at the cursor explaining what selections are required.

• 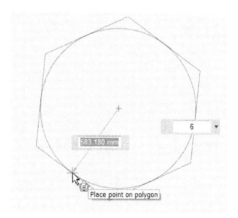 (Circumscribed Polygon)

When creating a sketched entity, you can enter dimensions in the entry fields and press <Tab> to lock them. Once locked, the dimensions automatically display with the entity complete.

Figure 6–18

- ⬡ (Inscribed Polygon)

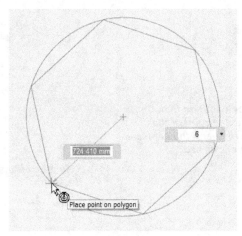

Figure 6–19

- ⬠ (Edge Polygon)

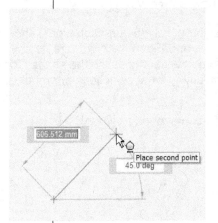
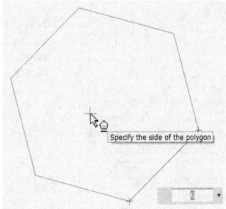

Figure 6–20

Ellipse

Use the **Ellipse** tool to create a predefined shape, as shown in Figure 6–21. To start the **Ellipse** tool, click ⬭ (Ellipse) in the *SKETCH* contextual tab>CREATE panel.

To create an ellipse, select three points to fully define the shape. Tooltips display at the cursor explaining what selections are required.

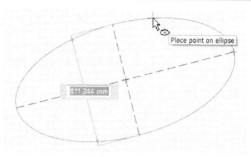

Figure 6–21

Construction lines are automatically created along the major and minor axes of the ellipse.

Tangent Arc Using a Line

The 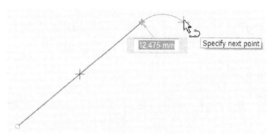 (Line) tool also enables you to sketch tangent arcs, as shown in Figure 6–22. When locating the endpoint of a line, press and hold the left mouse button and drag the cursor. A tangent arc will extend from the end of the line. After you locate the endpoint of the tangent arc, the next entity reverts back to a line unless you hold the left mouse button down again.

A Tangency constraint is automatically created at the intersection of the line and the arc.

Figure 6–22

Tangent Line Between Two Circles or Arcs

To sketch a line that is tangent to two circles or arcs:

1. Start the (Line) tool.
2. Click and hold the cursor over one of the circles or arcs.
3. While holding the left mouse button, drag the cursor to the next circle until the Tangent constraint displays.
4. Release the mouse button to locate the tangent line, as shown in Figure 6–23.

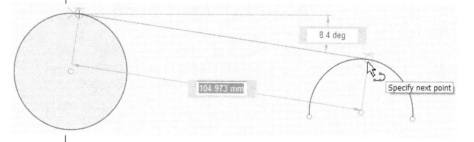

Figure 6–23

Fillets

The ⌐ (Fillet) command modifies the intersection of two lines in a 2D sketch, as shown in Figure 6–24. The fillet rounds corners in a sketch by placing an arc at the intersection of two lines. The fillet arc is always tangent to the intersecting entities.

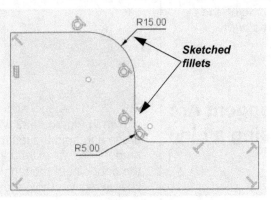

Figure 6–24

To create multiple fillets that are driven with the same dimension value, continue to select vertices prior to entering the value for the fillet.

Use the following steps, to create a fillet:

1. In the *SKETCH* contextual tab>CREATE panel, click

   ⌐ (Fillet).

2. Select the lines or arcs between which the fillet will be created or click directly on the intersection point to create the fillet. The dimension is added to the fillet arc and Tangency constraints are applied.

Construction Entities

Construction entities are used as references and aid in sketching. They do not create solid geometry as they are not considered to be a boundary of the resulting profile. It is common to use construction lines when sketching to indicate that arcs or circles lie along the same line or to indicate the midpoint of a line.

To create a construction entity:

1. Select a entity in the sketch.

2. In the SKETCH PALETTE, click ⫷ (Normal/Construction) to convert it to a construction entity. Alternatively, in the graphics window, right-click and select **Normal/Construction**, or press <X>.

Construction entities are dashed and you can add dimensions and constraints to them. An example of construction entities used as dimension and constraint references is shown in Figure 6–25.

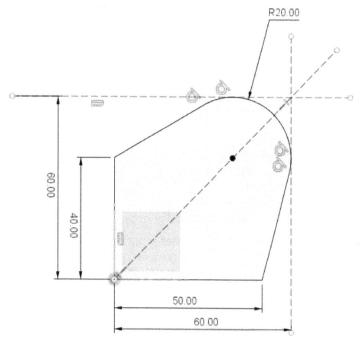

Figure 6–25

6.3 Dimensioning

Dimensions define the size and location of objects in the sketch.

Dynamic Input

When creating entities, a dynamic input line displays when you move the cursor in the graphics window. This line provides you with a heads-up display for the input fields. These fields enable you to enter explicit values for the start location of an entity, values to extend the entity, and angular values to position the entity, as shown in Figure 6–26. The field highlighted in blue is the active value, indicating that you can enter a value in the field.

To place an entity without creating the dimension, simply click to place the entity. You can assign dimensions after the entity has been created.

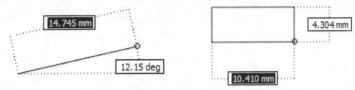

Figure 6–26

After entering a value in a dynamic input field, press <Tab> to toggle to the next field to enter its value. After all of the values have been entered, finalize the entity by pressing <Enter>. A dimension is automatically created.

Adding Sketch Dimensions

Use the following steps to create a dimension:

1. In the *SKETCH* contextual tab>CREATE panel, click

   ⊢ (Sketch Dimension). Alternatively, you can press <D>.
2. Select the entity or entities.
3. Move the cursor to the dimension's placement location and click to place the dimension.

A fully dimensioned sketch is shown in Figure 6–27.

Linear dimensions locate the circle with respect to the origin point

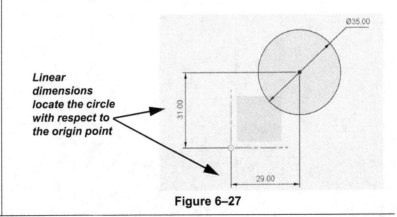

Figure 6–27

- The dimension type that is created depends on whether you select an entity or its endpoints. For example, selecting two non-parallel lines creates an angular dimension, while selecting two end points creates a linear dimension.

- Where you place the dimension can also impact the dimension type. Consider the inclined line shown in Figure 6–28. The dimension type will default to horizontal or vertical, depending on where the dimension is placed.

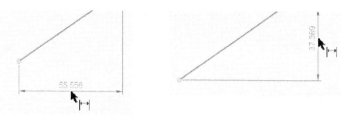

Figure 6–28

- To control the dimension type, right-click in the graphics window to access the marking and context menus. In the context menu (bottom), you can access options to lock the dimension type to **Horizontal**, **Vertical**, or **Aligned**, as shown in Figure 6–29.

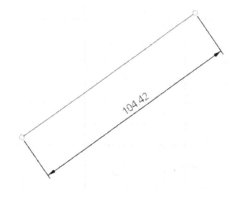

Figure 6–29

- When dimensioning a sketch to be used to create a revolved feature, you can create a diameter dimension. To dimension, select the centerline for the revolved cross-section, select the geometry, and then right-click and select **Diameter Dimension**. Place the dimension, as shown in Figure 6–30.

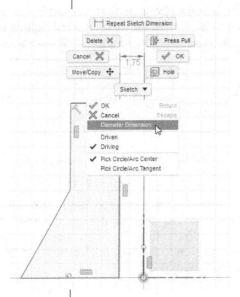
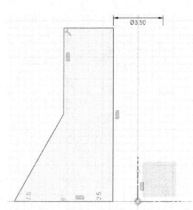

Figure 6–30

Modifying Sketch Dimensions

As soon as a dimension is placed, the entry field activates, enabling you to enter a value for the dimension. Press <Enter> to complete the placement. To edit a placed dimension, double-click on a dimension to change its value. The sketched geometry updates to reflect the new value.

Deleting Sketch Dimensions

To delete a dimension, select the dimension, right-click, and then select ✕ (Delete). You can also select the dimension and press <Delete>.

6.4 Sketch Constraints

Sketch constraints force a positional relationship between two or more entities and control what changes can be made to the sketch. For example, you can force two sketched lines to be parallel by applying a Parallel constraint, which is then indicated by a symbol adjacent to both lines, as shown in Figure 6–31.

In this example, the lower line was selected first, so its orientation is applied to the upper line to make them parallel.

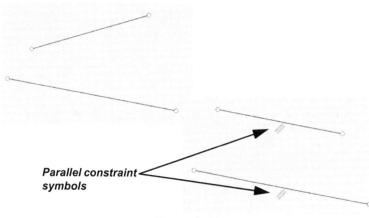

Parallel constraint symbols

Figure 6–31

- When sketching entities, constraints are automatically applied as you place entities in the sketch.

- If the automatically assigned constraints do not capture your intent, you can explicitly assign additional constraints using the CONSTRAINTS panel in the *SKETCH* contextual tab.

Constraint Types

When explicitly assigning constraints to your sketched entities, the order of selection can affect the positioning of the resulting entities. For the example shown in Figure 6–31, the lower line was selected first and the second entity was made parallel to it.

The icons beside the constraint names in the CONSTRAINTS panel are the same symbols that display on the geometry when the constraint is applied. The following table lists all of the constraint types, their icons, and a description for each.

Constraint	Icon	Description
Coincident		Connects a point or vertex with other sketch geometry. Can also be used to constrain linear entities. Coincident constraints only display when you hover the cursor over the entities that are coincident. To assign this constraint, select two points/vertices.

Colinear		Forces two lines to be colinear. The lines do not need to be in contact to have this constraint applied. To assign this constraint, select two lines.
Concentric		Forces two arcs, two circles, or an arc and a circle to share the same center point. To assign this constraint, select the center point of two entities.
Curvature		Creates a curvature continuous condition between a spline and another entity. To assign this constraint, select a spline and a second entity.
Equal		Forces two entities (such as two lines or two circles) to have the same size.
Fix/UnFix		Grounds the geometry, fixing it in place regardless of the constraints or dimensions applied to the geometry. Fixed vertices or entities display in green, showing they are fixed.
Horizontal/ Vertical		Forces lines to be horizontal or vertical in the 2D plane of the sketch. It can also force two points or vertices to remain horizontally or vertically aligned to each other. To assign this constraint, select the two linear entities/points.
Midpoint		Snaps a point or vertex to the midpoint of another entity. To assign this constraint, select a linear entity first, and then select the point/vertex that will snap to the midpoint.
Parallel		Forces two lines to be parallel. To assign this constraint, select the two linear entities.
Perpendicular		Forces two lines to remain at a 90° angle to each other. The lines do not need to be in contact to have this constraint applied. To assign this constraint, select the two linear entities.
Symmetry		Creates a symmetrical relationship about a selected line, commonly referred to as a mirrored relationship. To assign this constraint, select the two entities/points that are to be symmetric, and then select the symmetry line.
Tangent		Forces an arc or circle to be tangent to another entity. To assign this constraint, select the two entities.

Deleting Constraints

To delete a constraint (whether it was created during sketching or explicitly assigned), select the constraint icon in the graphics window and press <Delete>.

Projected Geometry

Incorporating the use of projected geometry into a sketch enables you to build relationships between features. In Figure 6–32, the edges of the hole were projected onto a sketch on the front face. The sketch was completed by adding lines between the points and the sketch was extruded as shown on the right. The projected edges create a relationship between the hole and the extrusion so that if the diameter of the hole changes, the height of the extrusion changes accordingly.

The **Project** option with the **Specified Entities** filter selected will only project entities such as lines, arcs, and points. It does not project silhouette edges.

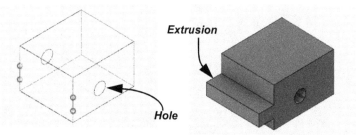

Figure 6–32

Use either of the following methods to start the **Project** tool:

- In the *SKETCH* contextual tab>CREATE panel, click

  Project/Include> (Project).

- In the graphics window, right-click and select **Sketch>**

  Project> (Project).

- Once edges are selected, they are immediately projected onto the sketch and are displayed in a purple color. To temporarily toggle off the display of all projected references in a sketch, clear the **Show Projected Geometries** option in the SKETCH PALETTE.

6.5 Construction Features

Construction features consist of planes, axes, or points. These features are used in a design when the existing geometry or the default origin planes, axes, and origin point do not provide a needed reference for geometry creation. For example, if geometry is required at an angle to the orthogonal origin planes, you must create a construction plane to provide the required sketch plane.

Figure 6–33 shows a series of sketches that are used to create geometry. A circular sketch was created on the YZ plane, but additional planes were required to create the remaining sketches. Four planes were created (as shown in the BROWSER) and each was used to create a sketch or support the creation of another plane.

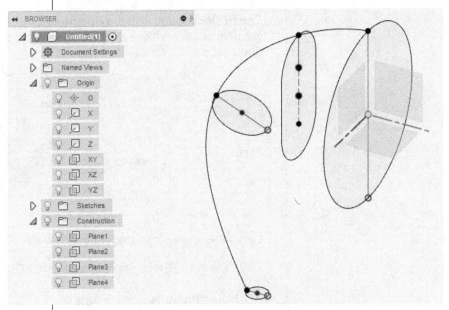

Figure 6–33

Consider the following uses for construction features:

Construction features have no mass or volume and extend infinitely in all directions.

- Construction planes can be used as placement planes for sketches, dimension references, and used in the creation of other construction features.

- Construction axes can be used as references in creating geometry or other construction features.

- Construction points can be used as references in creating geometry or other construction features.

Tip

Construction features can be created in either the SOLID or the FORM environments, but there are key differences between the resulting features:

- Construction features created in the SOLID environment are listed in the Timeline and can be modified.

- Construction features created in a form feature in the FORM environment are listed in the BROWSER, but they cannot be modified (i.e., their offset or angular values cannot be changed).

For this reason, you should consider creating construction features in the SOLID environment, unless you are sure that no changes will be required.

Origin Features

Each new design automatically includes the following (as shown in Figure 6–34):

- Three orthogonal construction planes at the origin (i.e., the YZ, XZ, and XY planes).

- Three orthogonal construction axes at the origin (i.e., the X-, Y- and Z-axes).

- A point at which the three Origin planes and three Origin axes intersect, called the Origin.

In a new design that is using the default Home orientation, the Y-direction is up. Using the default ViewCube orientation, the XZ represents the **Front**, the YZ represents the **Right** and the XY represents the **Top**, as shown in Figure 6–34. Note that since you can edit the views on the ViewCube, this default configuration might not be true for every design.

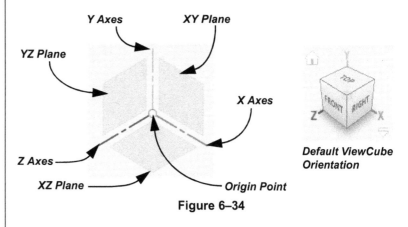

Default ViewCube Orientation

Figure 6–34

Construction Planes

The Construction plane options are located in the CONSTRUCT panel and are shown in Figure 6–35 to Figure 6–42:

Timeline icon:

- 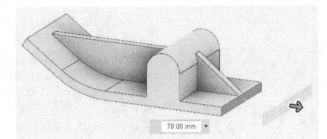 (Offset Plane)

70.00 mm

Figure 6–35

Timeline icon:

- (Plane at Angle)

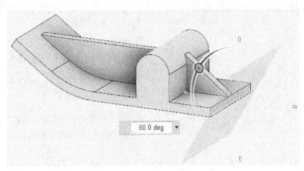

60.0 deg

Figure 6–36

Timeline icon:

- (Tangent Plane)

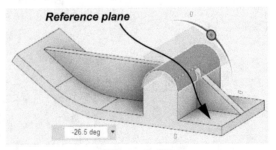

Reference plane

-26.5 deg

Figure 6–37

- 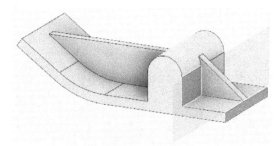 (Midplane)

Timeline icon:

Figure 6–38

- (Plane Through Two Edges)

Timeline icon:

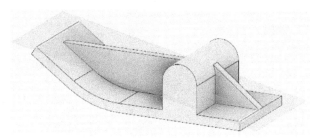

Figure 6–39

- (Plane Through Three Points)

Timeline icon:

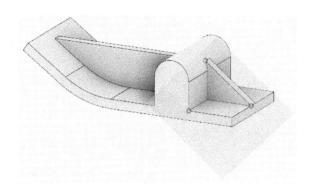

Figure 6–40

- (Plane Tangent to Face At Point)

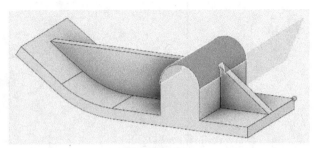

Figure 6–41

- (Plane Along Path)

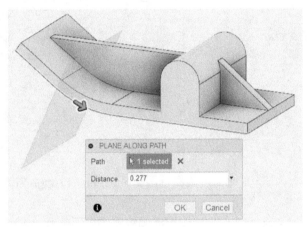

Figure 6–42

Construction Axes

The construction axis options are located in the CONSTRUCT panel. To create a construction axis, you must select references on the model to locate it. Once the option is active, a tooltip displays at the cursor indicating the type of references you need to select to fully locate the construction axis.

The construction axis features are shown in Figure 6–43 to Figure 6–48:

- 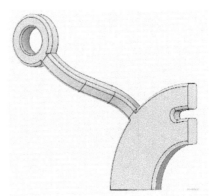 (Axis Through Cylinder/Cone/Torus)

Timeline icon:

Figure 6–43

- (Axis Perpendicular at Point)

Timeline icon:

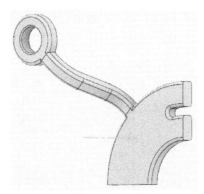

Figure 6–44

- (Axis Through Two Planes)

Timeline icon:

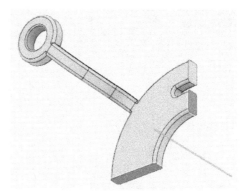

Figure 6–45

Timeline icon:

-  (Axis Through Two Points)

Figure 6–46

- 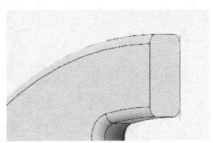 (Axis Through Edge)

Timeline icon:

Figure 6–47

- 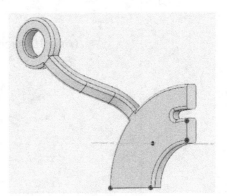 (Axis Perpendicular to Face at Point)

Timeline icon:

A sketched point can be used to place the axis.

Figure 6–48

Construction Points

The construction point options are located in the CONSTRUCT panel. To create a construction point, you must select references on the model to locate it. Once the option is active, a tooltip displays at the cursor indicating the type of references you need to select to fully locate the construction point.

The construction point features are shown in Figure 6–49 to Figure 6–54:

- (Point at Vertex)

Timeline icon:

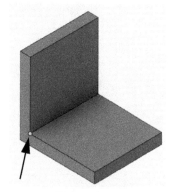

Figure 6–49

- 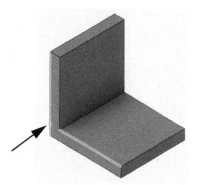 (Point Through Two Edges)

Timeline icon:

The edges do not need to physically intersect.

Figure 6–50

Timeline icon:

Construction planes can be used as a planar reference.

- (Point Through Three Planes)

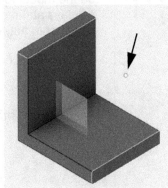

Figure 6–51

- (Point at Center of Circle/Sphere/Torus)

Timeline icon:

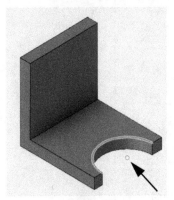

Figure 6–52

- (Point at Edge and Plane)

Timeline icon:

Construction axes can be used as an edge reference.

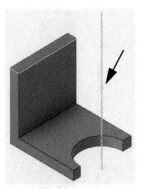

Figure 6–53

- 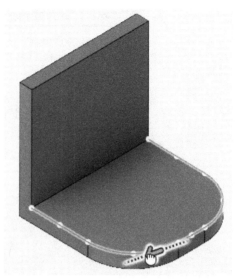 (Point Along Path)

Timeline icon:

Points along a path can be snapped to a vertex, or be located at a defined distance along the edge.

Figure 6–54

Editing Construction Features

Construction features are listed in the BROWSER in the **Construction** folder. Consider the following when working with construction planes:

- You can modify construction planes that are created with a rotational angle or distance position. To do this, right-click on the plane name in the BROWSER, Timeline, or graphics window and select **Edit Feature**. You can drag the manipulators or use the EDIT FEATURE palette to enter a new value, as required.

- To delete a construction feature, right-click on the plane,

  axes, or point you wish to delete and select ✕, or you can simply select it and press <Delete>. You can also use <Ctrl> or <Shift> to select multiple construction features for deletion at one time.

If you delete a construction feature that is referenced by another feature, you are prompted to confirm the deletion. If the construction feature is deleted, the child feature remains, and you are prompted to redefine it.

Practice 6a

Sketch Creation

Practice Objectives

- Create construction planes.
- Create sketches that can be used as a series of profiles to create a sculpted loft form.

In this practice, you will start a new design and create the four sketches shown in Figure 6–55. To create the sketches, you will create and use origin planes and construction planes.

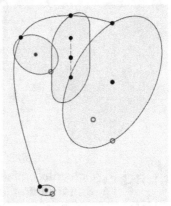

Figure 6–55

Task 1 - Create a new design and create a sketch on the YZ plane.

1. Click ▾ (File)>**New Design** to create a new design.

2. In the BROWSER, adjacent to the *Origin* folder, select (Show/Hide) to make the origin features visible.

3. Expand the *Origin* folder and select the YZ plane.

4. In the SKETCH panel, click (Create Sketch). Alternatively, you can start the command first, and then select the YZ Plane as the sketching plane.

5. In the SKETCH panel, click **Circle>** (Center Diameter Circle), or press <C> to start the Circle command.

6. Hover the cursor over the Origin Point at the center of the sketch. The cursor should snap to this reference. Start the sketch by clicking on the Origin Point, as shown in Figure 6–56.

The SKETCH PALETTE has checkbox options that enable you to toggle the sketch grid and the ability to snap to the grid.

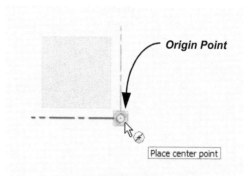

Origin Point

Place center point

Figure 6–56

7. Drag to define the diameter of the circle. In the entry field, enter **12** to assign a specific diameter value and press <Enter>. Click on the sketch diameter to confirm the creation. A circular entity and a diameter dimension is created, as shown in Figure 6–57.

- The circular sketch displays in black because it is fully constrained. The Coincident constraint was automatically assigned when the origin point was selected as the centerpoint, and the diameter dimension fully defines its size.

Dimensions are only automatically created if you enter a value in the entry field. A sketch can be created by initially placing entities and then dimensioning them as a separate step.

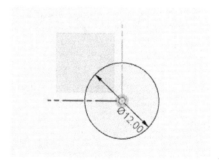

Figure 6–57

8. In the toolbar, click (Finish Sketch).

9. In the BROWSER, expand the *Sketches* folder and note that **Sketch1** is now listed. Additionally, the sketch is added to the Timeline ( ).

Task 2 - Create a second sketch on a new construction plane.

In this task, you will create a new construction plane and then use it to create a second sketch. The sketch that will be created is shown in Figure 6–58.

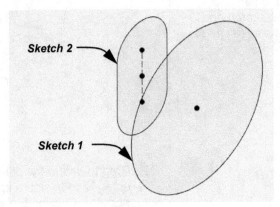

Figure 6–58

1. Return the design to the default **Home** view.

2. In the CONSTRUCT panel, click (Offset Plane).

3. Select the YZ plane as the plane to offset from. Enter **-5.00 mm** as the offset *Distance* value. The new construction plane should display as shown in Figure 6–59. Click **OK**.

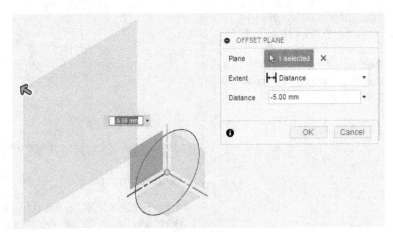

Figure 6–59

4. In the BROWSER, expand the *Construction* folder and note that **Plane1** is now listed. Additionally, the offset plane icon is added to the Timeline (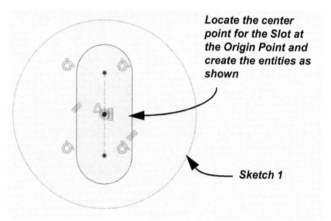).

5. Right-click on **Plane1** and select **Create Sketch** to start the creation of the new sketch for the next profile.

6. Hide the display of the Origin entities by clicking ◉ adjacent to the *Origin* folder.

7. In the SKETCH panel, click **Slot>** ⬭ (Center Point Slot).
   - Select the Origin point to define the center of the slot.
   - Drag the construction line straight up to a distance of approximately **2 mm**. Click again to locate the point.
   - Drag to define the size of the slot so that it displays similar to that shown in Figure 6–60.

Locate the center point for the Slot at the Origin Point and create the entities as shown

Sketch 1

Figure 6–60

8. Note that while some constraints are automatically added to the sketch, it is not fully defined (as indicated by its blue color). In the SKETCH panel, click ⊢⊣ (Sketch Dimension) or press <D>. Dimension the slot as shown in Figure 6–61:

   - Select the arc at the top of the slot radius and then click away from the entity to place the dimension. When prompted for the radius value, enter **2.3 mm**.
   - Select the two points at the ends of the construction line and then click away from the entities to place the dimension. When prompted for the linear value, enter **4.0 mm**.
   - The sketch should appear as shown in Figure 6–61. Note that the sketch is black, indicating that it is fully constrained.

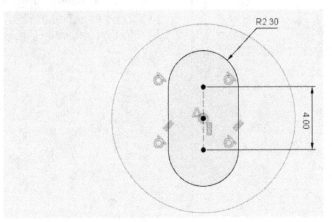

Figure 6–61

9. In the toolbar, click ✓ (FINISH SKETCH). **Sketch2** is added to the BROWSER and the Timeline.

Task 3 - Create a third sketch on a new construction plane.

In this task, you will create two new construction planes and then use them to create a third sketch. The sketch that you will create is shown in Figure 6–62.

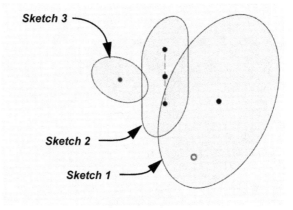

Figure 6–62

1. Return the design to the default **Home** view, if not already set.

2. Show the display of the Origin entities by clicking adjacent to the *Origin* folder.

3. In the CONSTRUCT panel, click (Plane at Angle). Select the Z axis as the *Angle* reference and enter **-25.0 deg**. The construction plane should display as shown in Figure 6–63. Click **OK**.

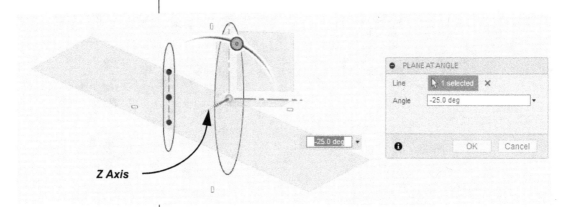

Figure 6–63

4. In the CONSTRUCT panel, click 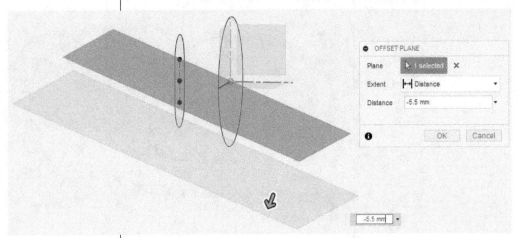 (Offset Plane). Select the plane that you just created and offset the new plane. For the offset *Distance*, enter **-5.5 mm**, as shown in Figure 6–64. Click **OK**.

Figure 6–64

5. Right-click on **Plane3** and select **Create Sketch** to start the creation of the new sketch for the next profile.

6. Hide the display of the Origin entities for clarity.

7. In the SKETCH panel, click **Circle>** (Center Diameter Circle), or press <C> to start the Circle command.

8. Sketch and dimension the circle shown in Figure 6–65. Note that the circle remains blue, indicating that it is not fully constrained.

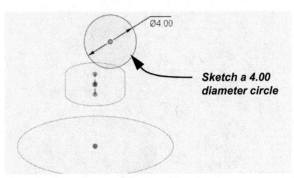

Figure 6–65

9. In the SKETCH panel, select **Project/Include>** (Project) and select the Origin Point (O) in the BROWSER. The point projects onto the sketch plane so that it can be used as a reference to locate the sketch entity. Click **OK**.

10. In the SKETCH PALETTE, click (Horizontal/Vertical) and then select the center of the sketched circle and the Origin Point. This aligns the two vertically, as shown in Figure 6–66.

11. In the SKETCH panel, click (Sketch Dimension) or press <D>. Create a dimension between the projected Origin Point and the sketched circle, as shown in Figure 6–66.

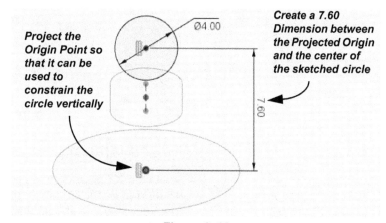

Project the Origin Point so that it can be used to constrain the circle vertically

Ø4.00

Create a 7.60 Dimension between the Projected Origin and the center of the sketched circle

7.60

Figure 6–66

12. Note that the sketch now displays in black, indicating that it is fully constrained.

13. In the toolbar, click (FINISH SKETCH). **Sketch3** is added to the BROWSER and the Timeline.

Task 4 - Create a fourth sketch on a new construction plane.

In this task, you will create a new construction plane and then create the sketch shown in Figure 6–67.

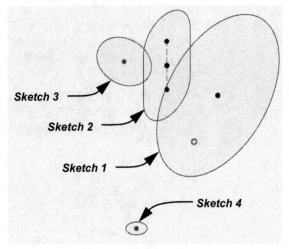

Figure 6–67

1. In the CONSTRUCT panel, click ▯ (Offset Plane).

2. Select the XZ plane as the plane to offset from and enter **-15.00 mm** as the *Distance* offset value. The new construction plane should display as shown in Figure 6–68. Click **OK**.

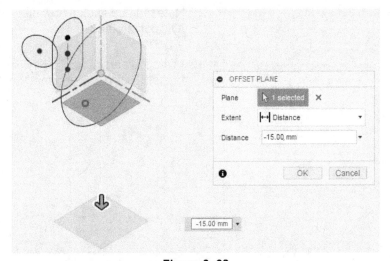

Figure 6–68

3. Note that **Plane4** is now listed in the BROWSER and the Timeline. Right-click on **Plane4** and select **Create Sketch** to start the creation of the new sketch for the last profile.

4. Sketch a **1.50 mm** diameter circle that is aligned horizontally with the Origin Point. Set the offset between the Origin Point and the circle as **8.00 mm**. The completed sketch is shown in Figure 6–69.

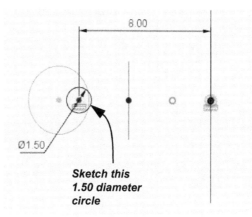

Figure 6–69

5. Once the sketch is fully constrained (i.e., displayed as black), click 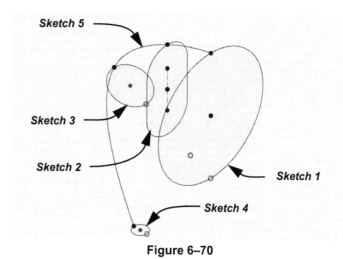 (FINISH SKETCH) to finish the sketch.

Task 5 - Create a fifth sketch on the XY plane.

In this task, you will create the sketched spline shown in Figure 6–70. This is created on the XY plane.

Figure 6–70

1. Right-click on XY plane and select **Create Sketch** to start the creation of the new sketch. This sketch will connect all of the sections to one another.

2. In the SKETCH panel, select **Project/Include>** ✈ (Intersect).

3. Rotate the sketch so that you can see each section, as shown in Figure 6–71.

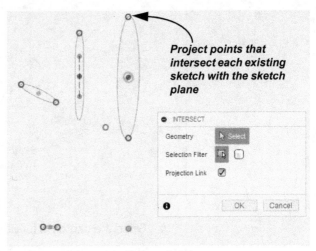

Project points that intersect each existing sketch with the sketch plane

Figure 6–71

4. Select each section to project a reference point onto the sketch plane, and then select the top arc in the slot, as shown in Figure 6–71. Click **OK**.

   • Two points will display on a circular entity because the entity intersects the sketch plane in two locations.

   • The purple circular entities indicate projection points.

5. In the SKETCH PALETTE, click 📷 (Look At). This returns the sketch to a 2D orientation looking at the sketch plane.

6. In the SKETCH panel, click ⁀ (Fit Point Spline). Select the projected points from each sketch (as shown in Figure 6–72) to define the spline. Once you have selected the fourth point, right-click and click **OK**.

Each spline point should be displayed in black, indicating that it has snapped to the projected entity. The sketch should also display in black, indicating that it is fully constrained.

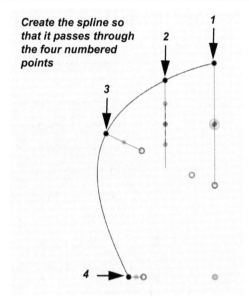

Create the spline so that it passes through the four numbered points

Figure 6–72

7. Click (FINISH SKETCH) to finish the sketch. The design consists of five sketches and the construction planes that were used to create them. In a future exercise you will use these sketches to create the geometry shown in Figure 6–73.

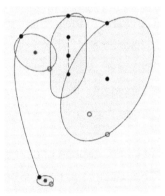

Sketched profiles that will be used to create a sculpted loft

Solid geometry created from sketched entities

Figure 6–73

8. Save the design with the name **Earbud** to your project.

9. Close the file.

Chapter Review Questions

1. Which of the following is required to begin the creation of a new sketch?

   a. Sketch Plane

   b. Sketch References

   c. Constraints

   d. Dimensions

2. An Origin Plane cannot be selected as a sketch plane.

   a. True

   b. False

3. Which of the following can be made equal using the

   $=$ (Equal) constraint? (Select all that apply.)

   a. Angles between lines

   b. Line Lengths

   c. Arc Radii

   d. Circle Diameters

4. Which of the following constraints could be used to create two circles with the same center? (Select all that apply.)

   a. Concentric

   b. Colinear

   c. Coincident

   d. Tangent

5. What is the purpose of using the ⬚ (Fix) constraint?

   a. To position one point exactly on another.

   b. To edit an existing constraint.

   c. To resolve conflicts among other constraints.

   d. To fix a point relative to the default coordinate system of the sketch.

6. Based on the constraint symbols shown in Figure 6–74, which constraint types are applied to the bottom horizontal entity? (Select all that apply.)

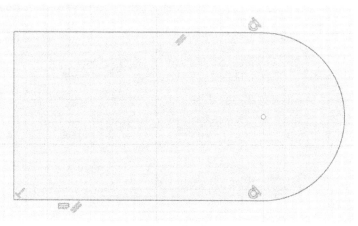

Figure 6–74

a. Symmetric

b. Parallel

c. Perpendicular

d. Tangent

e. Collinear

f. Coincident

g. Horizontal

h. Vertical

Command Summary

Button	Command	Location
	2-Point Circle	• **Toolbar:** *DESIGN* Workspace>*SKETCH* contextual tab>CREATE panel
	2-Point Rectangle	• **Toolbar:** *DESIGN* Workspace>*SKETCH* contextual tab>CREATE panel • **Context Menu:** Right-click in the graphics window and select **Sketch>2-Point Rectangle**.
	2-Tangent Circle	• **Toolbar:** *DESIGN* Workspace>*SKETCH* contextual tab>CREATE panel
	3-Point Arc	• **Toolbar:** *DESIGN* Workspace>*SKETCH* contextual tab>CREATE panel
	3-Point Circle	• **Toolbar:** *DESIGN* Workspace>*SKETCH* contextual tab>CREATE panel
	3-Point Rectangle	• **Toolbar:** *DESIGN* Workspace>*SKETCH* contextual tab>CREATE panel
	3-Tangent Circle	• **Toolbar:** *DESIGN* Workspace>*SKETCH* contextual tab>CREATE panel
	Axis Perpendicular at Point	• **Toolbar:** *DESIGN* Workspace> CONSTRUCT panel
	Axis Perpendicular to Face at Point	• **Toolbar:** *DESIGN* Workspace> CONSTRUCT panel
	Axis Through Cylinder/ Cone/Torus	• **Toolbar:** *DESIGN* Workspace> CONSTRUCT panel
	Axis Through Edge	• **Toolbar:** *DESIGN* Workspace> CONSTRUCT panel
	Axis Through Two Planes	• **Toolbar:** *DESIGN* Workspace> CONSTRUCT panel
	Axis Through Two Points	• **Toolbar:** *DESIGN* Workspace> CONSTRUCT panel
	Center Diameter Circle	• **Toolbar:** *DESIGN* Workspace>*SKETCH* contextual tab>CREATE panel • **Context Menu:** Right-click in the graphics window and select **Sketch>Center Diameter Circle**
	Center Point Arc	• **Toolbar:** *DESIGN* Workspace>*SKETCH* contextual tab>CREATE panel
	Center Rectangle	• **Toolbar:** *DESIGN* Workspace>*SKETCH* contextual tab>CREATE panel

	Coincident Constraint	• CONSTRAINTS panel
	Colinear Constraint	• CONSTRAINTS panel
	Concentric Constraint	• CONSTRAINTS panel
	Create Sketch	• **Toolbar:** *DESIGN* Workspace>*SOLID* contextual tab>CREATE panel • **Toolbar:** *DESIGN* Workspace>*FORM* contextual tab>CREATE panel
	Curvature Constraint	• CONSTRAINTS panel
	Delete	• **Context Menu:** Right-click in the graphics window with the entity or constraint selected • Press <Delete>
	Equal Constraint	• CONSTRAINTS panel
	Fix/UnFix Constraint	• CONSTRAINTS panel
	Horizontal/ Vertical Constraint	• CONSTRAINTS panel
	Line	• **Toolbar:** *DESIGN* Workspace>*SKETCH* contextual tab>CREATE panel • **Context Menu:** Right-click in the graphics window and select **Sketch>Line**
	Midplane	• **Toolbar:** *DESIGN* Workspace> CONSTRUCT panel
	Midpoint Constraint	• CONSTRAINTS panel
	Offset Plane	• **Toolbar:** *DESIGN* Workspace> CONSTRUCT panel
	Parallel Constraint	• CONSTRAINTS panel
	Perpendicular Constraint	• CONSTRAINTS panel
	Plane Along Path	• **Toolbar:** *DESIGN* Workspace> CONSTRUCT panel
	Plane at Angle	• **Toolbar:** *DESIGN* Workspace> CONSTRUCT panel
	Plane Tangent to Face At Point	• **Toolbar:** *DESIGN* Workspace> CONSTRUCT panel
	Plane Through Three Points	• **Toolbar:** *DESIGN* Workspace> CONSTRUCT panel

	Plane Through Two Edges	• **Toolbar**: *DESIGN* Workspace> CONSTRUCT panel
	Point	• **Toolbar**: *DESIGN* Workspace>*SKETCH* contextual tab>CREATE panel
	Point Along Path	• **Toolbar**: *DESIGN* Workspace> CONSTRUCT panel
	Point at Center of Circle/Sphere/ Torus	• **Toolbar**: *DESIGN* Workspace> CONSTRUCT panel
	Point at Edge and Plane	• **Toolbar**: *DESIGN* Workspace> CONSTRUCT panel
	Point at Vertex	• **Toolbar**: *DESIGN* Workspace> CONSTRUCT panel
	Point Through Three Planes	• **Toolbar**: *DESIGN* Workspace> CONSTRUCT panel
	Point Through Two Edges	• **Toolbar**: *DESIGN* Workspace> CONSTRUCT panel
	Sketch Dimension	• **Toolbar**: *DESIGN* Workspace>*SKETCH* contextual tab>CREATE panel • **Context Menu**: Right-click in the graphics window and select **Sketch Dimension**
	Fit Point Spline	• **Toolbar**: *DESIGN* Workspace>*SKETCH* contextual tab>CREATE panel • **Context Menu**: Right-click in the graphics window and select **Sketch>Fit Point Spline**
	Symmetry Constraint	• CONSTRAINTS panel
	Tangent Arc	• **Toolbar**: *DESIGN* Workspace>*SKETCH* contextual tab>CREATE panel
	Tangent Constraint	• CONSTRAINTS panel
	Tangent Plane	• **Toolbar**: *DESIGN* Workspace> CONSTRUCT panel

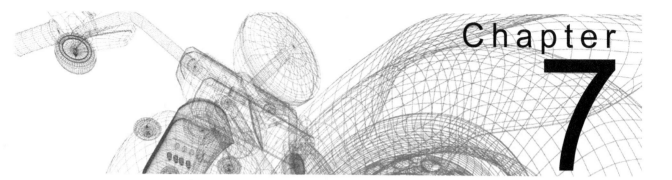

Sculpted T-Spline Extrudes and Revolves

In addition to using quick shapes to create T-Spline surface geometry, you can also create shapes that reference a sketch. Using the Extrude and Revolve options, you can create T-Spline surface geometry that is extruded normal to a sketch plane or that revolves a sketch about a centerline.

Learning Objectives in this Chapter

- Create T-Spline surface geometry by extruding a sketch.
- Create T-Spline surface geometry by revolving a sketch around a centerline.

7.1 Sculpted Extrude

The form quick shape options (e.g., Box, Cylinder, etc.) provide an efficient way to create T-Spline geometry. However, in situations where the required shape varies significantly from the available quick shape options, an **Extrude** might be a better method of creating geometry. The **Extrude** option enables you to reference a profile and then extend it by a defined distance, as shown in the examples in Figure 7–1. By referencing a sketch profile, you can more closely represent the required shape.

Sculpted extrudes create T-Spline geometry that can be manipulated using the options in the MODIFY panel.

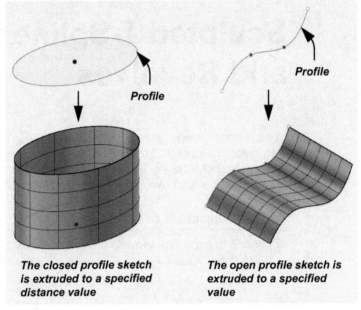

The closed profile sketch is extruded to a specified distance value

The open profile sketch is extruded to a specified value

Figure 7–1

To create extruded T-Spline geometry, complete the following in the FORM contextual environment.

1. Start the creation of the extruded T-Spline by clicking

    (Extrude) in the CREATE panel. The EXTRUDE palette displays as shown in Figure 7–2.

Figure 7–2

2. Select the profile that is to be extruded, as shown in Figure 7–3.

- The profile can be a sketched section, faces from existing T-Spline surfaces, or a planar face from an existing solid. An edge loop from another T-Spline body cannot be used as a profile reference.

- The sketched profile that is extruded can be an open or closed loop sketch.

- Consider enabling the **Profile Chain Selection** option in the palette to select all of the adjacent edges in the profile at once. To select individual edges when defining the profile, you must clear this option.

The profile sketch used to create a T-Spline extruded surface can be created in either the SOLID or FORM environments.

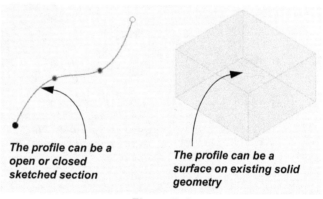

The profile can be a open or closed sketched section

The profile can be a surface on existing solid geometry

Figure 7–3

3. Ensure that the *Direction* setting of the extrude correctly defines the direction in which the geometry is to be created. The options include: **One Side**, **Two Side**, and **Symmetric**.

- Consider entering negative or positive *Distance* values to extrude in the required direction when using **One Side**.

- The **Two Side** option enables you to enter unique *Distance* values for both sides of the profile.

- The **Symmetric** option assigns the same *Distance* value on both sides of the extrude.

Once the profile is selected, the EXTRUDE palette updates to include additional options for defining the extruded T-Spline.

4. Enter a *Distance* value in the EXTRUDE palette. This defines the distance the profile is extruded. The profile is always extruded normal to the sketch plane on which the profile was created or the plane on which all entities lie, as shown in Figure 7–4.

- Alternatively, you can drag the manipulator arrow (⮕) to define the value or enter a value in the entry field in the graphics window.

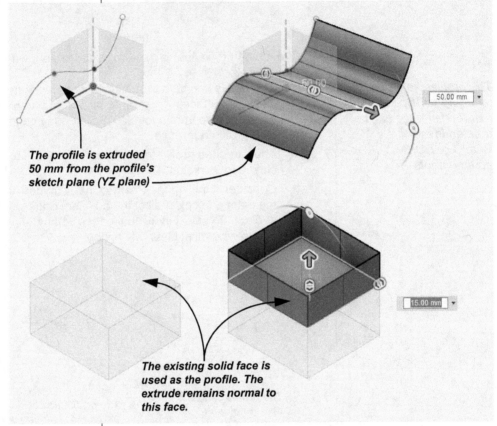

The profile is extruded 50 mm from the profile's sketch plane (YZ plane)

The existing solid face is used as the profile. The extrude remains normal to this face.

Figure 7–4

5. If the profile should be extruded at an angle to the normal axis, enter an *Angle* value, as shown for the two profiles in Figure 7–5.

- Alternatively, you can drag the rotator manipulator

(⟋) to define the value or enter a value in the entry field on the graphics window.

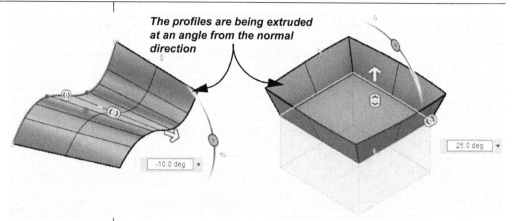

The profiles are being extruded at an angle from the normal direction

Figure 7–5

These options affect how closely the T-Spline geometry matches a sketched profile.

You can drag the manipulators to manually manipulate the number of Faces or Front Faces that are used to create the T-Spline geometry.

6. Define the control frame that will be generated on the extruded T-Spline geometry. The options include *Faces*, *Front Faces*, and *Spacing*, as described below and shown in Figure 7–6.

   • Enter the number of *Faces* that will extend around or along the profile.

   • Enter the number of *Front Faces* to be added along the extruded distance.

   • The two spacing options, **Curvature** and **Uniform**, can be used to customize the resulting control frame and help ensure that the profiles shape is matched as closely as possible, as shown in Figure 7–6. **Uniform** spaces the number of faces evenly along a profile. **Curvature** spaces the number of faces based on a profile's curvature. The greater the amount of curvature, the more faces that will be assigned to that area.

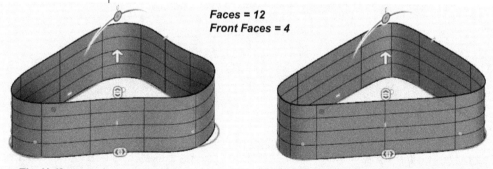

Faces = 12
Front Faces = 4

The Uniform option spaces the number of faces evenly along the entire profile

The Curvature option spaces the number of faces based on the curvature of the profile. Areas of higher curvature have more faces.

Figure 7–6

7. Click **OK** to complete the sculpted extrude.

7.2 Sculpted Revolve

Similar to a sculpted extrude, the **Revolve** option also enables you to reference a sketched profile to create sculpted T-Spline geometry. As opposed to extending along a single direction, a revolve is rotated about an axis of revolution, as shown in Figure 7–7. Once the T-Spline geometry is created, it can be further manipulated to create a design.

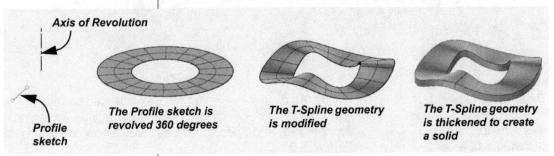

The Profile sketch is revolved 360 degrees

The T-Spline geometry is modified

The T-Spline geometry is thickened to create a solid

Figure 7–7

To create revolved T-Spline geometry, click 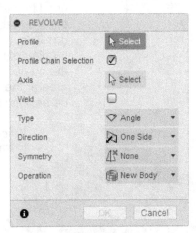 (Revolve) in the CREATE panel. The REVOLVE palette displays as shown in Figure 7–8.

Figure 7–8

1. Select the profile that is to be revolved.
   - The profile can be a sketched section, edges from existing T-Spline surfaces, or a planar face from an existing solid.
   - A sketched profile that is revolved can be an open or closed loop sketch.

The profile sketch used to create a T-Spline revolved surface can be created in either the SOLID or FORM environments.

- Consider enabling the **Profile Chain Selection** option in the palette to select all of the adjacent edges in the profile, at once. To select individual edges when defining the profile you must clear this option.

2. Select the *Axis* field in the REVOLVE palette and then select the axis around which the profile will be rotated. The axis can be an origin axis, a linear sketched entity, or a sculpted or solid edge.

Once the profile is selected, the REVOLVE palette updates to include some additional options for defining the extruded T-Spline.

3. Define the extent of the revolution as shown in Figure 7–9.
   - Set the *Type* option to **Full** to rotate the geometry fully through 360 degrees.
   - Set the *Type* option to **Angle** to define the extent of the revolve by entering an angular value. Alternatively, you can drag the rotation manipulator ( ) to define the angular value or enter a value in the entry field on the graphics window.

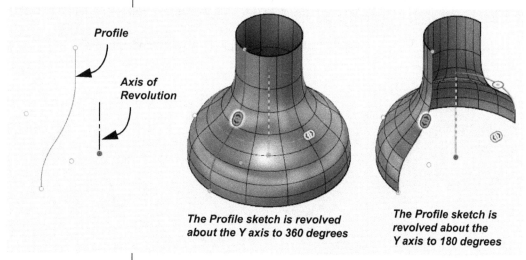

The Profile sketch is revolved about the Y axis to 360 degrees

The Profile sketch is revolved about the Y axis to 180 degrees

Figure 7–9

4. Ensure that the *Direction* setting of the revolve correctly defines the direction in which the geometry is to be created. The options include: **One Side**, **Two Side**, and **Symmetric**.
   - Consider entering negative or positive *Distance* values to revolve in the required direction when using **One Side**.
   - The **Two Side** option enables you to enter unique *Distance* values for both sides of the profile.
   - The **Symmetric** option assigns the same *Distance* value on both sides of the revolve.

5. Define the control frame that will be generated on the revolved T-Spline geometry.

   - Enter the number of *Faces* that will be generated around and along the length of the revolved profile. These are two separate entries.

   - The two spacing options, **Curvature** and **Uniform**, can be used to customize the resulting control frame and help ensure that the profiles shape is matched as closely as possible. **Uniform** spaces the number of faces evenly along a profile. **Curvature** spaces the number of faces based on a profile's curvature. The greater the amount of curvature, the more faces that will be assigned to that area.

   Symmetry can also be assigned separately using the Symmetry options, as required.

   - Set the *Symmetry* option to **Circular** to assign symmetry between adjacent faces as they are revolved. Otherwise leave the *Symmetry* option as **None**.

   - Enable the **Weld** option if faces or edges overlap as they are rotated. This forces overlapping entities to weld together.

6. Click **OK** to complete the sculpted revolve.

Practice 7a | Creating a Sculpted Extrude

Practice Objective

- Create extruded T-Spline surface geometry using sketched geometry.

In this practice, you will work in the FORM contextual environment to create T-Spline geometry that cannot be created using the quick shape tools. You will create the geometry by extruding an elliptical sketched profile. The final T-Spline geometry is shown in Figure 7–10.

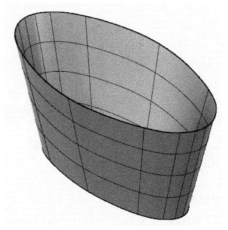

Figure 7–10

Task 1 - Create a sketch that will be used as the profile for the extrude.

1. Click ▯▾ (File)>**New Design** to create a new design.

2. Save the design as **Ellipse**.

3. In the SKETCH panel, click ▯ (Create Sketch).

4. Expand the *Origin* folder and select the **XZ** plane, or select the plane directly in the graphics window.

5. In the SKETCH panel, click ⬭ (Ellipse).

6. Select the Origin Point to start the creation of the ellipse.

7. Drag the cursor mouse horizontally to the right to locate the centerline at approximately **75 mm**, as shown in Figure 7–11. Click to locate the centerline.

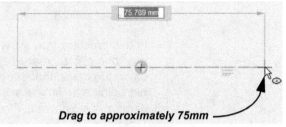

Drag to approximately 75mm

Figure 7–11

8. Drag the cursor up to locate the vertical centerline at approximately **30 mm**, as shown in Figure 7–12. Click to locate the vertical centerline and complete the ellipse.

Do not worry about fully constraining the sketch. It will be used as the basis for sculpted geometry, so the sketch's size will change when edits are made to the T-Spline shape.

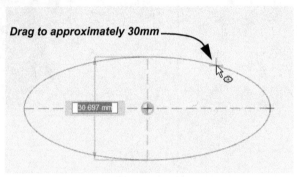

Drag to approximately 30mm

Figure 7–12

9. Click **FINISH SKETCH** to complete the sketch.

Task 2 - Create the sculpted extruded geometry.

---

1. Create a new form feature to enter the FORM contextual environment.

2. In the CREATE panel, click ▮ (Extrude).

3. Select the sketched ellipse as the profile that is to be extruded. The EXTRUDE palette and profile display as shown in Figure 7–13.

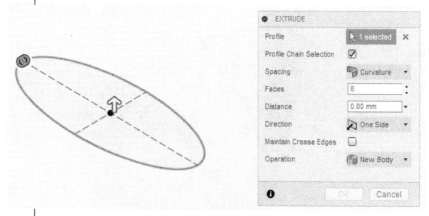

Figure 7–13

4. Ensure that the *Direction* field is set as **One Side**, and then extrude the profile up to **50mm**. The T-Spline geometry previews based on the defaults in the EXTRUDE palette, similar to that shown in Figure 7–14.

- To assign the *Distance* value, you can enter the value in the EXTRUDE palette, or drag the distance manipulator (arrow) in the graphics window.

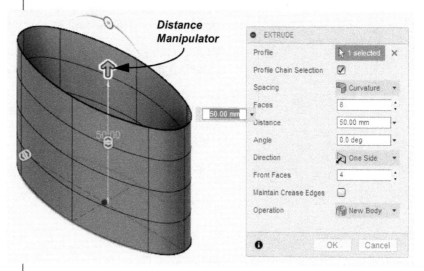

Figure 7–14

5. Change the *Angle* value to **15 deg**. The geometry updates as shown in Figure 7–15.

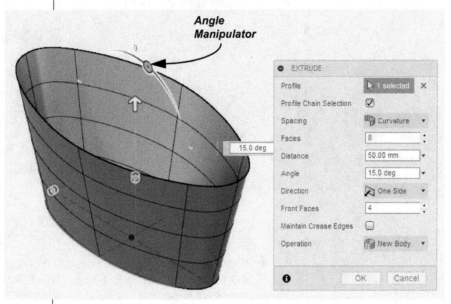

Figure 7–15

6. Ensure that the *Spacing* setting is set to **Uniform**. This evenly spaces the faces around the elliptical profile.

7. In the *Faces* field, enter **4**. Note how the elliptical shape is poorly matched to the profile when using four faces.

8. Change the *Faces* value to **8**. Note that the shape more closely matches the elliptical profile.

9. Change the *Spacing* setting to **Curvature**. This spaces the number of faces based on the profile's curvature. Note that the faces are closer together in the two areas of higher curvature.

10. Change the *Faces* value to **16**.

11. Set the *Front Faces* value to **4**, if not already set. Note that the shape now matches the elliptical profile, and that there are more faces in the areas of high curvature, as shown in Figure 7–16.

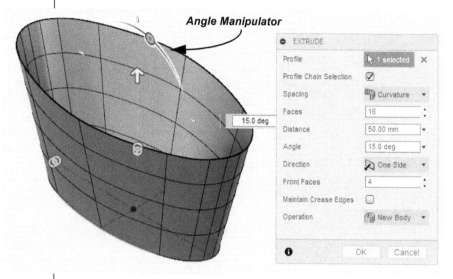

Figure 7–16

12. Click **OK** to create the sculpted extrude geometry shown in Figure 7–17. Extruding the profile using these settings provided a shape that could not be created using the quick shape options. The extrude can be edited to refine its shape and can then be thickened to create a solid.

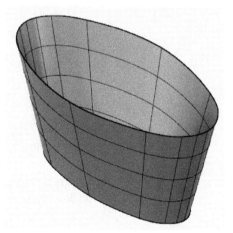

Figure 7–17

13. Save the design and close the file.

| Practice 7b | # Creating a Sculpted Revolve |

Practice Objective

- Create revolved T-Spline surface geometry using sketched geometry.

In this practice, you will work in the FORM contextual environment to create the surface of a wavy washer. You will begin by revolving a sketched line to create a flat, circular surface. Using the T-Spline faces that are generated in the FORM contextual environment, you will further edit the shape to create the wavy surface. This surface will then be thickened in the SOLID environment to create the solid geometry. The final geometry that you will create in this practice is shown in Figure 7–18.

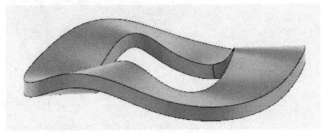

Figure 7–18

Task 1 - Create a sketch that will be used as the profile for the revolve.

1. Click (File)>**New Design** to create a new design.

2. Save the design as **Wavy Washer**.

3. In the SKETCH panel, click (Create Sketch).

4. Expand the *Origin* folder and select the **YZ** plane, or select the plane directly in the graphics window.

5. In the SKETCH panel, click (Line) or press <L> to access the **Line** command.

6. Sketch the **10mm** horizontal line shown in Figure 7–19. Ensure that the sketch is fully constrained (i.e., displayed in black) by assigning horizontal constraints to the line and constraints between an endpoint and the origin point.

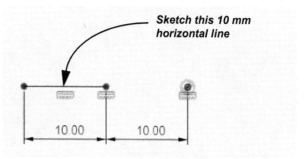

Sketch this 10 mm horizontal line

Figure 7–19

7. Finish the sketch. This line is the profile that will be used to create sculpted revolve geometry.

Task 2 - Create sculpted revolved geometry.

1. Create a new form feature to enter the FORM contextual environment.

2. In the CREATE panel, click 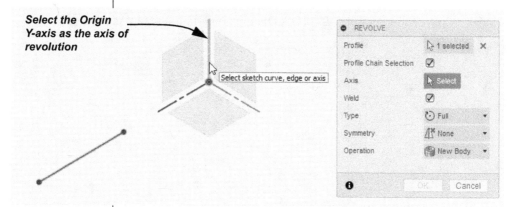 (Revolve).

3. Select the sketched 10mm line as the *Profile* that is to be revolved.

4. In the REVOLVE palette, select the *Axis* field. Once active, select the Y-axis, as shown in Figure 7–20. Once selected, a preview of the sculpted surface displays.

Select the Origin Y-axis as the axis of revolution

Figure 7–20

5. Set the number of faces that are to be used to create the geometry, as shown in the REVOLVE palette in Figure 7–21.

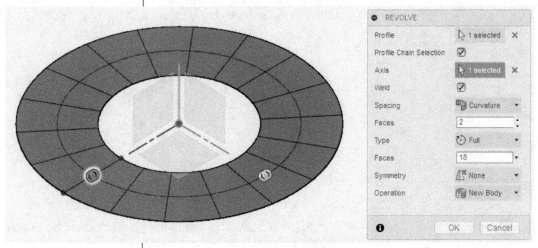

Figure 7–21

6. Set the *Type* option to **Angle** and enter **180** in the entry field in the REVOLVE palette or in the graphics window. With the **Angle** option selected, note how you can control the *Direction* setting to define the direction in which the geometry is to be created. The *Direction* options include, **One Side**, **Two Side**, or **Symmetric**.

7. Set the *Type* option to **Full** to rotate the line fully through 360 degrees.

8. Set the *Symmetry* option to **Circular**. This assigns symmetry between adjacent faces as they are revolved. Note that this type of symmetry does not create the required sculpted shape. Set the *Symmetry* option as **None**.

9. Click **OK** to complete the sculpted revolve.

10. Hide the *Origin* features if they are still displayed. The geometry displays as shown in Figure 7–22.

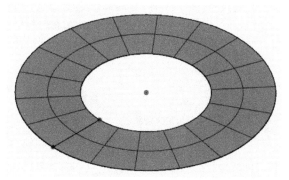

Figure 7–22

Task 3 - Modify the T-Spline to create a wavy shape.

---

1. Using the ViewCube, rotate the design to the **TOP** view.

2. In the MODIFY panel, click 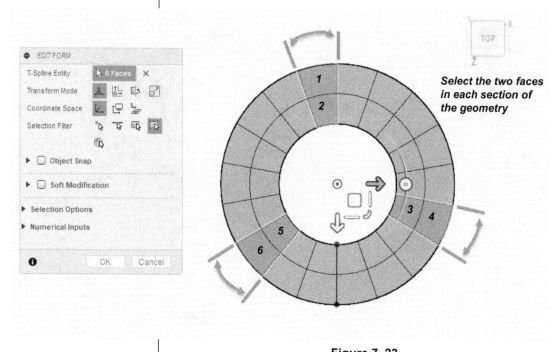 (Edit Form). The EDIT FORM palette displays.

3. Select the six faces shown in Figure 7–23.

Figure 7–23

4. Prior to transforming the selected faces, rotate the design to the **FRONT** view on the ViewCube.

5. Select the Y-axis manipulator arrow and drag it up to a value of **3.00 mm**, as shown in Figure 7–24. Alternatively, you can enter the value in the entry field in the graphics window.

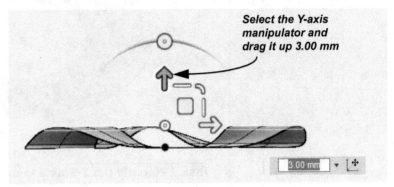

Select the Y-axis manipulator and drag it up 3.00 mm

Figure 7–24

6. Rotate the design back to the **TOP** view and add to the selection set by adding an additional 12 faces, as shown in Figure 7–25.

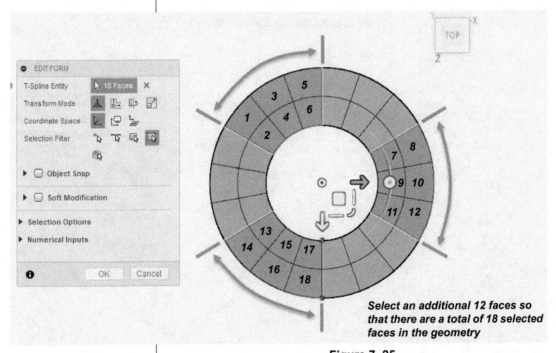

Select an additional 12 faces so that there are a total of 18 selected faces in the geometry

Figure 7–25

7. Rotate the design to the **FRONT** view on the ViewCube.

8. Select the Y-axis manipulator arrow and drag it up to a value of **1.5 mm**, as shown in Figure 7–26. Alternatively, you can enter the value in the entry field in the graphics window.

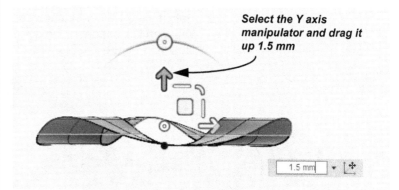

Select the Y axis manipulator and drag it up 1.5 mm

Figure 7–26

9. Click **OK** in the EDIT FORM palette to complete the edit. The T-Spline geometry should display as shown in Figure 7–27.

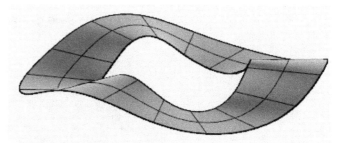

Figure 7–27

10. Click **FINISH FORM**. The design is returned to the SOLID environment.

Task 4 - Create solid geometry.

1. In the CREATE panel, click (Thicken). The THICKEN palette opens.

2. Select the T-Spline geometry and enter a **2.00 mm** *Thickness* value on the bottom of the surface. The geometry displays as shown in Figure 7–28.

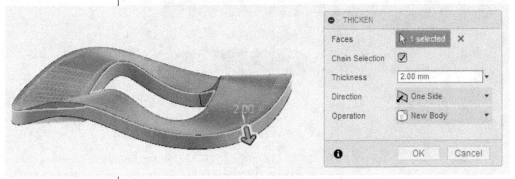

Figure 7–28

3. Click **OK**. The solid geometry updates as shown in Figure 7–29.

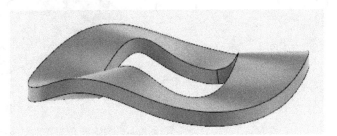

Figure 7–29

4. Save the design and close the file.

Practice 7c | Additional Sculpted Geometry

Practice Objective

- Create extruded and revolved T-Spline surface geometry using sketched geometry.

In this practice, use the skills you have learned to create sketches that support the creation of both extruded and revolved T-Spline geometry.

Task 1 - Create new parts.

1. Create each of the designs shown in Figure 7–30. These shapes can be created using a sketch as the profile for an extrude or a revolve. No additional edits are required.

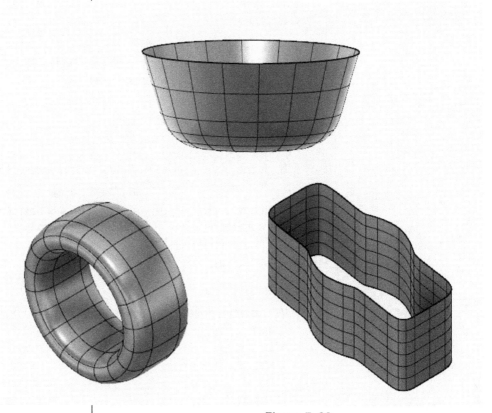

Figure 7–30

Chapter Review Questions

1. Which of the following can be selected as a profile reference for sculpted extrude geometry? (Select all that apply.)

   a. A open profile sketch.

   b. A closed profile sketch.

   c. A planar face on an existing solid.

   d. A loop of edges on existing T-Spline geometry.

   e. An edge on existing T-Spline geometry.

   f. A face on existing T-Spline geometry.

2. Sculpted T-Spline geometry that is extruded by referencing a closed profile is automatically capped at the top and bottom.

   a. True

   b. False

3. Which of the following *Direction* settings enables you to extrude a selected sketch profile on both sides of the sketch plane using unique values on each side.

   a. One Side

   b. Two Sides

   c. Symmetric

   d. None of the above. You must create separate extrude features in both directions.

4. Which of the following *Spacing* settings is best used so that the number of faces most accurately match the shape in a highly curved profile?

   a. Curvature

   b. Uniform

5. Which of the following three manipulators can be used in the graphics window to add faces to a sculpted revolve?

   a.

   b.

   c. ⟨⊹⟩

6. Unlike a profile for extruded T-Spline geometry, an edge on existing T-Spline geometry can be selected as the profile for revolved T-Spline geometry.

    a. True

    b. False

7. Which of the following can be selected as the *Axis* reference to define the axis of revolution for sculpted revolved geometry? (Select all that apply.)

    a. Origin Axis

    b. A curved sketched entity

    c. A linear sketched entity

    d. A solid edge

8. During T-Spline geometry creation, you can assign symmetry between selected faces in the REVOLVE palette.

    a. True

    b. False

Command Summary

Button	Command	Location
	Extrude	• **Toolbar:** *DESIGN* Workspace>*FORM* tab>CREATE panel
	Revolve	• **Toolbar:** *DESIGN* Workspace>*FORM* tab>CREATE panel

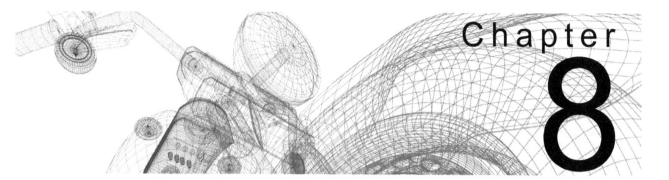

Sculpted T-Spline Sweeps and Lofts

You can use Sweep and Loft features to create specific geometry that cannot be created using standard extrusions. Sweeps enable you to sketch a cross-section and sweep it along a defined path, while a Loft enables you to create complex geometry that blends multiple profiles. Once the sweep or loft operation is complete, you can further manipulate the shape of the T-Spline geometry as required. Creating a sweep or loft in the same way as a solid does not enable you to manipulate the shape using a control frame.

Learning Objectives in this Chapter

- Create swept T-Spline geometry using path and profile entities.
- Create lofted T-Spline geometry using profile and reference entities.

8.1 Sculpted Sweeps

A Sweep feature creates geometry that is defined by sweeping a profile along a path. Sweeps are useful for geometry that have a uniform shape, but an irregular path. Similar to the other sketch-based feature types (e.g., Extrude and Revolve), the geometry is driven by a profile and the path along which the profile is swept. Both the profile and path must exist in the design prior to feature creation. Figure 8–1 shows an image of a pipe where a circular profile was swept along a curved path to generate the T-Spline geometry. A simple cylinder would require substantial modifications to create this shape, so a sweep is more efficient. Additionally, because T-Spline geometry generates a control frame, you can easily make edits to its shape once the sweep is created.

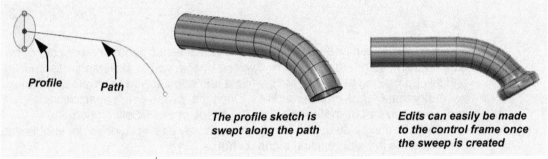

*The profile sketch is
swept along the path*

*Edits can easily be made
to the control frame once
the sweep is created*

Figure 8–1

Click 🗗 (Sweep) in the CREATE panel to start the **Sweep** tool in the FORM contextual environment.

To define how the geometry sweeps along a path, define the following using the SWEEP palette:

- The profile is selected to define the shape of the loft. The profile can be a sketched section or a planar face from an existing solid. An edge loop from another T-Spline body cannot be selected as a profile.
  - The profile that is swept along the path can be an open or closed loop sketch. Figure 8–2 shows an open sketch that is swept along an open path to create T-Spline geometry.

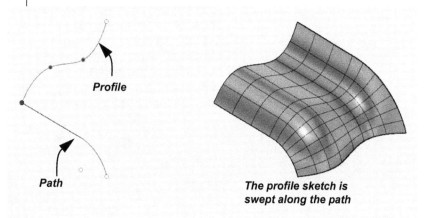

Profile

Path

The profile sketch is swept along the path

Figure 8–2

The profile and path sketches used to create a T-Spline sweep in the FORM environment can be created in either the SOLID or FORM environments.

- The path defines the path along which the profile is swept. The path can be a sketch, or it can be an edge in an existing solid or T-Spline geometry.

  - A sweep's path can be an open or a closed sketch and can be either 2D or 3D. The geometry shown in Figure 8–3 is a sweep that uses a closed path.

  - The geometry that is generated from the profile does not need to physically intersect the path.

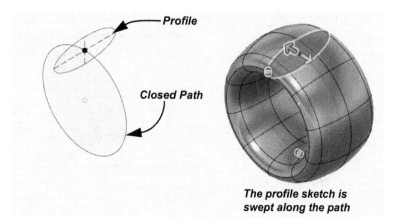

Profile

Closed Path

The profile sketch is swept along the path

Figure 8–3

- A profile can be swept a set distance along the path (as shown in Figure 8–4) using the *Distance* values in the SWEEP palette. The values are defined as a percentage of the overall path. One field represents the percentage from the beginning of the path and the other represents the percentage from the end of the path. Alternatively, you can drag the manipulator arrow to define the value, as required.

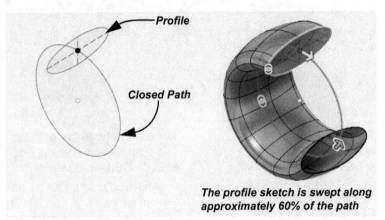

The profile sketch is swept along approximately 60% of the path

Figure 8–4

- A sweep's orientation can alter the shape of the final geometry. A **Perpendicular** orientation ensures that the profile remains perpendicular to the path, while a **Parallel** orientation keeps the profile parallel to the profile's sketch plane, as shown in Figure 8–5.

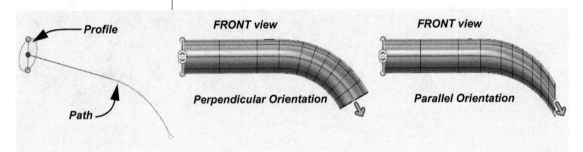

Figure 8–5

- The number of faces that are assigned to define the T-Spline geometry can affect how closely a highly curved profile is matched as it sweeps along the path. For example, fewer faces might not create the exact shape of the profile, as shown in Figure 8–6. Vary the number of faces as required to match the profile shape.

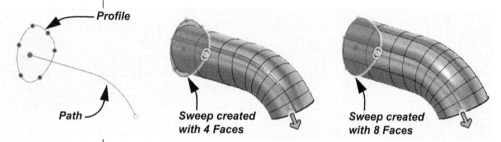

Figure 8–6

You can use the **Uniform** and **Curvature** spacing options to customize the resulting shape:

- **Uniform:** Spaces the number of faces evenly along a profile.

- **Curvature:** Spaces the number of faces based on a profile's curvature. The higher the curvature, the more faces that are generated. This option (in addition to the number of faces) affects how closely an T-Spline matches the sketch.

8.2 Sculpted Lofts

A loft feature enables you to create advanced geometry by blending between multiple profiles. Additionally you can assign reference curves between the profiles to define how the T-Spline geometry is created as the profiles blend with one another. Similar to the other sketched based feature types (e.g., Extrude and Revolve), the geometry is driven by sections that define the profile. With a loft, however, more than one section must be selected to define the geometry. Any profiles or reference curves that will be used to define the geometry must exist in the design prior to feature creation. Figure 8–7 shows two sweeps that were created by blending between three profiles: one with reference curves, and one without.

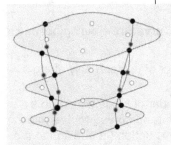  

3 sketched profiles and 4 reference curves (rails)	*The profiles are blended without reference curves*	*The profiles are blended with four reference curves*

Figure 8–7

Click  (Loft) in the CREATE panel to start the **Loft** tool in the FORM contextual environment.

To define how the geometry blends between profiles, define the following using the LOFT palette:

- Profiles are selected to define the shape of the loft. The profiles can be a sketch, point, or faces from existing solids. An edge loop from another T-Spline body cannot be selected as a profile.

- Set end conditions at the start and end profiles to control the shape of the loft, if required.

Using rails or a centerline is optional.

- Reference curves (rails and centerlines) can be selected to control how the geometry is shaped between the profiles. To use references, select an option in the *Guide Type* area.
  - A rail defines the path the geometry should take between profiles. Figure 8–8 shows a loft that blends three sketched profiles and uses rails to control the shape of the geometry between profiles.

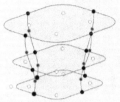 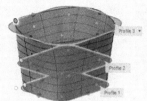 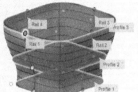 

| **Three sketched profiles and four rails** | **Loft created between the three profiles** | **The four rails are assigned** | **Completed T-Spline Loft with rails** |

Figure 8–8

When defining a loft feature, you can select multiple rails, but you can only select one centerline.

- A centerline sets the profiles so that they remain normal to a centerline reference as it blends between the profiles. Figure 8–9 shows a loft that blends four sketched sections and uses a centerline reference to ensure that the profiles remain normal to a centerline reference as it blends.

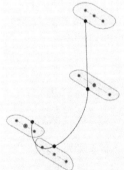 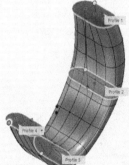 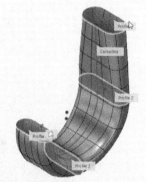 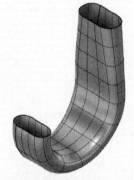

| **Four sketched profiles (slots) and a Centerline** | **Loft created between the four profiles** | **The Centerline is assigned** | **Completed T-Spline Loft with Centerline** |

Figure 8–9

- The spacing and number of faces can be controlled to define how closely the geometry matches the profile and how the geometry is shaped between the profiles.

- The number of faces that you assign to define the T-Spline geometry can affect how closely highly curved profiles are matched as they blend between one another and along any reference curves. For example, fewer faces might not create the exact shape of the profile, as shown in Figure 8–10. Vary the number of faces as required to match the profile shape.

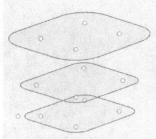 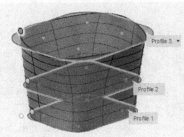 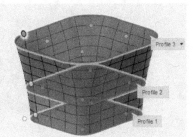

Three sketched profiles   *Sweep created with eight faces around the width*   *Sweep created with 20 faces around the width*

Figure 8–10

You can use the **Uniform** and **Curvature** spacing options to customize the resulting shape, as shown in Figure 8–11:

- **Uniform:** Spaces the number of faces evenly along a profile.
- **Curvature:** Spaces the number of faces based on a profile's curvature and a deviation value. The higher the amount of curvature, the more faces that will be generated.

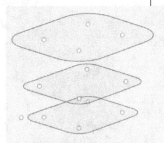 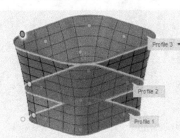 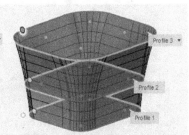

Three sketched profiles   *Sweep created using the Uniform option and 20 faces around the width*   *Sweep created using the Curvature option and 20 faces around the width*

Figure 8–11

- Control points (i.e., white vertices) control how sections blend. Control points can be selected and moved to change loft geometry, as shown in Figure 8–12.

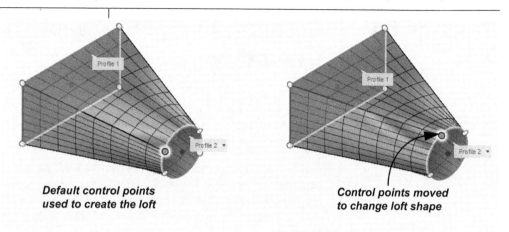

Default control points used to create the loft

Control points moved to change loft shape

Figure 8–12

Profiles are added in the order that they are selected. To change the order, in the graphics window, select the Profile [#] symbol and select a new number.

Figure 8–13 shows a loft created from sketched profiles, a point and an existing solid face. End conditions are assigned to control tangency into the existing solid (Connected (G0), Tangent (G1), and Curvature (G2)) and at the point (Sharp and Point Tangent).

In this example, a T-Spline was the best tool to use to simplify the number of profiles required to achieve the final geometry. With the control frame of the T-Spline, the shape can be further modified. To accomplish this with a solid, multiple profiles and rails would be required.

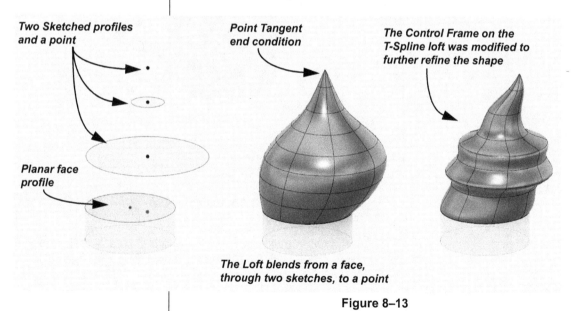

Two Sketched profiles and a point

Point Tangent end condition

The Control Frame on the T-Spline loft was modified to further refine the shape

Planar face profile

The Loft blends from a face, through two sketches, to a point

Figure 8–13

Practice 8a

Creating Sculpted Swept Geometry

Practice Objectives

- Create swept geometry using appropriate path and profile entities.
- Edit the T-Spline created from a sculpted sweep.

In this practice, you will create the handle for a mug using a sculpted sweep. You are provided with the solid geometry of the mug to begin the exercise and will sketch the required entities to define the handle. A sculpted sweep is being used to create the handle so that the T-Spline control frame can be used to modify its shape before completion. Using a solid sweep would not be possible to generate this shape without using a series of complex lofted sections. The final design is shown in Figure 8–14.

Figure 8–14

Task 1 - Start a new design.

1. Click ▮ ▾ (File)>**Open**. In the Open window, click **Open from my computer**.

2. In the Open dialog box, navigate to the *Autodesk Fusion 360 Surfacing Practice Files* folder. Select **Mug.f3d**, and click **Open**. The design displays as shown in Figure 8–15.

Figure 8–15

3. Review the Timeline and note that the model was created as a sketched revolve in the SOLID environment of the *DESIGN* workspace and that it was shelled.

Task 2 - Create the path and profile for the sweep.

---

1. Start the creation of a new sketch on the XY Plane.

2. In the SKETCH panel, click ⁀ (Fit Point Spline) and sketch a spline similar to that shown in Figure 8–16.
   - The spline represents the path that the sculpted sweep will take to create the handle of the mug.
   - Do not connect the path to the mug. This will be done once the sculpted handle is completed.

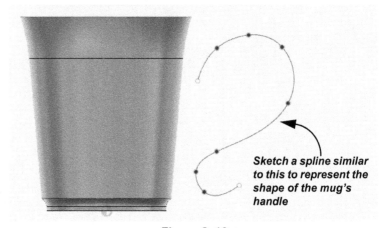

Sketch a spline similar to this to represent the shape of the mug's handle

Figure 8–16

---

3. Finish the sketch.

4. In the CONSTRUCT panel, click ✐ (Plane Along Path). Select the sketch of the Spline that was just created as the *Path* reference.

5. With the *Distance Type* set to **Proportional**, ensure that the *Distance* value is set to the required value to create the plane at the end, near the top of the mug (as shown in Figure 8–17). The required value depends on how the spline was sketched. Positioning the plane at the top end requires a value of **0** or **1**. Click **OK**.

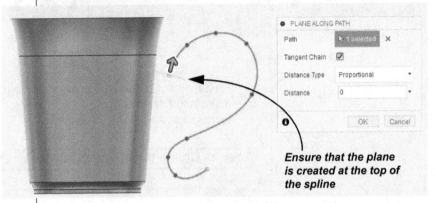

Ensure that the plane is created at the top of the spline

Figure 8–17

6. Start the creation of a new sketch on the plane just created.

7. In the SKETCH panel, click ⊘ (Center Diameter Circle) and sketch a **10mm** circle on the new workplane. Sketch the circle so that it is constrained to the start point of the spline, as shown in Figure 8–18. This will be the profile for the sweep. Finish the sketch.

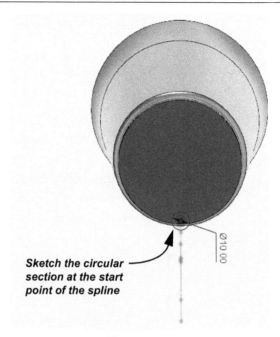

Sketch the circular section at the start point of the spline

⌀10.00

Figure 8–18

8. In the BROWSER, rename the previous two sketches as **Path** and **Profile**, respectively. The design should display as shown in Figure 8–19.

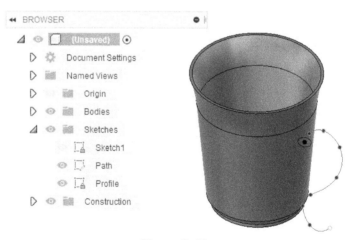

Figure 8–19

Task 3 - Create the sculpted sweep.

1. Create a new form feature to enter the FORM contextual environment.

   - Note how the solid body that represents the mug displays as light gray. This indicates that you are in the FORM contextual environment. You are unable to interact with the existing solid geometry while in this workspace.

2. In the CREATE panel, click 🗁 (Sweep). The SWEEP palette opens.

3. The *Profile* field is active by default. Select the circular sketch as the profile for the sculpted sweep.

4. Select the *Path* field to activate it. Select the sketched spline as the path for the sculpted sweep. The sculpted geometry displays on the model.

5. Maintain the default settings (as shown in Figure 8–20) and click **OK**.

Figure 8–20

Task 4 - Edit the sculpted sweep.

In this task, you will edit the T-Spline faces of the handle to create a unique shape that would not be possible to create using a solid sweep.

1. In the SYMMETRY panel, click ▲▲ (Mirror - Internal) and select two faces on the geometry (similar to that shown in Figure 8–21) to define a line of symmetry through the handle. Click **OK**.

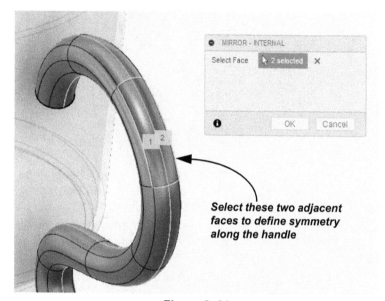

Select these two adjacent faces to define symmetry along the handle

Figure 8–21

2. Using the ◈ (Fill Hole) command with the **Fill Star** mode, close the hole at the bottom of the sculpted sweep as shown in Figure 8–22. Click **OK**.

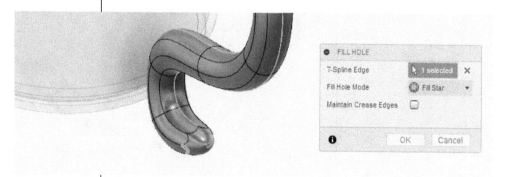

Figure 8–22

3. Click 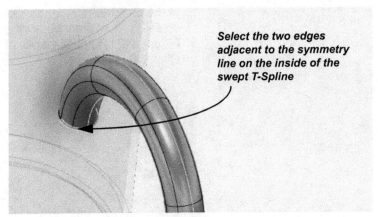 (Edit Form) and select the two edges shown in Figure 8–23. The edges on the opposite side of the symmetry line are also automatically selected. These edges are on the inside of the handle.

- Hint: To select multiple edges at once, hold <Ctrl>.

Select the two edges adjacent to the symmetry line on the inside of the swept T-Spline

Figure 8–23

4. Using the ViewCube, change to the **FRONT** view orientation and start the **Edit Form** command. Make the following edits to the edges.

- Use the Rotation manipulator and rotate clockwise **-45 deg** (as shown in Figure 8–24) to rotate the selected edges.

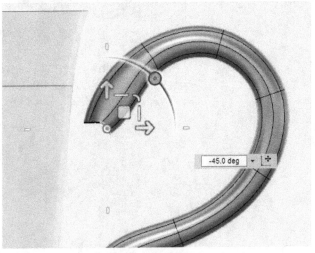

-45.0 deg

Figure 8–24

- Use the Y-direction manipulator and drag down **-10mm**, as shown in Figure 8–25.

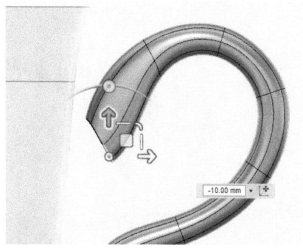

Figure 8–25

- Use the X-direction manipulator and drag to the left **-7mm**, as shown in Figure 8–26.

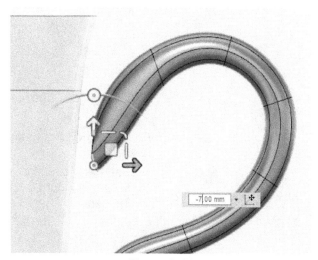

Figure 8–26

5. Click **OK** to complete the edit. The handle should display similar to that shown in Figure 8–27.

6. Select the face shown in Figure 8–27 for editing.

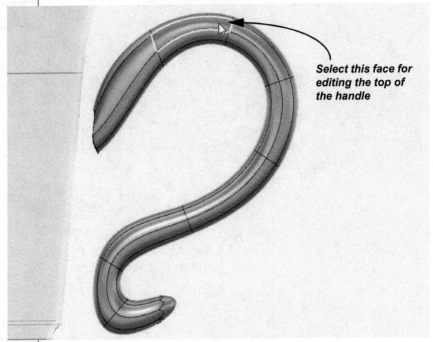

Select this face for editing the top of the handle

Figure 8–27

7. Using the ViewCube, change to the **TOP** view orientation.

8. Click 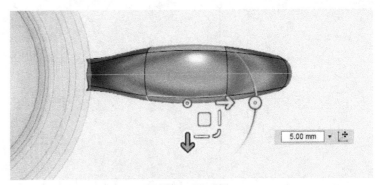 (Edit Form) and make the following edit to the faces:

   - Use the Z-direction manipulator and drag down **5mm** (as shown in Figure 8–28) to create a wider face at the top of the handle.

Figure 8–28

9. Click **OK** to complete the edit.

10. Using the **Fill Hole** command with the **Reduced Star** mode, close the hole at the top of the sculpted sweep. Click **OK**.

Task 5 - Relocate the handle.

1. Using the ViewCube, change to the **FRONT** view orientation.

2. In the MODIFY panel, click ✛ (Move/Copy). The MOVE/COPY palette opens.

3. By default, *Bodies* is selected as the type of object that will be moved. Select the sculpted sweep that you just created.

4. Using the X-direction manipulator that displays, drag the handle approximately **10 mm** towards the mug until the bodies intersect one another, as shown in Figure 8–29.

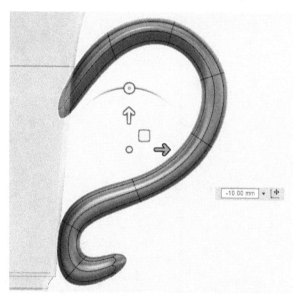

Figure 8–29

5. Click **OK** to finish the move.

6. Finish the form feature.

Task 6 - Complete the design in the SOLID environment.

1. In the MODIFY panel, click [Combine icon] (Combine). Complete the following in the COMBINE palette:
   - For the *Target Body* reference, select the initial mug geometry.
   - Select the *Tool Bodies* field to activate it, and then select the handle.
   - Ensure that *Operation* is set to **Join**.
   - Click **OK**. The two solid bodies are now merged.

2. Rotate the design and note that the handle protrudes into the mug, as shown in Figure 8–30.

Figure 8–30

3. In the MODIFY panel, click [Replace Face icon] (Replace Face). Complete the following in the REPLACE FACE palette. The resulting geometry should appear as shown in Figure 8–31.
   - Drag a selection window around the faces that protrude through the surface of the mug.
   - Select the *Target Faces* field to activate it and then select the inside face of the mug as the reference.

Use the Replace Face command to remove the handle geometry that extrudes through the mug

Figure 8–31

4. Save the design with the name **Mug** to your *Autodesk Fusion 360 Practice Files* project. Close the file.

Practice 8b

Creating a Sculpted Loft

Practice Objectives

- Create lofted geometry using profiles and a rail.
- Use the Edit Form command to make changes to the shape of the design.
- Complete the design by splitting it into two bodies and shelling the solid geometry.

In this practice, you will create the earbud model shown in Figure 8–32. You will start with a loft feature to create the initial T-Spline geometry, and then make additional edits to modify the shape of the design.

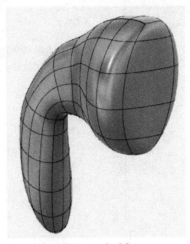

Figure 8–32

Task 1 - Open a part file and create a loft.

In this task, you will open a model that you created previously. It contains a number of sketches that will be used to create a solid loft feature. A model has been provided for you if you did not complete the previous sketch.

1. Open **Earbud** from your Fusion 360 project. The sections and rails required for the loft feature are shown in Figure 8–33.

   - If you did not complete the sketching exercise, click

     ▉ ▾ (File)>**Open** to access a model that has been created for you. In the Open window, click **Open from my computer**.

- In the Open dialog box, navigate to the *Autodesk Fusion 360 Practice Files* folder, select **Earbud.f3d**, and click **Open**.

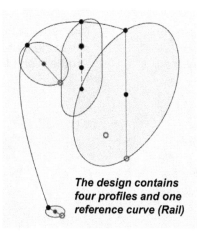

The design contains four profiles and one reference curve (Rail)

Figure 8–33

2. Activate the FORM contextual environment.

3. In the CREATE panel, click ◗ (Loft). The LOFT palette opens as shown in Figure 8–34.

Figure 8–34

4. Verify that the **Chain Selection** option is selected. This ensures that all of the entities in a closed loop are selected. If this option is disabled, you must select each entity separately in each loop.

The order in which you select the profiles defines how they are lofted together.

5. Select the *Profiles* area to activate it. In the graphics window, select the four profiles from top to bottom (**Profile1**, **Profile2**, **Profile3**, and **Profile 4**), as shown in Figure 8–35.

The location that is selected on the profile determines where the Profile [#] label displays.

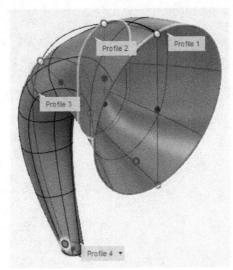

Figure 8–35

6. Note how the previewed T-Spline geometry closely matches the selected profiles using the default of eight faces. This is because the shapes of each profile are not highly curved. The addition of faces in the length and width directions will help ensure the required control frame for future modification. Set the number of *Faces* to **10** for both the length and width.

7. Change the *Width Spacing* to **Curvature**. Note the faces that are added to the geometry. This option spaces the number of faces based on a profile's curvature and a deviation value.

8. Return the *Width Spacing* setting to **Uniform**. The control frame that was generated with 10 faces is satisfactory to capture the shape of the design and provides the necessary control entities for editing.

9. Click **OK** to create the loft.

10. In the BROWSER, expand the *Sketches* folder and note that the display of the four profile sketches is automatically toggled off once they are used. The model displays as shown in Figure 8–36.

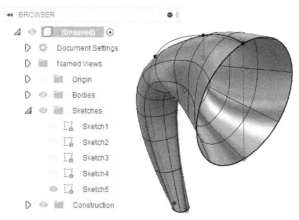

Figure 8–36

11. When the loft was created, the sketched rail was not assigned prior to completing the feature. With sculpted features, because there is no feature history that is added when geometry is created, you cannot edit the loft. Click

    ↰ (Undo) at the top of the graphics window.

12. The sketches should now be displayed. If not, toggle their display on in the BROWSER.

13. Start the creation of the Loft a second time.

14. Select **Profile 1**, **Profile 2**, and **Profile 3**. For the fourth profile, select the point shown in Figure 8–37 at the center of Sketch4 (instead of the circular sketch).

    - Previously, the circle was selected to leave an opening for wire to connect to the earbud. In this design, the earbud is wireless with a pointed end.

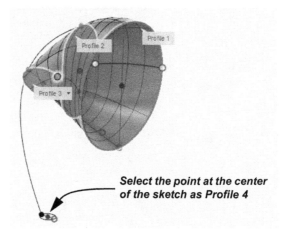

Select the point at the center of the sketch as Profile 4

Figure 8–37

15. In the LOFT palette, expand the end condition field for *Profile 4*, as shown in Figure 8–38. By default, **Sharp** is set as the end condition for points. Select **Point Tangent** to assign a tangent condition to obtain a smoother point.

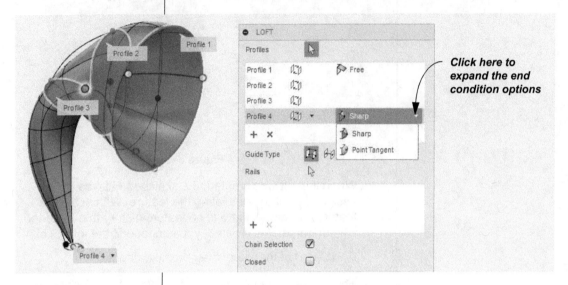

Click here to expand the end condition options

Figure 8–38

16. To refine the shape of the earbud between the profiles, assign a rail using the remaining sketch. In the LOFT palette, select 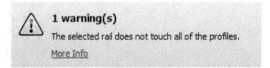 adjacent to the *Rails* heading to activate it.

17. Select the remaining sketch in the design (**Sketch5**). Note that a warning displays (shown in Figure 8–39), indicating that the rail does not touch all of the profiles. To correct this, you can redefine the sketch, or you can change the point that is used for Profile 4.

⚠ **1 warning(s)**
The selected rail does not touch all of the profiles.
More Info

Figure 8–39

18. In the Profiles list, ensure that Profile 4 is highlighted, and then click ✕ to delete it from the list of profiles.

19. In the *Profiles* area, click ✛ to add a new profile. Select the point shown in Figure 8–40. The point is at the intersection of the rail (Sketch5) and the circular sketched entity in Sketch4.

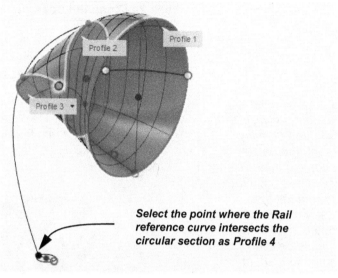

Select the point where the Rail reference curve intersects the circular section as Profile 4

Figure 8–40

20. Set the end condition for *Profile 4* to **Point Tangent**.

21. Reassign Sketch5 as the Rail reference.

22. Set the number of faces to **12** for both the length and width.

23. Click **OK** to create the lofted T-Spline geometry. The design should display as shown in Figure 8–41.

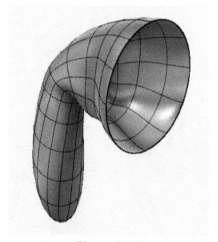

Figure 8–41

24. Ensure that all of the sketches are cleared from the display.

Task 2 - Close the opening for the design.

In this task, you will close the opening in the design by extruding and scaling the open edge to begin filling the hole. You will use the Bridge and Weld Vertices options to close the opening fully.

The process used to close the opening in this Task is one of many different approaches that you can use. This process was used to practice additional editing tools and create a good control frame that could be used if the face needed further shaping.

1. Use the ✎ (Edit Form) command to extrude the open edge loop. Enter an extrude distance of **2mm** so that the new edge loop is created 2 mm from the selected reference, as shown in Figure 8–42. Hint: Hold <Alt> to create a new extruded edge.

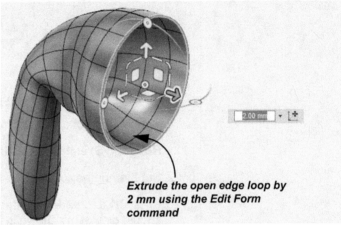

Extrude the open edge loop by 2 mm using the Edit Form command

Figure 8–42

2. Continue to use the **Edit Form** command while holding <Alt> to scale the same open edge loop. Release <Alt> each time to extrude a new edge with each scale operation. In total, create three new edges that extrude using a value of **0.75**, as shown in Figure 8–43.

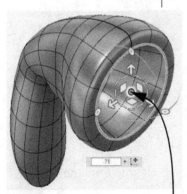 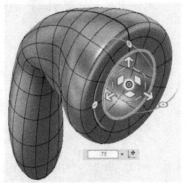 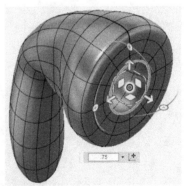

Use the scaling manipulator while holding <Alt> to scale the edge and close the opening

Figure 8–43

3. Use the 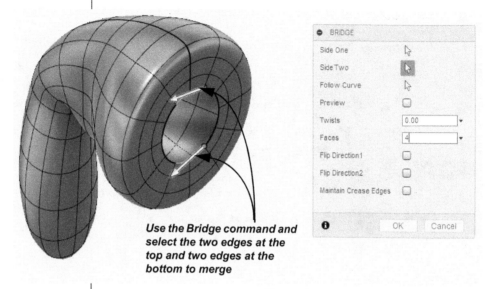 (Bridge) option to connect the two edges at the top and the two edges at the bottom to the opening, as shown in Figure 8–44. Set the number of *Faces* that are to be generated to **4**.

Use the Bridge command and select the two edges at the top and two edges at the bottom to merge

Figure 8–44

4. Click **OK** to create the bridge.

5. Use the 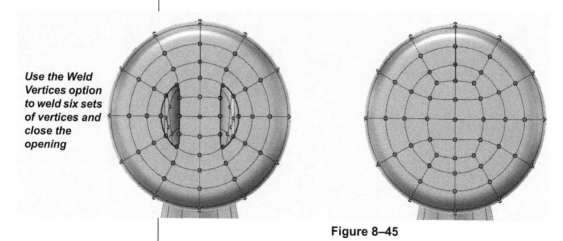 (Weld Vertices) option to weld vertices together to close the opening. There are six sets of vertices that should be welded. Ensure that the *Weld Mode* option is set to **Vertex to Midpoint** to obtain the control frame that is shown on the right in Figure 8–45.

Use the Weld Vertices option to weld six sets of vertices and close the opening

Figure 8–45

6. Click **OK**.

7. Switch to the **FRONT** view. Use the 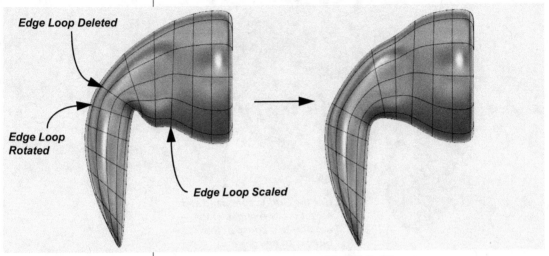 (Edit Form) and
   ✖ (Delete) options to smooth the design so that it is similar
   to that shown in Figure 8–46.

Edge Loop Deleted

Edge Loop
Rotated

Edge Loop Scaled

Figure 8–46

8. Switch to the **RIGHT** view. Use the (Edit Form) option to
   narrow the bottom portion of the earbud (i.e., lower three
   edge loops at one time), similar to that shown in Figure 8–47.

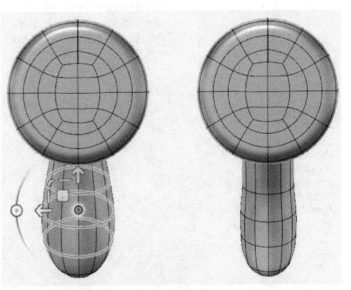

Figure 8–47

9. Click **OK.**

10. Click **Finish Form** to complete the design. Note that once in the SOLID environment, the T-Spline geometry is converted into a solid because it is completely airtight.

Task 3 - Complete the design in the SOLID environment.

In this task, you will complete the design in the SOLID environment by splitting the solid body and shelling the design.

1. In the MODIFY panel, click  (Split Body).

2. Select the solid body as the geometry to split.

3. In the SPLIT BODY palette, select the *Splitting Tool(s)* field to activate it and select the YZ plane. Click **OK**. The design displays as shown in Figure 8–48. Note how there are now two bodies in the design.

Figure 8–48

4. Hide the display of **Body2**.

---

5. In the MODIFY panel, click 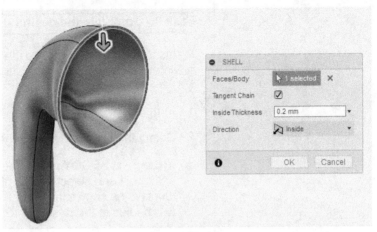 (Shell). Select the flat face on Body1 to be removed by the shell operation. Enter **0.2 mm** as the thickness value on the inside of the geometry, as shown in Figure 8–49. Click **OK** to complete the operation.

Figure 8–49

6. Hide the display of **Body1** and show **Body2**. Shell **Body2** using the same technique.

7. Toggle on the display of both solid bodies.

Task 4 - Apply materials and appearances to the design.

In this task, you will assign appearances to the two solid bodies in the design.

The name of the design will display as (Unsaved) if you have not saved it to your project yet.

1. Right-click on the name of the design at the top of the BROWSER and select **Appearance**, as shown in Figure 8–50. The APPEARANCE palette opens.

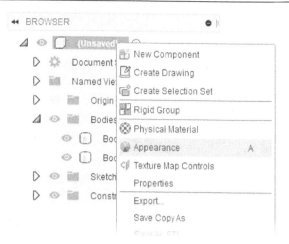

Figure 8–50

2. In the *Library* area at the bottom of the palette, expand the **Paint>Metallic** category.

3. Select the **Paint - Metallic (Dark Gray)** appearance and drag it onto the larger of the two solid bodies in the design. The color of the entire body updates to reflect this appearance. Alternatively, you can drop the appearance on the body name in the BROWSER.

4. Select the **Paint - Metallic (Green)** appearance and drag it onto the other solid body in the design. The color of the entire body updates to reflect the assigned appearance. The design should display as shown in Figure 8–51.

Earbud_Final.f3d has been included in your practice files folder to review the completed design.

Figure 8–51

5. Save the design with the name **Earbud** to your project.

6. Close the file.

Chapter Review Questions

1. Which sculpted form type would you use to create the T-Spline geometry shown in Figure 8–52?

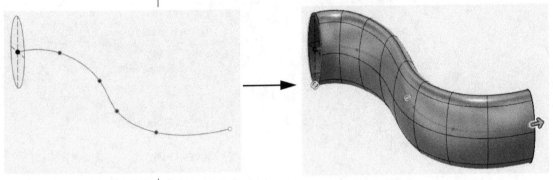

Figure 8–52

    a. **Loft**

    b. **Revolve**

    c. **Extrude**

    d. **Sweep**

2. Which elements must exist in a design before you can start the creation of a sculpted Sweep? (Select all that apply.)

    a. Profile

    b. Path

    c. Sections

    d. Start Point

3. For a sculpted sweep, which of the following statements are true? (Select all that apply.)

    a. A sculpted sweep creates a form whose geometry is blended between multiple profiles.

    b. A sculpted sweep creates a form whose geometry is swept along a defined path.

    c. The profile of a sculpted sweep can be an open or closed profile.

    d. The path of a sculpted sweep can be either 2D or 3D.

    e. The profile geometry must physically intersect the path.

4. Which *Orientation* option enables you to create the sculpted sweep shown in Figure 8–53?

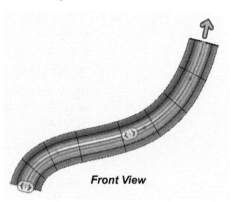

Front View

Figure 8–53

a. Perpendicular

b. Parallel

5. The *Distance* value that the sweep extends along the path is defined using the same units as the model.

a. True

b. False

6. Which of the following best describes the type of geometry that is created using a sculpted loft?

a. A sculpted loft creates a form whose geometry is swept along a defined path.

b. A sculpted loft creates a form where the geometry is blended between multiple profiles.

c. A sculpted loft creates a form that rotates a single profile around a selected centerline.

d. A sculpted loft creates a form that blends a profile along multiple paths.

7. Which of the following statements are true of sculpted lofts? (Select all that apply.)

   a. The profiles for sculpted lofts can only be sketched entities.

   b. Once you select the profiles for a loft feature, you cannot reorder them.

   c. To use an existing solid planar face as a section of a loft, you can select the solid face directly without creating a sketch.

   d. End conditions can be assigned to the second of three profiles.

   e. Control points are used to determine the twist of a sculpted loft.

8. Profiles for a sculpted loft can be a sketch, point, or an edge loop in existing T-Spline geometry.

   a. True

   b. False

9. If the profiles for a sculpted loft are highly curved, which of the following options is best to use so that the resulting T-Spline geometry closely matches the shapes of the profiles and so that additional faces are added where needed?

   a. Uniform

   b. Curvature

10. When referencing existing geometry as the start or end section for a loft, which of the following conditions provides access to the *Weight* settings to control its shape? (Select all that apply.)

   a. Free

   b. Tangent

   c. Smooth

Answers: 1.d, 2.(a,b), 3.(b,c), 4.a, 5.b, 6.b, 7.(c,e), 8.b, 9.b, 10.(a,b,c)

Command Summary

Button	Command	Location
	Loft	• **Toolbar:** *DESIGN* Workspace>*FORM* tab>CREATE panel
	Sweep	• **Toolbar:** *DESIGN* Workspace>*FORM* tab>CREATE panel

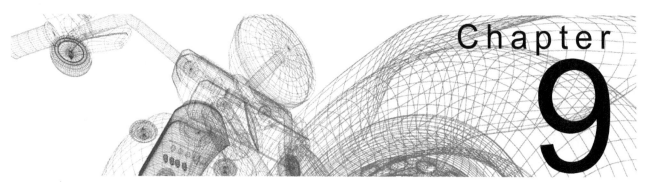

Chapter 9

Project Practices: Creating Sculpted Geometry

This project practice chapter is provided for you to practice your skills at creating and editing sculpted geometry using the tools that you have learned in this learning guide. While there is limited explanation provided, videos are available to guide you if you need additional help.

Practice 9a	# Blowdryer Design

Project Objective

- Use the tools available in the Autodesk Fusion 360 software to create a highly sculpted design.

In this practice, you will create the design shown in Figure 9–1. You will use both the SOLID and FORM environments of the *DESIGN* workspace, as required.

Figure 9–1

Project Video

A video (Sculpted Blowdryer Final 3XSpeed.avi) of the completed project is included in the *Practice Files/Project Videos/Blowdryer* folder.

Video Length: *2:34*

Task 1 - Set up a new design.

1. Create a new design in the current project.

2. In the BROWSER, expand **Document Settings**, hover the cursor over the **Units** node, and then select ☑ (Change Active Units).

3. In the CHANGE ACTIVE UNITS palette, for the *Unit Type* option, select **Inch**. Click **OK**.

Task 2 - Create a T-Spline cylinder.

In this task, you will create the form feature that will be used as the basic shape of the design.

Task Video

A video (02 Sculpt Cylinder.avi) of the completed task is included in the *Practice Files/Project Videos/Blowdryer* folder.

Video Length: *0:36*

1. Activate the FORM contextual environment of the *DESIGN* workspace.

2. Create the cylinder on the YZ plane, centered on the Origin point.
   - In the *Direction* area, select **One Side** to ensure that the T-Spline is extended on only one side of the sketch plane.
   - Set the dimensions to *Diameter*: **2.0 in** and *Height:* **-8 in**.
   - Ensure that no symmetry is set (**None**).
   - Set the number of faces to *Diameter Faces*: **8** and *Height Faces:* **9**, as shown in Figure 9–2.

Enter a negative Height value to ensure that the cylinder is extended on the negative side of the YZ plane.

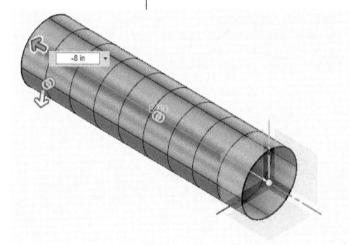

Figure 9–2

3. Complete the cylinder.

Task 3 - Insert a canvas image.

The overall size of the design was determined based on the cylinder that was created in the previous task. The image scale is unknown and will need to be set to match the cylinder.

Task Video

A video (03 Attach Canvas.avi) of the completed task is included in the *Practice Files/Project Videos/Blowdryer* folder.

Video Length: 1:03

1. In the INSERT panel, click (Canvas) to open the CANVAS palette.

   • Assign the canvas to the XY plane.

   • Click (Select Image) and use the Open dialog box to select **BlowDryer.jpg** from the practice files folder.

   • Enable the **Display Through** option.

2. Reorient the design to the **FRONT** view.

3. Note that the size of the image is much smaller than the cylinder. Use the manipulator handles shown in Figure 9–3 to scale and move the image to reposition it on the cylinder. Figure 9–3 shows the scale and move manipulators that you can use.

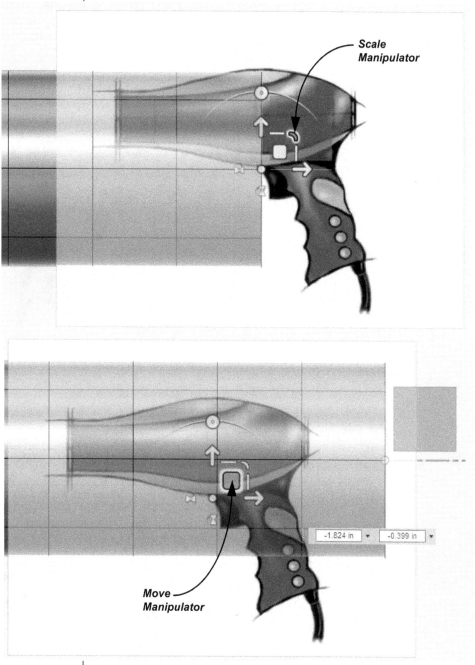

Figure 9–3

4. Continue to scale and move until the image displays similar to that shown in Figure 9–4. The scaling and positioning does not need to be exact, but you should overlay the cylinder as closely as possible.

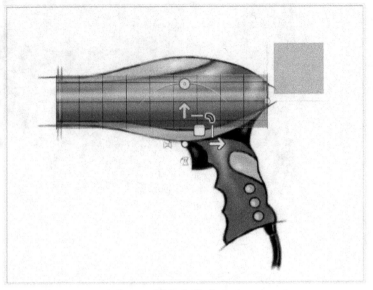

Figure 9–4

5. Complete the attachment of the image.

6. Save the design as **Blowdryer**.

Task 4 - Edit the shape of the cylinder to match the canvas image.

In this task, you will use the **Edit Form** command to modify the shape of the cylinder to closely match the conceptual design for the main body of the blowdryer.

Task Video

A video (**04 Edit Cylinder.avi**) of the completed task is included in the *Practice Files/Project Videos/Blowdryer* folder.

Video Length: *1:29*

1. Start the (Edit Form) command to edit the shape of the cylinder.

2. Select the entire edge loop that defines the right end of the cylinder. Translate and scale the edge as shown in Figure 9–5.

1. Translate the edge loop up.

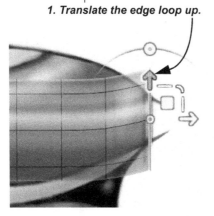 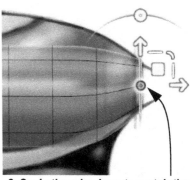

2. Scale the edge loop to match the sketched image. Additional translation might be required to match the edges.

Figure 9–5

It might take multiple iterations to match the canvas. Ensuring smooth edges that closely match the conceptual sketch is acceptable.

3. Use the same technique of translating and scaling the edge loops shown in Figure 9–6.

- Translate and scale the edge loops to match the canvas.
- Ensure that the control edge loops that align with the handle match the relative locations both horizontally and vertically to help ease handle creation.

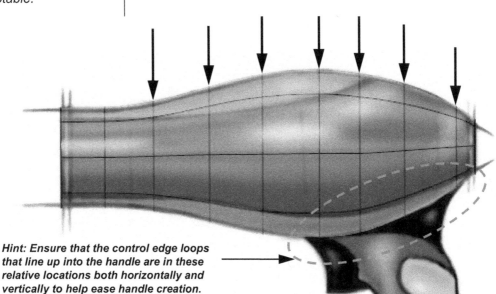

Hint: Ensure that the control edge loops that line up into the handle are in these relative locations both horizontally and vertically to help ease handle creation.

Figure 9–6

4. Using <Ctrl>, select the two remaining edge loops at the left end of the cylinder, as shown in Figure 9–7. Manipulate these loops at the same time to obtain a smoother transition to the nozzle.

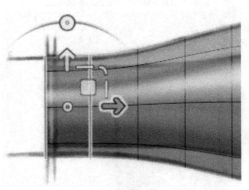

Figure 9–7

5. As each edge loop is adjusted, changes might need to be made to previous edges. Adjust the edges as required and complete the edits.

6. Save the design.

Task 5 - Assign symmetry to the design and prepare the area where the handle attaches.

In this task, you will assign symmetry to the design so that each side of the blowdryer body is created as a mirror image. Symmetry will be tested by deleting faces to create what will become the handle. Additionally, you will begin to create the top of the handle.

<table>
<tr><td></td><td>

Task Video

A video (05 Symmetry and Delete Add Faces.avi) of the completed task is included in the *Practice Files/Project Videos/Blowdryer* folder.

Video Length: *3:49*
</td></tr>
</table>

1. In the SYMMETRY panel, click ⚓ (Mirror - Internal).

2. Return to the **Home** view and temporarily toggle off the display of the canvas image.

3. Select the references shown in Figure 9–8 to define symmetry along the canvas plane.

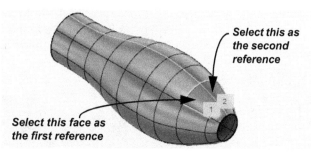

Select this as the second reference

Select this face as the first reference

Figure 9–8

4. Delete the faces shown in Figure 9–9. Because of the symmetry, the faces on the opposite side of the symmetry line are automatically selected.

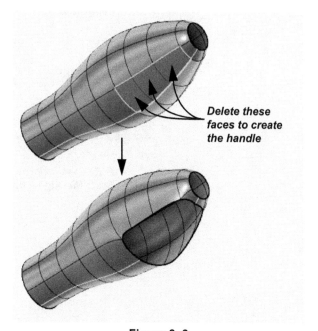

Delete these faces to create the handle

Figure 9–9

5. Return to the **FRONT** view and toggle on display of the canvas image on this plane.

6. Use the 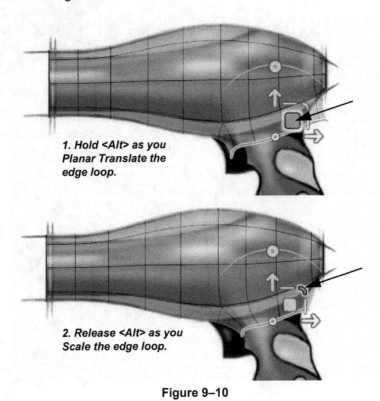 (Edit Form) command to create the handle. Ensure that you hold <Alt> to create each control frame edge loop. Release <Alt> to manipulate and reposition the new edge loop relative to the canvas sketch. The edits to first edge loop can be made similar to those shown in Figure 9–10 and Figure 9–11.

1. Hold <Alt> as you Planar Translate the edge loop.

2. Release <Alt> as you Scale the edge loop.

Figure 9–10

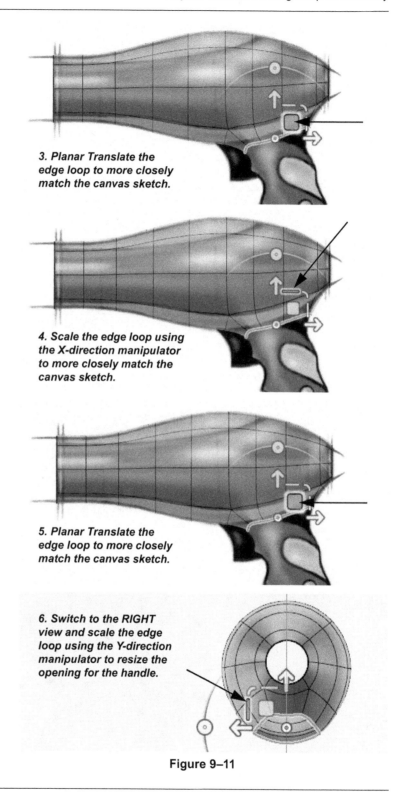

3. *Planar Translate the edge loop to more closely match the canvas sketch.*

4. *Scale the edge loop using the X-direction manipulator to more closely match the canvas sketch.*

5. *Planar Translate the edge loop to more closely match the canvas sketch.*

6. *Switch to the RIGHT view and scale the edge loop using the Y-direction manipulator to resize the opening for the handle.*

Figure 9–11

7. Refine the shape of the narrower edge at the back end of the blowdryer design to improve the handle shape, as shown in Figure 9–12.

1. Select the narrow edge on the left of the canvas plane.

2. Scale the edge using the Y-direction manipulator to widen it.

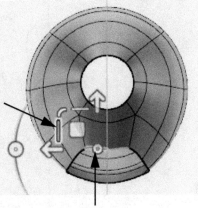

3. Return to the FRONT view.

4. Select the two points at the right side of the edge.

5. Planar Translate these two points to more closely match the sketch.

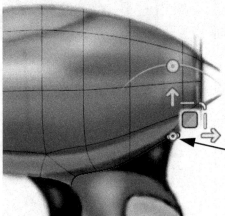

6. Planar Translate the remaining points along the edge to more closely match the sketch.

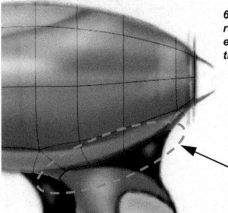

Figure 9–12

8. Create an additional edge and shape it similar to that shown in Figure 9–13.

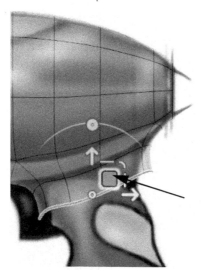

1. Hold <Alt> as you use Planar Translate to move the edge loop.

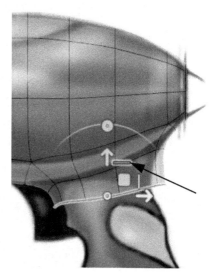

2. Release <Alt> and scale the edge loop using the X-direction manipulator.

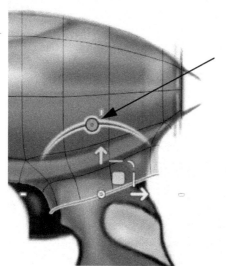

3. Rotate the edge loop to more closely match the canvas image.

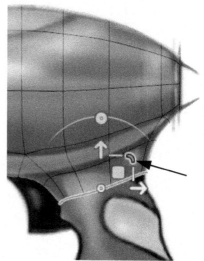

4. Scale the edge loop to more closely match the canvas image.

Figure 9–13

Task 6 - Continue the design of the handle.

In this task, you will complete the design of the handle using the same technique of adding and modifying a loop of edges.

1. Continue with the same technique of adding a loop of edges and modifying these new edges and points to match the canvas sketch. The completed handle should be similar to that shown in Figure 9–14. As you add new edges, you might need to go back to previous edges and further edit them. Multiple iterations might be required to create an acceptable handle.

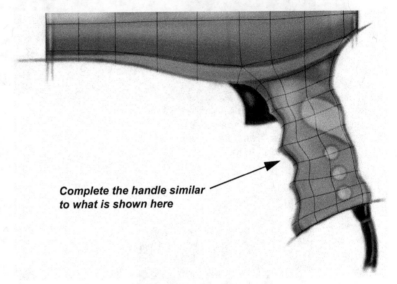

Complete the handle similar to what is shown here

Figure 9–14

Task Video

A video (06 Create Handle.avi) of the completed task is included in the *Practice Files/Project Videos/Blowdryer* **folder.**

Video Length: *2:10*

2. Select the last three edge loops on the bottom of the handle (as shown in Figure 9–15), rotate to the **RIGHT** view, and scale them.

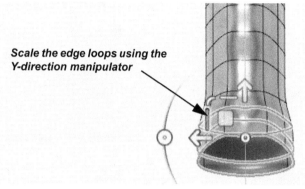

Scale the edge loops using the Y-direction manipulator

Figure 9–15

3. Use the ☖ (Fill Hole) option to close the bottom of the handle. Hint: Use the **Reduced Star** *Fill Hole Mode* to create a rounded face between the last edge and the flat bottom.

4. Hide the canvas image from the display and review the design. The design should be similar to that shown in Figure 9–16.

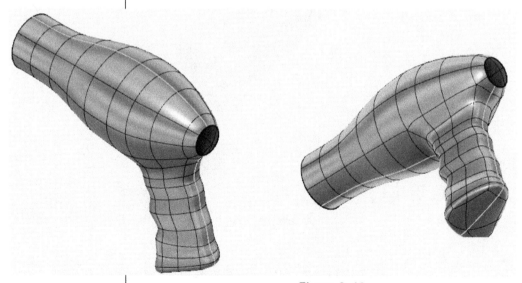

Figure 9–16

To continue with a model that has been completed for you, open **Blowdryer_Task6_Complete.f3d** from the practice files folder.

Task 7 - Create a solid referencing the surface geometry.

In this task, you will use the **Thicken** command to create solid geometry from the surface geometry that has been modeled.

Task Video

A video (07 Thicken.avi) of the completed task is included in the *Practice Files/Project Videos/Blowdryer* folder.

Video Length: *0:46*

1. Finish the form feature to return to the SOLID environment of the *DESIGN* workspace.

2. In the CREATE panel, click ✏️ (Thicken). Select the body of the blowdryer to be thickened and enter a *Thickness* value of **0.063 in**, as shown in Figure 9–17.

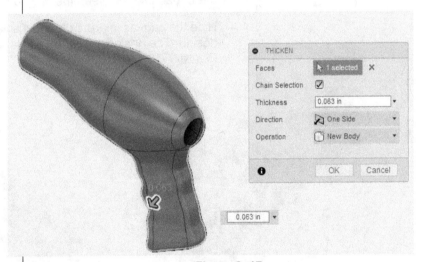

Figure 9–17

3. Review the design and verify that the design is now a solid body.

Task 8 - Make modifications to the form feature.

In this task, you will return to the form feature and make additional edits to the shape of the finger grips on the handle. Once completed, you will verify that the solid geometry reflects the changes that were made.

Task Video

A video (08 Modify Form Feature.avi) of the completed task is included in the *Practice Files/Project Videos/Blowdryer* folder.

Video Length: *1:02*

1. Edit the form feature in the design.

2. Use the 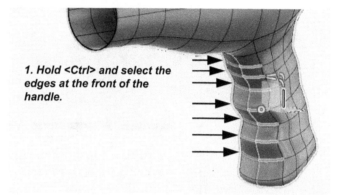 (Edit Form) command to scale the shape of the finger grips on the handle, as shown in Figure 9–18.

1. Hold <Ctrl> and select the edges at the front of the handle.

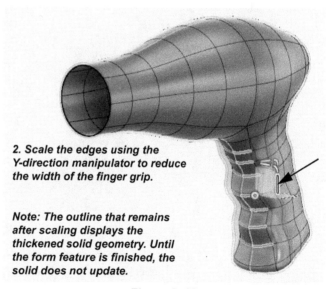

2. Scale the edges using the Y-direction manipulator to reduce the width of the finger grip.

Note: The outline that remains after scaling displays the thickened solid geometry. Until the form feature is finished, the solid does not update.

Figure 9–18

3. Finish the form feature and ensure that the solid geometry updates to reflex the change.

Task 9 - Split faces in the design.

In this task, you will create sketches that will be used to split faces on the model. This will be done so that separate appearances can be assigned to the faces.

Task Video 1

A video (09 Split Face1.avi) of the completed task is included in the *Practice Files/Project Videos/Blowdryer* folder.

Video Length: *2:00*

Task Video 2

A video (09 Split Face2.avi) of the completed task is included in the *Practice Files/Project Videos/Blowdryer* folder.

Video Length: *1:30*

1. Create a construction plane that is offset by **2.5 in** from the XY origin plane, as shown in Figure 9–19.

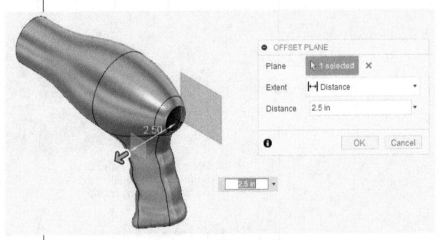

Figure 9–19

2. Begin the creation of a sketch on the new plane. This sketch will be used to define the split. Sketch a Spline that traces the sketched edge of the canvas image, as shown in Figure 9–20.

Sketch the edge on the canvas —
image using a Spline

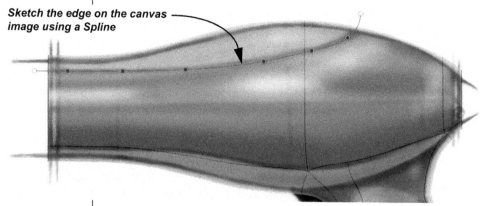

Figure 9–20

3. Complete the sketch.

4. In the MODIFY panel, click ⬚ (Split Face). Define the split as shown in Figure 9–21.

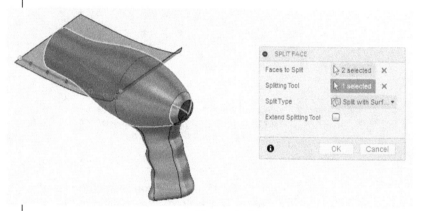

Figure 9–21

The design should display similar to that shown in Figure 9–22.

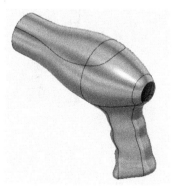

Figure 9–22

5. The control frame that was generated when creating the form feature does not create a smooth edge to divide the body for color assignment. Create a second sketch on the same sketch plane and use a Spline to create a smooth path to split the body, as shown in Figure 9–23.

- Sketch the spline above any of the existing control frame entities. If they overlap, you will generate unwanted faces after the split.

- The spline might not exactly match the sketch. This split is for assigning color and is not a key design criteria.

- As sketching, you might notice that the spline is snapping to existing entities. To avoid this, hold <Ctrl> as you are placing the spline points.

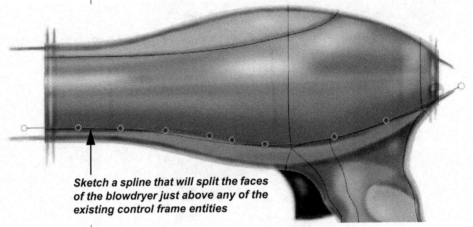

Sketch a spline that will split the faces of the blowdryer just above any of the existing control frame entities

Figure 9–23

6. Use the spline to split the faces of the design. The model should display similar to that shown in Figure 9–24. The canvas image has been toggled off in the image for clarity.

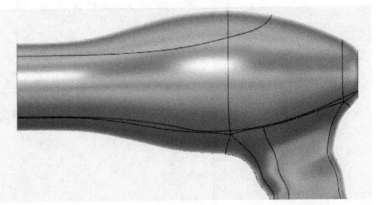

Figure 9–24

7. Create two additional sketches and use them to split the faces of the design similar to that shown in Figure 9–25. The canvas image has been toggled off in the image for clarity. Note that the thumb rest sketch on the handle only splits the front face.

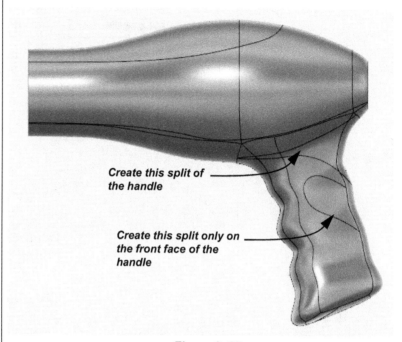

Create this split of the handle

Create this split only on the front face of the handle

Figure 9–25

To continue with a model that has been completed for you, open **Blowdryer_Task9_Complete.f3d** from the practice files folder.

Task 10 - Apply materials and appearances to the design.

In this task, you will assign a plastic material to the design. Then, you will assign a unique appearance to faces of the design to improve its display for imagery that might be required for product.

Task Video 1

A video (10 Apply Material.avi) of the completed task is included in the *Practice Files/Project Videos/Blowdryer* folder.

Video Length: *0:21*

Task Video 2

A video (10 Add Appearances.avi) of the completed task is included in the *Practice Files/Project Videos/Blowdryer* folder.

Video Length: 1:14

1. Right-click on the solid body in the BROWSER and select **Physical Material** as shown in Figure 9–26. The PHYSICAL APPEARANCE palette opens.

Figure 9–26

2. In the *Library* area at the bottom of the palette, expand the **Plastic** category.

3. Select the **ABS Plastic** material and drag and drop it onto the design. The color of the entire body updates to reflect the appearance that is assigned with this material. Close the PHYSICAL APPEARANCE palette.

4. Right-click on the solid body in the BROWSER and select **Appearance**. The APPEARANCE palette opens.

5. In the *Library* area, expand the **Plastic>Opaque** categories.

6. Select the **Plastic - Matt (Yellow)** appearance and drag and drop it onto the design. The color of the entire body updates to reflect the assigned appearance, replacing the appearance of the ABS Plastic material.

7. In the design, hold <Ctrl> and select the faces that should be assigned as black.

8. In the **Opaque** category, select the **Plastic - Matte (Black)** appearance and drag and drop it onto the selected faces. The design should display as shown in Figure 9–27.

   • Consider assigning appearances to individual faces or to a smaller selection set if you are having trouble selecting faces. Changing the zoom level can also make it easier to select small faces.

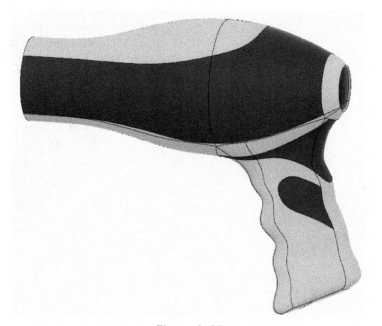

Figure 9–27

Task 11 - Complete the design of the button.

In this final task, you will create the button between the handle and the body of the blowdryer design. Minimal instructions are provided to test your knowledge of the sculpting design tools.

Task Video

A video (11 Button Design.avi) of the completed task is included in the *Practice Files/Project Videos/Blowdryer* **folder.**

Video Length: 2:32

1. In the SOLID environment, create a sketch on the XY plane to represent the shape of the button. Once the sketch is completed, extrude the sketch symmetrically on both sides of the sketch plane to a total thickness of **0.5 in** and cut the existing solid. The completed cut is shown in Figure 9–28.

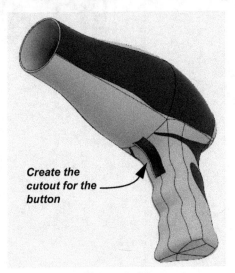

Create the cutout for the button

Figure 9–28

2. Reuse the same sketch that you just created and create the button as a new extruded solid body, as shown in Figure 9–29.

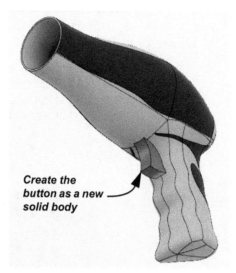

Create the button as a new solid body

Figure 9–29

3. To complete the design, change the appearance of the button solid body to **Plastic - Matte (Black)**. The design should display similar to that shown in Figure 9–30.

Figure 9–30

A completed model (**Blowdryer_Complete.f3d**) has been provided for you in the practice files folder.

4. Save the design.

Practice 9b

Controller Design

Project Objective

- Use the tools available in the Autodesk Fusion 360 software to create a highly sculpted design.

In this practice, you will create the design shown in Figure 9–31 using the FORM contextual environment. You will be provided three image files to attach to the origin planes to provide you with the overall shape of the design.

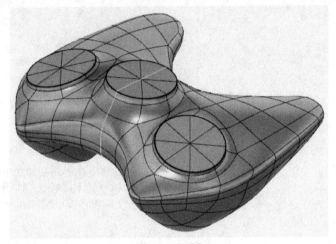

Figure 9–31

Project Video

A video (Sculpted Controller Final 3XSpeed.avi) of the completed project is included in the *Practice Files/Project Videos/Controller* folder.

***Video Length:** 9:20*

Task 1 - Set up a new design.

1. Create a new design in the current project.

2. In the BROWSER, expand **Document Settings**, hover the cursor over the **Units** node, and then select 🗓 (Change Active Units).

3. In the CHANGE ACTIVE UNITS palette, for the *Unit Type* option, select **Inch**. Click **OK**.

Task 2 - Attach canvas images.

In this task, you will attach three canvas images to the origin planes to provide conceptual sketches that will be used to create the geometry in the design.

Task Video

A video (02 Attach Canvases.avi) of the completed task is included in the *Practice Files/Project Videos/Controller* **folder.**

Video Length: 4:47

1. In the INSERT panel, click  (Canvas) to open the CANVAS palette.

   - Assign the canvas to the **XZ** plane.
   - Using the ViewCube, reorient the design to the **TOP** view.

   - Click (Select Image) and use the Open dialog box to select **Gaming_Controller_Top.jpg** from the practice files folder.
   - For the *Z Angle* value, enter **-90.0 deg**.
   - For the *Scale Plane XY* value, enter **6.00**. The image should display as shown in Figure 9–32.

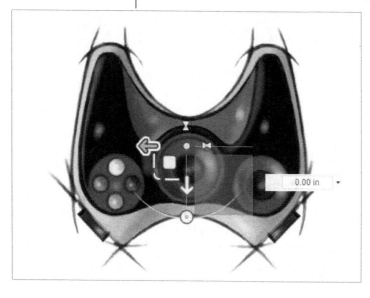

Figure 9–32

2. Click **OK**.

3. In the BROWSER, expand the *Canvases* folder. Right-click on **Gaming_Controller_Top** and click ⊢⊣ (Calibrate).

4. Select the two points on the controller image shown in Figure 9–33 to measure the current size of the image. The size displays once the second point is selected. This value will vary depending on your selection location, but should be approximately **2.8 in**.

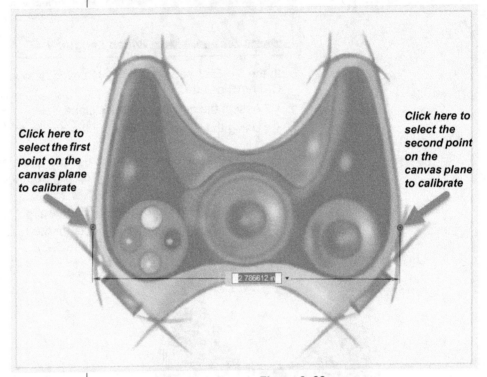

Click here to select the first point on the canvas plane to calibrate

Click here to select the second point on the canvas plane to calibrate

2.786612 in

Figure 9–33

5. Enter **6** as the new value and press <Enter>. This resizes the image. This value was used because the design intent requires the controller to be approximately 6 inches wide.

6. In the *Origin* folder, hide the display of all but the center point. The center point is required to help center the image.

7. Right-click on **Gaming_Controller_Top** and click 🖼 (Edit Canvas).

8. Select the planar manipulator (shown in Figure 9–34) and drag the image so that the Origin Point lines up as closely as possible with the center of the button in the middle of the controller image.

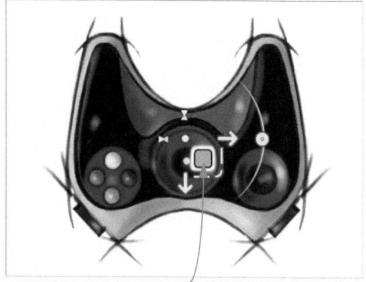

Select the planar manipulator and position the image so that the Origin Point is centered on the controller button in the center of the image

Figure 9–34

9. Click **OK**.

10. Return all of the *Origin* features to the display.

11. In the INSERT panel, click (Canvas) to open the CANVAS palette.

   • Assign the next canvas to the **XY** plane.

   • Reorient the design to the **BACK** view using the ViewCube.

   • Click (Select Image) and use the Open dialog box to select **Gaming_Controller_Front.jpg** from the practice files folder.

12. Click **OK**.

13. In the BROWSER, expand the *Canvases* folder. Right-click on **Gaming_Controller_Front** and click (Calibrate).

14. Select the two points on the controller image shown in Figure 9–35 to measure the current size of the image. The size displays once the second point is selected.

15. Enter **6** as the new value and then press <Enter> to resize the image to match the **Gaming_Controller_Top** image.

Click here to select the first point on the canvas plane to calibrate

Click here to select the second point on the canvas plane to calibrate

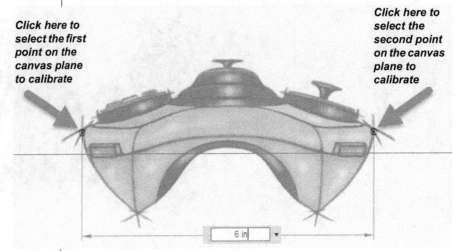

6 in

Figure 9–35

16. Right-click on **Gaming_Controller_Top** and click ⊢ (Edit Canvas). Set the *Canvas opacity* value to **50** and click **OK**.

17. For the **Gaming_Controller_Front** image, set the *Canvas opacity* value to **50**.

18. In the *Origin* folder, hide the display of all but the YZ plane. This plane is required to help align the image with the top image.

19. Edit **Gaming_Controller_Front**.

20. Ensure that the **BACK** view is being displayed on the ViewCube.

21. Select the planar or directional manipulators and drag the image so that the YZ plane aligns down the middle of the controller image and the outside edges of the image lie on the **Gaming_Controller_Top** image, as shown in Figure 9–36.

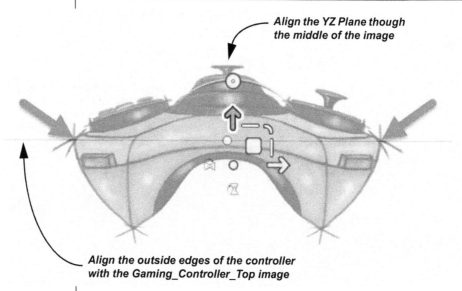

*Align the YZ Plane though
the middle of the image*

*Align the outside edges of the controller
with the Gaming_Controller_Top image*

Figure 9–36

22. Click **OK**.

23. Rotate the design. Note how you can see both images in all views now that the canvas' are set at 50% opacity.

24. Using the same techniques that were used in this task, complete the following:

- Attach the **Gaming_Controller_Side** image to the **YZ** plane.

- Calibrate the distance between the outside-most edges to **5.00 in**, as shown in Figure 9–37.

*Click here to select the
first point on the canvas
plane to calibrate*

*Click here to select the
second point on the
canvas plane to calibrate*

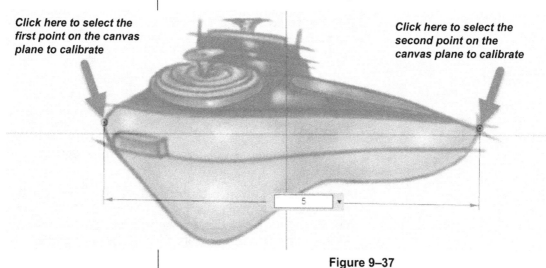

Figure 9–37

- Set the *Canvas opacity* to **50%**.
- Reposition the image so that it aligns with the other two images, as shown in Figure 9–38.

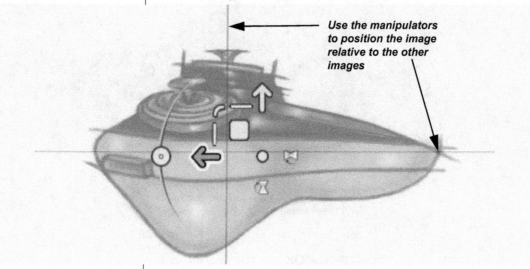

Use the manipulators to position the image relative to the other images

Figure 9–38

25. Save the design as **Controller**.

To continue with a model that has been completed for you, open **Controller_Task2_Complete.f3d** from the practice files folder.

Task 3 - Create reference features that will be used for geometry creation.

In this task, you will create construction planes and a sketch that are required as references in geometry creation.

1. In the CONSTRUCT panel, click ▥ (Offset Plane). Select the **XZ** plane in the BROWSER or in the graphics window and enter **1.25 in** as the offset value to offset the new plane above the XZ plane. Click **OK**.

2. Right-click on the new plane and select **Create Sketch**.

3. In the SKETCH panel, click **Project/Include>** ▱ (Project) and select the X origin axis in the BROWSER. This projects the axis onto the new offset plane as a linear entity. It will be used in the next step to create another construction plane. Complete the sketch.

4. Hide the three canvas images from the display. This will help to simplify the display to create the next plane.

5. In the CONSTRUCT panel, click 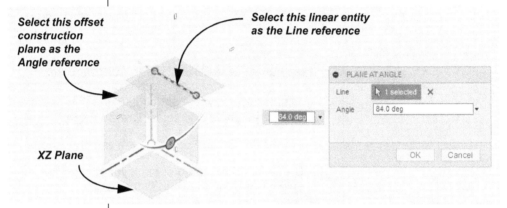 (Plane at Angle). The PLANE AT ANGLE palette displays.

   - Select the linear entity shown in Figure 9–39 that was created by projecting the axis in the previous step.
   - Select the Offset Plane shown in Figure 9–39 that was created at the beginning of this task.
   - Enter **84.0 deg** to create the angular plane.
   - Click **OK** to create the construction plane.

Select this offset construction plane as the Angle reference

Select this linear entity as the Line reference

XZ Plane

Figure 9–39

6. Hide the *Origin* features, Offset Plane (**Plane1**), and **Sketch1** from the display.

7. Display the three canvas images. Note that the new plane was created so that it aligns with a top face on the controller button (from the **RIGHT** view), as shown in Figure 9–40.

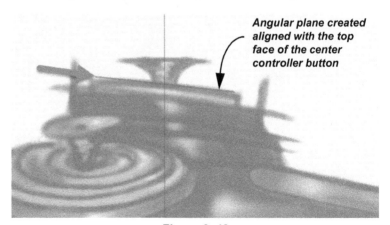

Angular plane created aligned with the top face of the center controller button

Figure 9–40

Task 4 - Create T-Spline geometry to represent the controller buttons on the top face.

In this task, you will create the three buttons that lie on the top face of the controller. You will use two different techniques to create the T-Spline bodies and can compare the processes for each. To complete the task, you will use the **Edit Form** option to refine the shape of the buttons.

Task Video

A video (04 Top Face Controller Buttons.avi) of the completed task is included in the *Practice Files/Project Videos/Controller* folder.

Video Length: 6:28

1. Right-click on the construction plane that was created at the 84 degree angle and select **Create Sketch**.

2. Project the Origin Point onto the sketch plane.

3. Create a **1.5 in** diameter circle located on the projected Origin Point, as shown in Figure 9–41.

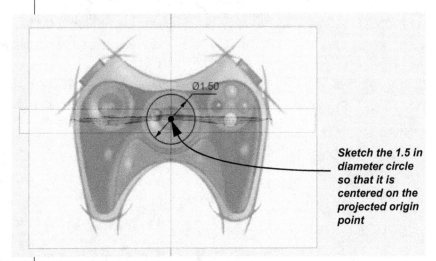

Sketch the 1.5 in diameter circle so that it is centered on the projected origin point

Figure 9–41

4. Stop the sketch.

5. Activate the FORM contextual environment.

6. Create extruded geometry that references the circular sketch as shown in Figure 9–42. This extruded T-Spline geometry will form the geometry of the center controller button.

Extruded controller button

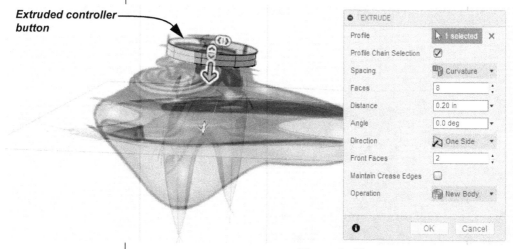

Figure 9–42

7. The angle of the cylinder is correct, but it needs to be repositioned slightly relative to the canvas images. You can do this by moving the images, but it is more efficient if you move the body on its own.

8. In the MODIFY panel, click ✛ (Move/Copy). Once the MOVE/COPY palette is open, select the extruded T-Spline body. Use the manipulator handles to move the body similar to that shown in Figure 9–43.

Move the body to match with the canvas image

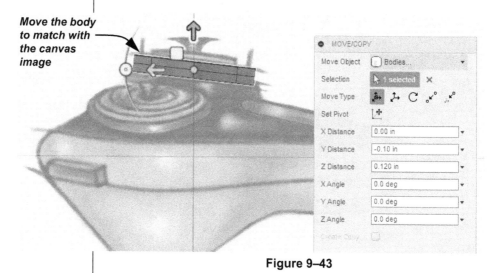

Figure 9–43

9. Click **OK** once the body has been successfully moved.

To create the second and third bodies to represent the remaining two buttons on the top of the controller, you will use a different method, rather than extruding another sketch.

10. Create a new body using the **Cylinder** quick shape option. Use the XZ Origin Plane as the placement plane, and locate the cylinder as shown in Figure 9–44.

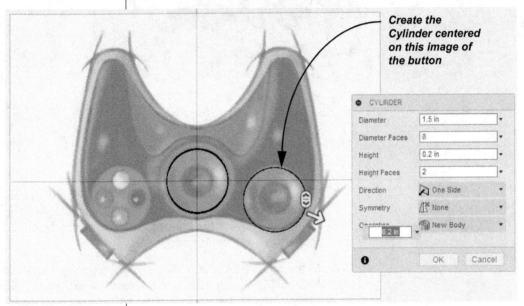

Create the Cylinder centered on this image of the button

Figure 9–44

11. Use the (Edit Form) option to relocate the body.

- To select all entities for editing, you can activate the All ( ) filter and draw a selection box around the geometry, or you can activate the Body ( ) filter and select the body on its own with a single selection.
- Change between the three views shown in Figure 9–45 to position the body.

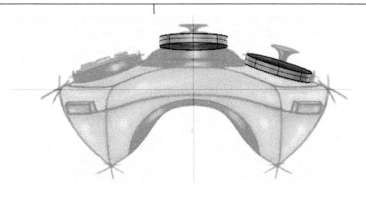

Use the TOP, FRONT, and RIGHT views on the ViewCube to reorient the design as you are changing the form's location

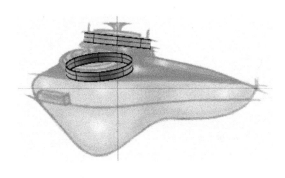

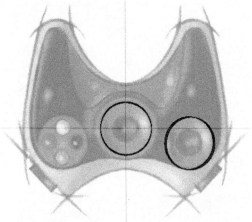

Figure 9–45

12. To create the body to represent the third button, you can mirror the one you just created. In the SYMMETRY panel, click ▲▲ (Mirror Duplicate).

13. For the body to be mirrored, select the second body that you just created using the cylinder, and then select the YZ plane as the mirror plane, as shown in Figure 9–46.

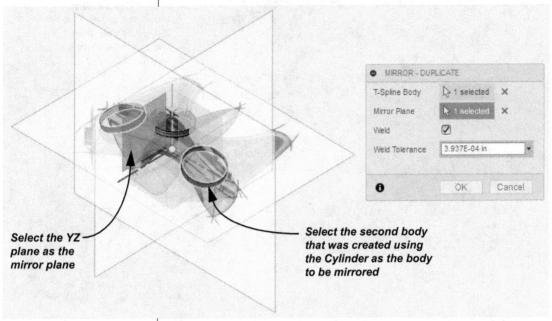

Select the YZ plane as the mirror plane

Select the second body that was created using the Cylinder as the body to be mirrored

Figure 9–46

14. Click **OK**. A mirrored T-Spline body is created.

15. Use the 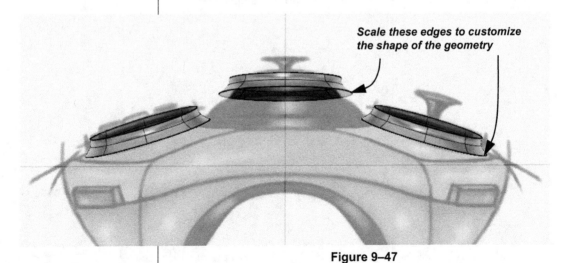 (Edit Form) option to scale the lower edges of the two bodies shown in Figure 9–47. When scaling the mirrored body, its mirror also updates.

Scale these edges to customize the shape of the geometry

Figure 9–47

16. in the SYMMETRY panel, assign symmetry using the
    (Mirror - Internal) option, as shown in Figure 9–48.

Select the two faces on either side of the YZ plane

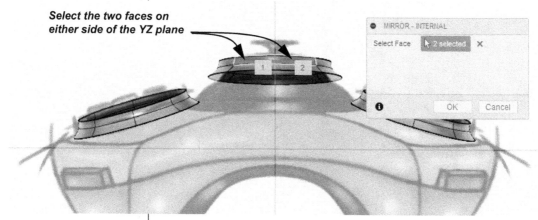

Figure 9–48

17. Use (Edit Form) to refine the shape of the middle button as shown in Figure 9–49 to Figure 9–53.

Translate this edge

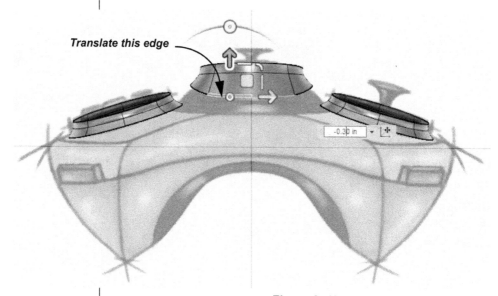

Figure 9–49

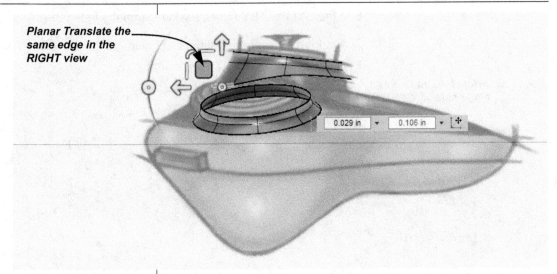

Planar Translate the same edge in the RIGHT view

Figure 9–50

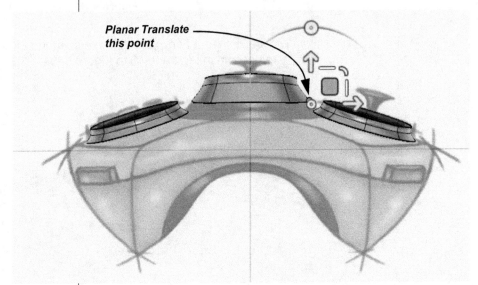

Planar Translate this point

Figure 9–51

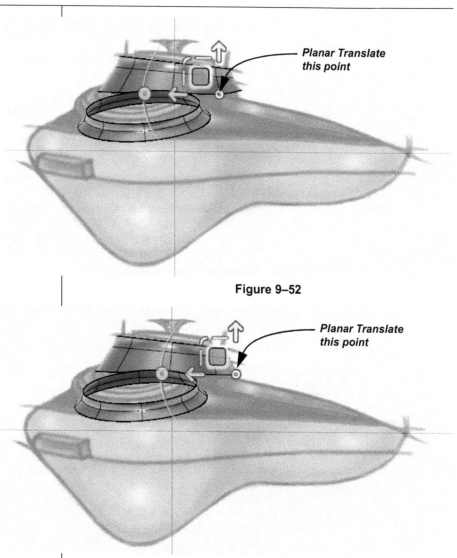

Figure 9–52

Figure 9–53

18. Complete the edit and save the design.

To continue with a model that has been completed for you,
open **Controller_Task4_Complete.f3d** from the practice files
folder.

Task 5 - Create Bridge geometry between the buttons.

In this task, you will create geometry that connects the buttons to one another using the **Bridge** option.

Task Video

A video (05 Bridge Geometry.avi) of the completed task is included in the *Practice Files/Project Videos/Controller folder.*

Video Length: *1:16*

1. Rotate the design similar to that shown in Figure 9–54. Note that the side and top canvas images have been hidden from the display for image clarity.

2. Start the (Bridge) tool and select the edge references shown in Figure 9–54. Ensure that the *Faces* value is set to **1**.

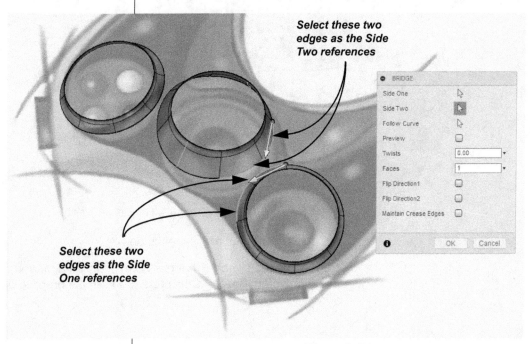

Select these two edges as the Side Two references

Select these two edges as the Side One references

Figure 9–54

3. Click **OK**.

4. Note how due to the symmetry settings in the design, geometry is also created on the other side of the center button and a warning message displays. Click 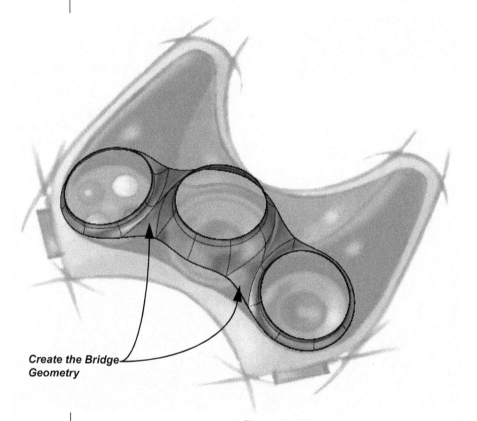 (Undo) to remove the Bridge operation.

5. In the SYMMETRY panel, click (Clear Symmetry) and select the T-Spline geometry representing the middle button. Do this again to clear the symmetry associated between the right and left buttons.

6. Use the (Bridge) tool to create the T-Spline geometry that connects the middle button to both side buttons. The final geometry should display similar to that shown in Figure 9–55.

Create the Bridge Geometry

Figure 9–55

7. Save the design.

Task 6 - Create a sketch that represents the overall top profile of the controller.

In this task, you will create extruded T-Spline geometry to represent the top profile of the controller. You will do this by creating a sketch that traces the canvas sketch.

Task Video

A video (06 Extruded Top Profile.avi) of the completed task is included in the *Practice Files/Project Videos/Controller* folder.

Video Length: 4:44

1. Return to the SOLID environment. Rotate the design to the **TOP** view.

2. Begin the creation of a sketch on the XZ plane.

3. Use the sketch tools (e.g., line, 3-point arc, fillets, etc.) to create the sketch shown in Figure 9–56. Add Vertical constraints to vertically align endpoints with the Origin Point and use the Tangent constraints between arcs.

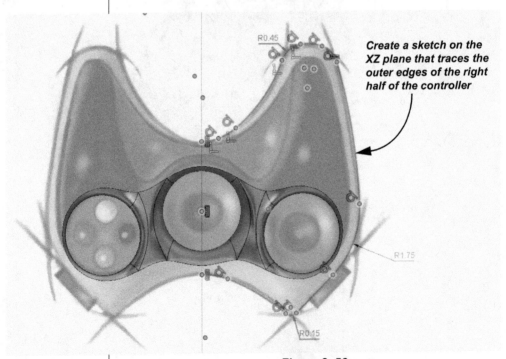

Create a sketch on the XZ plane that traces the outer edges of the right half of the controller

Figure 9–56

4. Stop the sketch. In the Timeline, drag the last Sketch icon
   (⌑) prior to the form feature icon (▣).

5. Double-click on the ▣ in the Timeline to open the form
   feature and access the FORM contextual environment.

6. Create extruded T-Spline geometry using the sketch that was
   just created. In the EXTRUDE palette, use the settings
   shown in Figure 9–57 to define the *Distance* value and
   number of faces on the geometry. In the *Direction* field,
   ensure that you have selected the **Symmetric** option.

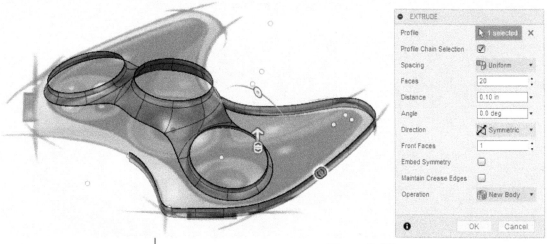

Figure 9–57

7. In the SYMMETRY panel, click ▲ (Mirror Duplicate). Select
   the extruded body that you just created as the body to be
   mirrored and select the YZ plane as the mirror plane. Click
   OK to complete the mirror, as shown in Figure 9–58.

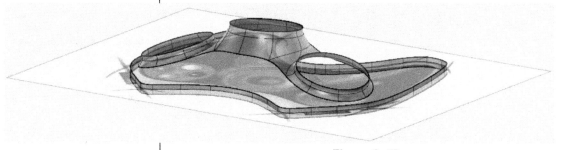

Figure 9–58

8. Use the **Clear Symmetry** option in the SYMMETRY panel to clear the symmetry between the two halves of the extrude.

9. Save the design.

To continue with a model that has been completed for you, open **Controller_Task6_Complete.f3d** from the practice files folder.

Task 7 - Create T-Spline geometry to merge faces between the extrude and the buttons.

In this task, you will complete the T-Spline geometry on the top of the controller, as shown in Figure 9–59.

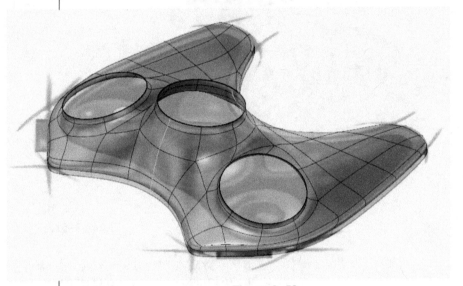

Figure 9–59

Task Video

A video (07 Completed Top Profile.avi) of the completed task is included in the *Practice Files/Project Videos/Controller* **folder.**

Video Length: *2:56*

1. Use the 🔄 (Bridge) tool to merge the two sets of edges shown in Figure 9–60. Ensure that the *Faces* value is set to **1**.

Select the six edges between these two top arrows as the Side One references

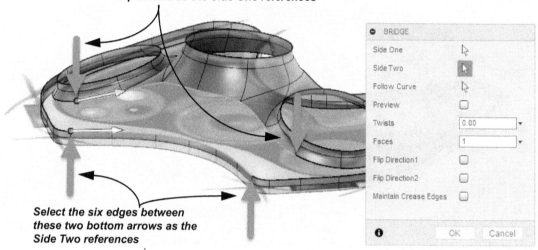

Select the six edges between these two bottom arrows as the Side Two references

Figure 9–60

2. The completed bridge geometry displays as shown in Figure 9–61.

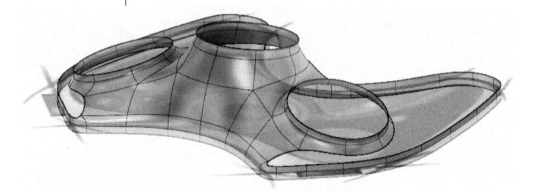

Figure 9–61

3. The remainder of the geometry that will be created on the top of the model should be symmetric. Assign symmetry as shown in Figure 9–62.

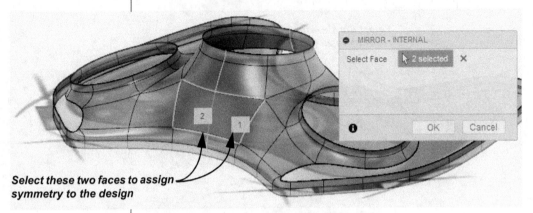

Select these two faces to assign symmetry to the design

Figure 9–62

4. Use 🔄 (Bridge) to merge the geometry shown in Figure 9–63. Because symmetry was assigned, the bridge will also be generated on the opposite side.

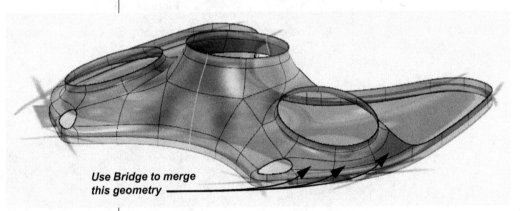

Use Bridge to merge this geometry

Figure 9–63

5. To fill the hole between the two bridged areas, you can use the 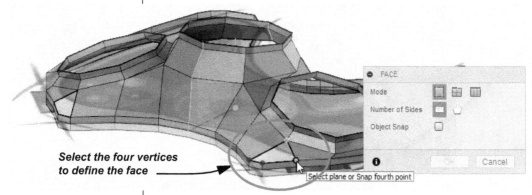 (Face) option in the CREATE panel. Set the options as shown in Figure 9–64 to create a **Simple**, **Four Sided** face by selecting the four vertices that exist around the hole.

Select the four vertices to define the face

Figure 9–64

6. The completed bridge geometry is shown in Figure 9–65.

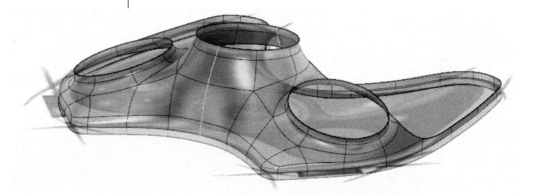

Figure 9–65

7. Rotate the model to the front of the design.

8. To use the 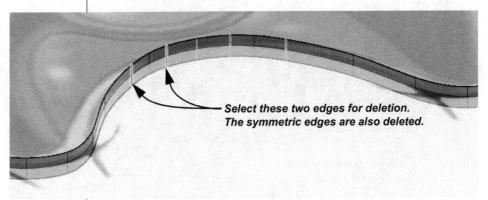 (Bridge) tool, the number of entities that are selected on the edges must be equal. Note that the number of faces is larger in the extruded T-Spline. Delete the edges shown in Figure 9–66.

Select these two edges for deletion. The symmetric edges are also deleted.

Figure 9–66

9. Use the (Bridge) tool to merge the edges as shown in Figure 9–67. Note that there are three faces created between the selected edges.

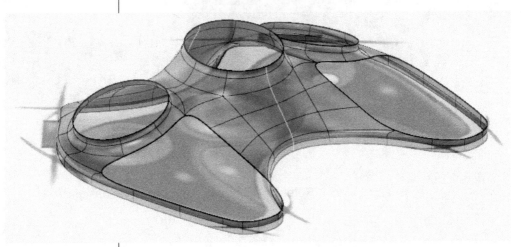

Figure 9–67

10. Use the 🖐 (Bridge) tool as shown in Figure 9–68 to begin to close the open areas that remain on the model.

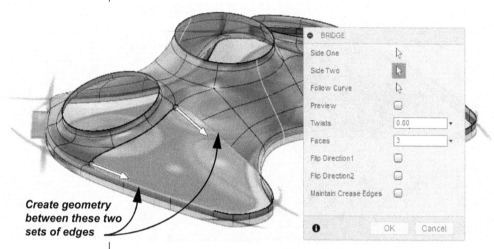

Create geometry between these two sets of edges

Figure 9–68

11. Review the area between the button and the body of the controller, as shown in Figure 9–69. Your geometry might vary depending on how you created your T-Spline bodies. It might display with an open hole, or be similar to Figure 9–69 where the geometry is overlapping itself.

12. Double-click on an edge in this area and note how it reveals a loop similar to that shown. This is an indication that it is open.

Next, you will use 🖐 (Weld Vertices) to close the hole.

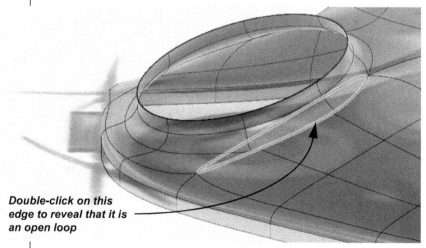

Double-click on this edge to reveal that it is an open loop

Figure 9–69

13. To prepare for welding the vertices, an open hole should be displayed to make selection easier. If your geometry does not reveal a hole, use the 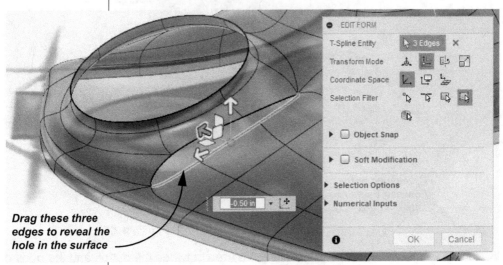 (Edit Form) option to drag the edge similar to that shown in Figure 9–70.

Drag these three edges to reveal the hole in the surface

Figure 9–70

14. Use the 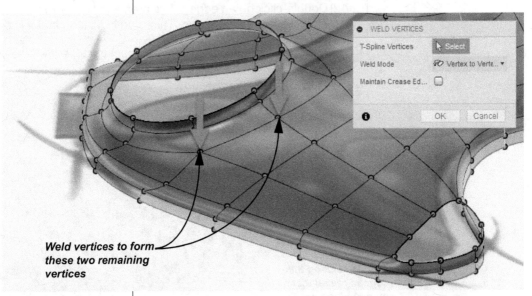 (Weld Vertices) tool to close the hole by matching two sets of vertices, as shown in Figure 9–71.

Weld vertices to form these two remaining vertices

Figure 9–71

15. To fill the remaining hole on the top of the controller, you will use the 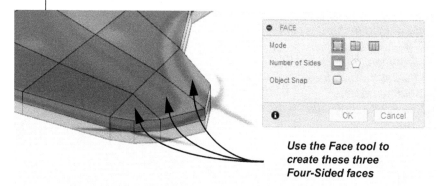 (Face) tool. Set the options to create **Simple**, **Four-Sided** faces and select three sets of four vertices to fill the hole as shown in Figure 9–72.

Use the Face tool to create these three Four-Sided faces

Figure 9–72

16. The completed geometry is shown in Figure 9–73.

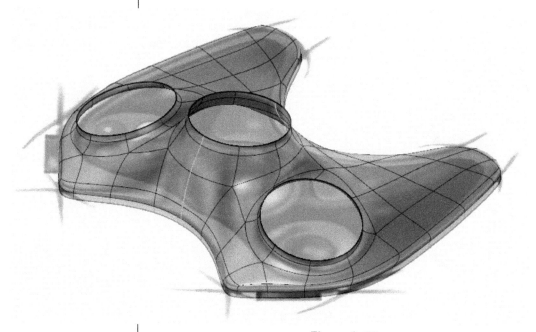

Figure 9–73

17. Save the design.

To continue with a model that has been completed for you, open **Controller_Task7_Complete.f3d** from the practice files folder.

The remaining tasks in this project assume that you are now familiar with all of the tools that can be used in the FORM contextual environment, and understand which tools should be used to successfully complete the tasks.

Task 8 - Adjust the top of the controller to match the sketch.

In this task, adjust the faces, edges, and points on the top of the controller using **Edit Form**. This is required to accurately match the canvas image. The final edited geometry that should be completed by the end of this task is shown in Figure 9–74.

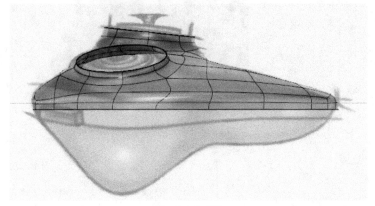

Figure 9–74

To continue with a model that has been completed for you, open **Controller_Task8_Complete.f3d** from the practice files folder.

Task Video

A video (08 Adjusted Top Profile.avi) of the completed task is included in the *Practice Files/Project Videos/Controller* folder.

Video Length: *8:21*

Task 9 - Begin the creation of the bottom of the controller.

In this task, create an additional row of T-Spline faces that will begin to form the lower portion of the controller. The row of faces that should be completed by the end of this task are shown in Figure 9–75.

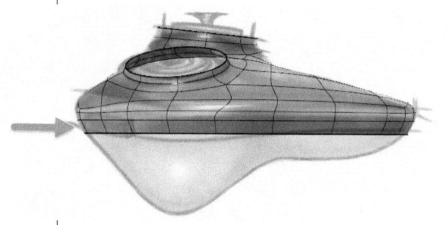

Figure 9–75

To continue with a model that has been completed for you, open **Controller_Task9_Complete.f3d** from the practice files folder.

Task Video

A video (**09 Adding Faces to Bottom.avi**) of the completed task is included in the *Practice Files/Project Videos/Controller* folder.

Video Length: *1:55*

Task 10 - Complete the bottom of the controller.

In this task, complete the bottom of the controller using the **Bridge**, **Weld Edges**, and **Edit Form** options. The completed geometry should be similar to that shown in Figure 9–76.

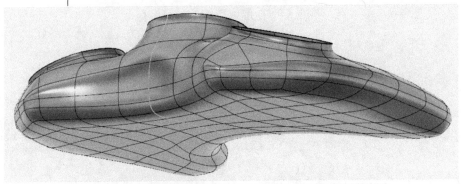

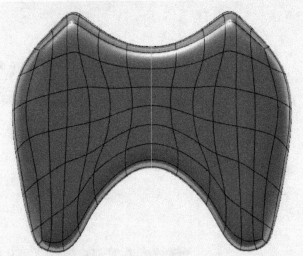

Figure 9–76

To continue with a model that has been completed for you, open **Controller_Task10_Complete.f3d** from the practice files folder.

Task Video

A video (10 Controller Bottom.avi) of the completed task is included in the *Practice Files/Project Videos/Controller* folder.

Video Length: 3:55

Task 11 - Complete the bottom of the controller.

In this task, complete the bottom of the controller by adjusting the shape of the T-Spline geometry to match the canvas image. The completed geometry should be similar to that shown in Figure 9–77.

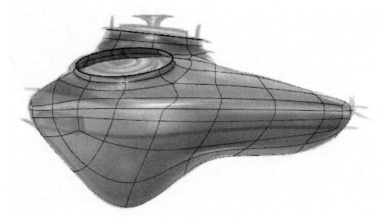

Figure 9–77

To continue with a model that has been completed for you, open **Controller_Task11_Complete.f3d** from the practice files folder. As time permits, continue to design the entire controller using multiple bodies.

Task Video

A video (11 Adjusted Bottom Profile.avi) of the completed task is included in the *Practice Files/Project Videos/Controller* **folder.**

Video Length: 6:44

Task 12 - Complete the controller.

In this task, complete the controller by closing the three holes on the top of the design. The completed geometry should be similar to that shown in Figure 9–78.

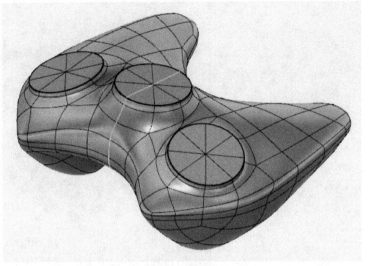

Figure 9–78

To continue with a model that has been completed for you, open **Controller_Complete.f3d** from the practice files folder.

Task Video

A video (12 Fill Holes.avi) of the completed task is included in the *Practice Files/Project Videos/Controller* **folder.**

Video Length: 1:12

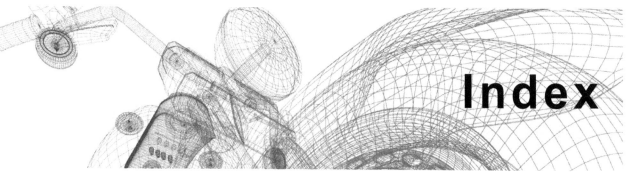

Index